Encyclopedia of Drugs, Narcotics, Drug Abuse, Drug Addiction and Drug Peddling/Trafficking

About the Book

The aims of this book to shed light on the lesser-known drug abuse, drug addiction and drug Peddling/Trafficking in all over the world. The book deals with different essential topics on drugs, narcotics, drug Abuse, drug addiction and drug Peddling/trafficking. The aim of this book is to provide a generalized survey of drug abuse in the world. This book is very important in understanding social empacts of drug addiction. The book explains all aspects of addictive behavior.

About the Author

Adam Felman was born in June 17, 1952 in Scotland. He completed his graduation degree in Psychology from Herriot-Watt University, Edinburgh Campus and did post graduation in Psychology from same university .He worked as an Assistant Professor in different department. His writing style is unique and creative. He tried to aware the people about social issues by his writing.His books and stories have been bestsellers in different state even his work being translated into 50 regional languages and selling thousands of copies. He has extensively participated in various conferences, seminars, symposia, Training Programmers and workshop related to prohibiting of drugs use. He has a great interest in organizing rehabilitation centers for drug addicts.

Encyclopedia of Drugs, Narcotics, Drug Abuse, Drug Addiction and Drug Peddling/Trafficking

Adam Felman

AMIGA PRESS INC.
Delhi: - 110051 (India)

AMIGA PRESS INC.
H.O:- 28-A, Indra Park, St.No-9
Chander Nagar, Krishna Nagar
Delhi: - 110051 (India)
Tel: - 011-22504028, +91-98736-57000
Email: - amigapress@gmail.com
info@amigapress.co.in
amigaeditorial@gmail.com
amigapub@gmail.com

Website: - www.amigapress.co.in

This edition is published by Amiga Press Inc.

ISBN: 978-93-84533-63-2

Printed and bound by Amiga Press Inc.

Preface

For much of the past century, scientists studying drugs and drug use labored in the shadows of powerful myths and misconceptions about the nature of addiction. When scientists began to study addictive behavior in the 1930s, people addicted to drugs were thought to be morally flawed and lacking in willpower. Those views shaped society's responses to drug use, treating it as a moral failing rather than a health problem, which led to an emphasis on punishment rather than prevention and treatment.

Today, thanks to science, our views and our responses to addiction and the broader spectrum of substance use disorders have changed dramatically. Groundbreaking discoveries about the brain have revolutionized our understanding of compulsive drug use, enabling us to respond effectively to the problem.

As a result of scientific research, we know that addiction is a medical disorder that affects the brain and changes behavior. We have identified many of the biological and environmental risk factors and are beginning to search for the genetic variations that contribute to the development and progression of the disorder. Scientists use this knowledge to develop effective prevention and treatment approaches that reduce the toll drug use takes on individuals, families, and communities.

–Author

Contents

1

Introduction of Drug

A drug is any substance that causes a change in an organism›s physiology or psychology when consumed.

Drugs are typically distinguished from food and substances that provide nutritional support. Consumption of drugs can be via inhalation, injection, smoking, ingestion, absorption via a patch on the skin, or dissolution under the tongue.

In pharmacology, a drug is a chemical substance, typically of known structure, which, when administered to a living organism, produces a biological effect. A pharmaceutical drug, also called a medication or medicine, is a chemical substance used to treat, cure, prevent, or diagnose a disease or to promote well-being. Traditionally drugs were obtained through extraction from medicinal plants, but more recently also by organic synthesis. Pharmaceutical drugs may be used for a limited duration, or on a regular basis for chronic disorders.

Pharmaceutical drugs are often classified into drug classes—-groups of related drugs that have similar chemical structures, the same mechanism of action (binding to the same biological target), a related mode of action, and that are used to treat the same disease. The Anatomical Therapeutic Chemical Classification System (ATC), the most widely used drug classification system, assigns drugs a unique ATC code, which is an alphanumeric code that assigns it to specific drug classes within the ATC system. Another major classification system is the Biopharmaceutics Classification System. This classifies drugs according to their solubility and permeability or absorption properties.

Psychoactive drugs are chemical substances that affect the function of the central nervous system, altering perception, mood or consciousness. These drugs are divided into different groups like: stimulants, depressants, antidepressants, anxiolytics, antipsychotics, and hallucinogens. These psychotropic drugs have been proven useful in treating wide range of medical conditions including mental disorders around the world. The most widely used drugs in the world include caffeine, nicotine and alcohol, which are also considered recreational drugs, since they are used for pleasure rather than medicinal purposes. Abuse of several psychoactive drugs can cause psychological or physical addiction. It's worth noting that all drugs can have potential side effects. Excessive use of stimulants can promote stimulant psychosis. Many recreational drugs are illicit and international treaties such as the Single Convention on Narcotic Drugsexist for the purpose of their prohibition

Drug Manufacturing

Drug manufacturing is the crime of being involved in any step in the drug production process. Similar to drug trafficking, drug manufacturing requires that the defendant had knowing possession of a drug, or the chemicals necessary to manufacture a drug, and that he or she had an intent to manufacture. Thus, drug manufacturing requires more than simple drug possession. With the rise of synthetic drugs and the rise in domestic production of methamphetamines, charges of drug manufacturing have increased significantly in recent years.

What is Manufacturing?

The term manufacturing encompasses a broad range of activities related to the production of drugs. While producing illegal substances in an in-house lab is clearly drug manufacturing, the crime also targets those who sell necessary precursor chemicals, specialized drug production equipment, or provide other operational support. In many states, merely offering to assist in drug manufacturing is enough to be prosecuted for the crime. Because many precursor chemicals are legal substances, prosecution for drug manufacturing requires that a seller knew, or had reason to know, that the purchaser of the chemicals intended to use them to make illegal drugs. Thus, for instance, a home supply store that sells certain chemicals to the general public would not be charged with drug manufacturing unless a prosecutor could show that they knew, or should have known, that their customers were purchasing the chemicals for drug production.

Additionally, under federal law, the cultivation of marijuana is also treated as drug manufacturing. The government regards it as equivalent to the manufacture of any Schedule I illegal drug. This means that individuals who grow marijuana plants for use may technically be charged for drug production, a much more serious crime than simple drug possession. Some states that allow recreational use of marijuana, or medical marijuana possession, have carved out exceptions to this federal law, allowing users to legally cultivate a certain number of marijuana plants for their personal use.

Intent to Manufacture

Unlike drug possession, drug manufacturing requires not only that a defendant possessed illicit materials or drugs, but also that he or she clearly intended to manufacture illegal substances. This is an important distinction, and many defendants caught with common drug chemicals argue a lack of intent as a defense to the crime of drug manufacturing. Intent to manufacture is typically proven through possession of other circumstantial evidence, such as drug manufacturing equipment, a home drug lab, or a stockpile of precursor chemicals. Thus, for instance, while possession of common cold medicines (often used in methamphetamine production) may not be enough to charge an individual with drug production, possession of these medicines in tandem with other methamphetamine chemicals, can result in a charge of drug manufacturing. Similarly, a man who is found in possession of marijuana may be subject only to a charge of drug possession. However, if he is also found to have multiple plants, or grow lights, on his property, he may be charged with drug manufacturing instead.

Drug Manufacturing Penalties

Punishment for the crime of drug manufacturing can be quite significant. Drug manufacturing is typically prosecuted as a felony, and often results in at least one year of prison, although sentences can be as high as ten years. Defendants may also face substantial fines, up to $25,000 or more. Under federal laws, punishment for the cultivation of marijuana plants can range from five years in prison for 50 plants to more than 25 years for 1,000 or more plants.

One common defense to drug manufacturing is that the defendant was a permit or license holder who is authorized to be in possession of certain precursor chemicals. Thus, for instance, many factories and businesses that use industrial chemicals common in drug production may be protected from a drug manufacturing charge because they possess permits allowing them to purchase and use these chemicals.

Drug Crimes

Laws regulating drug crimes are an area of intense interest in the United States right now. Many states have contemplated drug law reforms, including the increasing legalization of medical marijuana, and, in a few states, general marijuana use. These efforts reveal the complicated interplay between federal and state drug laws.

Controlled Substances Act

Drug crimes laws primarily target the use and distribution of controlled substances. Federal drug laws are governed by the Controlled Substances Act, 21 U.S.C. § 801 et seq., ("the CSA") and most states model their own drug laws after the CSA. The CSA places drugs in five different categories, ranging from Schedule I to Schedule V drugs. Schedule I drugs are those drugs typically prohibited by drug laws as they have been deemed to have no safe accepted use. Schedule I drugs include marijuana, LSD, MDMA (also known as ecstasy), heroin, and other serious drugs. Schedule II drugs have an accepted medical use, but are also drugs for which there is a high potential for abuse. Accordingly, Schedule II drug use is permitted only with a prescription.

Schedule II drugs include cocaine, methamphetamine, morphine and other amphetamines. Schedules III-V classify other drugs of varying degrees of severity and impose certain restrictions on their use, such as requiring that the user has a prescription or is over 21. Unlike Schedule I drugs, drugs in Schedules II-V are not per se illegal, but require that the patient use them in a regulated manner.

State Drug Laws

Although most states follow the CSA in setting forth their own drug laws, there are some important differences. While federal laws tend to focus on the movement of drugs across state borders, such as drug trafficking, state laws tend to focus on the means and methods of manufacture and distribution within the state itself. Thus, for instance, states most often enforce the crimes of drug possession and drug manufacturing. When targeting larger criminal operations, however, it is not uncommon for federal and state officials to utilize both state laws and the CSA in pursuing criminal charges against high profile drug operations.

Another distinction between state and federal drug laws is the increasing trend toward state legalization of medical marijuana and general marijuana use. In recent years, several states have made the decision to decriminalize these offenses, or lesser versions of these offenses (such as simple possession). Federal laws have not yet followed suit on this issue and there remains some tension between state and federal enforcement objectives.

Drug Sentencing Laws

Individuals convicted of federal drug crimes are subject to sentencing under a scheme of federal mandatory minimum sentencing laws. These laws can dictate a defendant's sentence based on the type and amount of drug in the defendant's possession, as well as any prior convictions that a defendant may have. They severely limit the ability of a judge to make discretionary decisions based on the context in which the crime occurred or the background of the defendant. As a result, these federal mandatory minimums have resulted in lengthy sentences for many drug criminals and have been criticized for contributing to prison overcrowding. For this reason, they remain a topic of considerable debate.

Etymology

In English, the noun "drug" is thought to originate from Old French "drogue", possibly deriving later into "droge-vate" from Middle Dutch meaning "dry barrels", referring to medicinal plants preserved in them. The transitive verb «to drug» (meaning intentionally administer a substance to someone, often without their knowledge) arose later and invokes the psychoactive rather than medicinal properties of a substance.

Medication

A medication or medicine is a drug taken to cure or ameliorate any symptoms of an illness or medical condition. The use may also be as preventive medicine that has future benefits but does not treat any existing or pre-existing diseases or symptoms. Dispensing of medication is often regulated by governments into three categories—over-the-counter medications, which are available in pharmacies and supermarkets without special restrictions; behind-the-counter medicines, which are dispensed by a pharmacist without needing a doctor›s prescription, and prescription only medicines, which must be prescribed by a licensed medical professional, usually a physician.

In the United Kingdom, behind-the-counter medicines are called pharmacy medicines which can only be sold in registered pharmacies, by or under the supervision of a pharmacist. These medications are designated by the letter P on the label. The range of medicines available without a prescription varies from country to country. Medications are typically produced by pharmaceutical companies and are often patented to give the developer exclusive rights to produce them. Those that are not patented (or with expired patents) are called generic drugs since they can be produced by other companies without restrictions or licenses from the patent holder.

Pharmaceutical drugs are usually categorised into drug classes. A group of drugs will share a similar chemical structure, or have the same mechanism of action, the same related mode of action or target the same illness or related illnesses. The Anatomical Therapeutic Chemical Classification System (ATC), the most widely used drug classification system, assigns drugs a unique ATC code, which is an alphanumeric code that assigns it to specific drug classes within the ATC system. Another major classification system is the Biopharmaceutics Classification System. This groups drugs according to their solubility and permeability or absorption properties.Lifestyle drug

Lifestyle drug is an imprecise term commonly applied to medications which treat non–life-threatening and non-painful conditions such as baldness, wrinkles, erectile dysfunction, or acne, which the speaker perceives as either not medical problems at all or as minor medical conditions relative to others. It is sometimes intended as a pejorative, bearing the implication that the scarce medical research resources allocated to develop such drugs were spent frivolously when they could have been better spent researching cures for more serious medical conditions. Proponents, however, point out that improving the patient's subjective quality of life has always been a primary concern of medicine, and argue that these drugs are doing just that. It finds broad use in both media and scholarly journals.

Concept and impact on society

There is direct impact of lifestyle drugs on society, particularly in the developing world. Implications associated with labeling of indications and products sales of these lifestyle drugs may be varied. Drugs can, over time, switch from 'lifestyle' to 'mainstream' use.

Bioethics and medical policy debate

Though no precise widely accepted definition or criteria are associated with the term, there is much debate within the fields of pharmacology and bioethics around the propriety of developing such drugs, particularly after the commercial debut of Viagra.

The German government's health insurance scheme has denied insurance coverage for some Lebensstildroge («lifestyle drugs») which they deem spurious.

Critics of pharmaceutical firms claim that pharmaceutical firms actively medicalize; that is, they invent novel disorders and diseases which were not recognized as such before their «cures» could be profitably marketed, in effect pathologizing what were widely regarded as normal conditions of human existence. The consequences are said to include generally greater worries about health, misallocation of limited medical research resources to comparatively minor conditions while many serious diseases remain uncured, and needless health care expenditure. This medicalization of some element of human condition has significance, in principle, as a matter for political discourse or dialogue in civil societyconcerning values or morals.

Social critics also question the propriety of devoting huge research budgets towards creating these drugs when far more dangerous diseases like cancer and AIDS remain uncured. It is sometimes claimed that lifestyle drugs amount to little more than medically sanctioned recreational drug use.

Spiritual and religious use

Some religions, particularly ethnic religions are based completely on the use of certain drugs, known as entheogens, which are mostly hallucinogens,—psychedelics, dissociatives, or deliriants. Some drugs used as entheogens include kava which can act as a stimulant, a sedative, a euphoriant and an anesthetic. The roots of the kava plant are used to produce a drink which is consumed throughout the cultures of the Pacific Ocean.

Some shamans from different cultures use entheogens, defined as «generating the divine within»to achieve religious ecstasy. Amazonian shamans use ayahuasca (yagé) a hallucinogenic brew for this purpose. Mazatec shamans have a long and continuous tradition of religious use of Salvia divinorum a psychoactive plant. Its use is to facilitate visionary states of consciousness during spiritual healing sessions.

Silene undulata is regarded by the Xhosa people as a sacred plant and used as an entheogen. Its root is traditionally used to induce vivid (and according to the Xhosa, prophetic) lucid dreams during the initiation process of shamans, classifying it a naturally occurring oneirogen similar to the more well-known dream herb Calea ternifolia.

Peyote a small spineless cactus has been a major source of psychedelic mescaline and has probably been used by Native Americans for at least five thousand years. Most mescaline is now obtained from a few species of columnar cacti in particular from San Pedro and not from the vulnerable peyote.

The entheogenic use of cannabis has also been widely practised for centuries. Rastafari use marijuana (ganja) as a sacrament in their religious ceremonies.

Psychedelic mushrooms (psilocybin mushrooms), commonly called magic mushrooms or shrooms have also long been used as entheogens.

Smart drugs and designer drugs

Nootropics, also commonly referred to as "smart drugs", are drugs that are claimed to improve human cognitive abilities. Nootropics are used to improve memory, concentration, thought, mood, and learning. An increasingly used nootropic among students, also known as a study drug, is methylphenidate branded commonly as Ritalin and used for the treatment of attention deficit hyperactivity disorder (ADHD) and narcolepsy. At high doses methylphenidate can become highly addictive. Serious addiction can lead to psychosis, anxiety and heart problems, and the use of this drug is related to a rise in suicides, and overdoses. Evidence for use outside of student settings is limited but suggests that that it is commonplace. Intravenous use of methylphenidate can lead to emphysematous damage to the lungs, known as Ritalin lung.

Some nootropics are also now beginning to be used to treat medical conditions such as Parkinson's disease, and Alzheimer's disease. They are also commonly used to regain brain function lost during aging.

Other drugs known as designer drugs are produced. An early example of what today would be labelled a ‹designer drug› was LSD, which was synthesised from ergot. Other examples include analogs of performance-enhancing drugs such as designer steroids taken to improve physical capabilities and these are sometimes used (legally or not) for this purpose, often by professional athletes. Other designer drugs mimic the effects of psychoactive drugs. Since the late 1990s there has been the identification of many of these synthesised drugs. In Japan and the United Kingdom this has spurred the addition of many designer drugs into a newer class of controlled substances known as a temporary class drug.

Synthetic cannabinoids have been produced for a longer period of time and are used in the designer drug synthetic cannabis.

Recreational drug use

Recreational drug use is the use of a drug (legal, controlled, or illegal) with the primary intention of altering the state of consciousnessthrough alteration of the central nervous system in order to create positive emotions and feelings. The hallucinogen LSD is a psychoactive drug commonly used as a recreational drug.

Some national laws prohibit the use of different recreational drugs; and medicinal drugs that have the potential for recreational use are often heavily regulated. However, there are many recreational drugs that are legal in many jurisdictions and widely culturally accepted. Cannabis is the most commonly consumed controlled recreational drug in the world (as of 2012). Its use in many countries is illegal but is legally usedin several countries usually with the proviso that it can only be used for personal use. It can be used in the leaf form of marijuana (grass), or in the resin form of hashish. Marijuana is a more mild form of cannabis than hashish.

There may be an age restriction on the consumption and purchase of legal recreational drugs. Some recreational drugs that are legal and accepted in many places include alcohol, tobacco, betel nut, and caffeine products, and in some areas of the world the legal use of drugs such as khat is common.

There are a number of legal intoxicants commonly called legal highs that are used recreationally. The most widely used of these is alcohol.

Administration of drugs

All drugs, can be administered via a number of routes, and many can be administered by more than one.

Bolus is the administration of a medication, drug or other compound that is given to raise its concentration in blood to an effective level. The administration can be given intravenously, by intramuscular, intrathecal or subcutaneous injection.

Inhaled, (breathed into the lungs), as an aerosol or dry powder. (This includes smoking a substance)

Injection as a solution, suspension or emulsion either: intramuscular, intravenous, intraperitoneal, intraosseous.

Insufflation, or snorted into the nose.

Orally, as a liquid or solid, that is absorbed through the intestines.

Rectally as a suppository, that is absorbed by the rectum or colon.

Sublingually, diffusing into the blood through tissues under the tongue.

Topically, usually as a cream or ointment. A drug administered in this manner may be given to act locally or systemically.

Vaginally as a pessary, primarily to treat vaginal infections.

Control of drugs

There are numerous governmental offices in many countries that deal with the control and oversee of drug manufacture and use, and the implementation of various drug laws. The Single Convention on Narcotic Drugs is an international treaty brought about in 1961 to prohibit the use of narcotics save for those used in medical research and treatment. In 1971, a second treaty the Convention on Psychotropic Substances had to be introduced to deal with newer recreational psychoactive and psychedelic drugs.

The legal status of Salvia divinorum varies in many countries and even in states within the United States. Where it is legislated against the degree of prohibition also varies.

The Food and Drug Administration (FDA) in the United States is a federal agency responsible for protecting and promoting public health through the regulation and supervision of food safety, tobacco products, dietary supplements, prescription and over-the-counter medications, vaccines, biopharmaceuticals, blood transfusions, medical devices, electromagnetic radiation emitting devices, cosmetics, animal foods and veterinary drugs.

2

The Impact of Drugs on Society

The negative consequences of drug abuse affect not only individuals who abuse drugs but also their families and friends, various businesses, and government resources. Although many of these effects cannot be quantified, ONDCP recently reported that in 2002, the economic cost of drug abuse to the United States was $180.9 billion.

The most obvious effects of drug abuse--which are manifested in the individuals who abuse drugs--include ill health, sickness and, ultimately, death. Particularly devastating to an abuser's health is the contraction of needle borne illnesses including hepatitis and HIV/AIDS through injection drug use. NSDUH data indicate that in 2004 over 3.5 million individuals aged 18 and older admitted to having injected an illicit drug during their lifetime. Of these individuals, 14 percent (498,000) were under the age of 25. Centers for Disease Control and Prevention (CDC) reports that 123,235 adults living with AIDS in the United States in 2003 contracted the disease from injection drug use, and the survival rate for those persons is less than that for persons who contract AIDS from any other mode of transmission. CDC further reports that more than 25,000 people died in 2003 from drug-induced effects.

Children of individuals who abuse drugs often are abused or neglected as a result of the individuals' preoccupation with drugs. National-level studies have shown that parents who abuse drugs often put their need to obtain and abuse drugs before the health and welfare of their children. NSDUH data collected during 2002 and 2003 indicate that 4.3 percent of pregnant women aged 15 to 44 report having used illicit drugs in the past month. Moreover, that same data show that 8.5 percent of new mothers report having used illicit drugs in the past month. Children whose parents and other family members abuse drugs often are physically or emotionally abused and often lack proper immunizations, medical care, dental care, and necessities such as food, water, and shelter.

The risk to children is even greater when their parents or guardians manufacture illicit drugs such as methamphetamine. Methamphetamine abusers often produce the drug in their own homes and apartments, using hazardous chemicals such as hydriodic acid, iodine, and anhydrous ammonia. Children who inhabit such homes often inhale dangerous chemical fumes and gases or ingest toxic chemicals or illicit drugs. These children commonly test positive for methamphetamine and suffer from both short- and long-term health consequences. Moreover, because many methamphetamine producers also abuse the drug, children commonly suffer from neglect that leads to psychological and developmental problems. NCLSS data show that U.S. law enforcement agencies report having seized 9,895 illicit methamphetamine laboratories in 2004. These agencies report that 2,474 children were affected by these laboratories (i.e., they were exposed to chemicals, they resided at laboratory sites, or they were displaced from their homes), while 12 children were injured and 3 children were killed.

The economic impact of drug abuse on businesses whose employees abuse drugs can be significant. While many drug abusers are unable to attain or hold full-time employment, those who do work put others at risk, particularly when employed in positions where even a minor degree of impairment could be catastrophic; airline pilots, air traffic controllers, train operators, and bus drivers are just a few examples. Quest Diagnostics, a nationwide firm that conducts employee drug tests for employers, reports that 5.7 percent of the drug tests they conducted on individuals involved in an employment-related accident in 2004 were positive. Economically, businesses often are affected because employees who abuse drugs sometimes steal cash or supplies, equipment, and products that can be sold to get money to buy drugs. Moreover, absenteeism, lost productivity, and increased use of medical and insurance benefits by employees who abuse drugs affect a business financially.

The economic consequences of drug abuse severely burden federal, state, and local government resources and, ultimately, the taxpayer. This effect is most evident with methamphetamine. Clandestine methamphetamine laboratories jeopardize the safety of citizens and adversely affect the environment. Children, law enforcement personnel, emergency responders, and those who live at or near methamphetamine production sites have been seriously injured or killed as a result of methamphetamine production. Methamphetamine users often require extensive medical treatment; some abuse, neglect, and abandon their children, adding to social services costs; some also commit a host of other crimes including domestic violence, assault, burglary, and identity theft. Methamphetamine producers tax strained law enforcement resources and budgets as a result of the staggering costs associated with the remediation of laboratory sites. According to DEA, the average cost to clean up a methamphetamine production laboratory is $1,900. Given that an average of 9,777 methamphetamine laboratory seizures were reported to NCLSS each year between 2002 and 2004, the economic impact is obvious. DEA absorbs a significant portion of such costs through a Hazardous Waste Cleanup Program and in 2004 administered over 10,061 state and local clandestine laboratory cleanups and dumpsites at a cost of over $18.6 million. Nonetheless, resources of state and local agencies also are significantly affected. For example, 69 percent of the county officials responding to a 2005 survey by the National Association of Counties report that they had to develop additional training and special protocols for county welfare workers who work with children exposed to methamphetamine. Moreover, the time and manpower involved in investigating and cleaning up clandestine laboratories increase the workload of an already overburdened law enforcement system.

10 Ways Drug Abuse Hurts You and Those Around Youlove you?

Most of us have heard countless times that drug abuse isn't beneficial – the word "abuse" is in the name, after all. But a lot of people don't realize just how dangerous it can be, both to the person using and the people that person loves and cares about.

One of the most effective ways you can work to prevent the dangers of drug abuse is by learning what, exactly, those dangers are so that you can better understand the nature of the problem and share that information with people around you.

Knowing is Half the Battle

To make it easier, we've outlined some of the most common ways drug abuse can be deeply hurtful to you, your community, and the people you love. With this knowledge, you'll be better equipped to protect yourself and your loved ones from danger.

It Hurts You Physically

First and foremost, drug abuse is very literally harmful to your body. Depending on the drug of choice, abuse can lead to lung and cardiovascular disease, stroke, various kinds of cancer, HIV/AIDS, and Hepatitis B and C, to name a few.

Unfortunately, these aren't only consequences that come from long-term use. For example, using just once can result in a fatal overdose, brain damage, and/or infect someone with diseases that will stay with them for the rest of their life.

It Hurts Your Job

No matter the type of drug you take, abusing that drug can have serious consequences when it comes to landing and maintaining a job. In the short term, impaired judgment and lack of sleep from drug use can make you perform poorly the duties you'd otherwise excel at. In the long run, desperation from addiction can lead to stealing, lying, excessive absences, and other undependable behaviors that an employer will find unacceptable.

It Hurts Your Mental Health

In addition to impacting your physical health, drug abuse can also take a serious toll on your mental health. Depression, anxiety, paranoia, hallucinations, delusions, and insomnia can all stem from drug abuse; or, if the person already had mental health problems before using the drug, those problems are often exacerbated by its use. In some cases, these issues can't be reversed once a person discontinues use of the drug.

It Hurts Your Finances

Simply put, drugs cost money. The more you abuse a drug, the more of it you need to get the same effect, and therefore, the more money you need to spend to support the habit. Combined with the aforementioned detriment drug abuse can have when it comes to maintaining a job, persisting with this habit can have serious negative impacts on your financial future.

It Hurts Your Freedom

Difficulty with finances, keeping a job, and mental health problems are all issues that can ultimately land a person in jail. Whether it's by pursuing unlawful means of financial gain, committing crimes due to paranoid delusions, stealing from others to support a habit, or any other of the myriad ways drug abuse can contribute to criminal activity, each of those paths leads to the same place—jail.

It Hurts Your Romantic Relationships

Healthy romantic relationships are built on a foundation of trust. Unfortunately, drug abuse commonly leads people to engage in deceitful behaviors that breach that trust. Dishonesty about money spent on the drug, lying about whereabouts, or not being forthcoming about the use of the drug are some of the ways trust, and ultimately relationships, can be destroyed due to drug abuse.

It Hurts Your Friendships

In addition to the deceit that commonly accompanies drug abuse, detrimental personality changes can arise, too. Having a short temper, lack of patience, decreased interest in others, and self-serving habits are all prevalent behaviors stemming from drug abuse that can negatively impact your friendships.

It Hurts Your Family Relationships

Generally, the more someone abuses drugs, the more their priorities shift toward their drug of choice. For instance, an important family event, such as a wedding or baby shower, will often take a backseat to a person's drug use. Prioritizing a drug over loved ones can very quickly lead to self-alienation and tarnished or broken family relationships.

It Hurts People You Don't Know

Even people with no relationship to the person abusing drugs can be severely impacted by that person's use. Car accidents as a result of driving under the influence, burglary, assault, and other harmful behaviors are much more common among those abusing drugs, and, as such, put innocent bystanders at a much greater risk of being harmed.

It Hurts Your Community

Communities rife with drug use and abuse tend to reflect the problem in negative ways. There are more drug dealers, break-ins, instances of prostitution, and other criminal behaviors that threaten the safety and security of a community.

How Drug Abuse Impacts Families

Those closest to a drug-addicted individual are the hardest hit. Common patterns emerge within families where at least one individual is addicted to drugs. These patterns include high levels of criticism or negativism within households, parental inconsistency, or in the case of parents coping with a drug-addicted child, denial. Misdirected anger between drug addicted and non-addicted family members is common as is self-medication as a strategy in coping with family dysfunction.

Co-dependent relationships often form between partners, where at least one partner is addicted to drugs and the majority of domestic disputes involve the use of alcohol or drugs. Children with one or more parents abusing drugs are more likely to take on the responsibility of the parental role, often functioning in denial of their parents' addiction or behaviors relating to the addiction. These children commonly lack necessities, including shelter, and have little to no health care. Similarly, families with at least one drug-addicted parent are more likely to end up homeless or in poverty, and are less likely to have adequate health care, representing a common barrier in obtaining treatment for the addiction.

Drug or alcohol abuse is the primary cause of more than 75 percent of all foster placements, and 80 percent of all child abuse and neglect cases cite drug or alcohol abuse as a primary factor. Rates of substance abuse among youth in foster care are significantly higher than comparative populations. Specific drug types are associated with higher rates of child custody losses. For example, fewer than 10 percent of babies born to untreated heroin addicted mothers reside their biological mothers at five years of age. And sadly, children of drug addicted individuals are eight times as likely to abuse drugs as adults.

Strain Of Drug Addiction On Employers And Co-Workers

A 2006 study estimated that around 19 million people drink alcohol while at work, just before leaving for work, or go to work with hangover symptoms. This staggering number does not necessarily reflect daily abuse of alcohol at the workplace, but it does suggest a prevalence of accepted use of the intoxicant, despite known risks. Losses in revenue from decreased productivity due to illicit drug use in the workplace totals nearly $200 billion annually.

Co-workers of drug-addicted people take on additional responsibilities at work to accommodate decreases in productivity. They also work longer hours "covering for" drug addicted individuals who fail to show up as scheduled. Someone working while under the influence of drugs and alcohol is at higher risk of workplace related injury, resulting in increased insurance premiums passed on to employers and co-workers.

A loss in productivity affects employers directly, and if drug-use is rampant, can result in loss of the business. Smaller to medium-sized businesses are most at risk of failure resulting from drug related decreases in productivity. Estimates suggest working drug users are a third less productive than their non-drug using co-workers.

Strain On Health Care System

Addiction is a chronic disease in this country. If you add up the annual accumulative costs of treatment for all brain-related diseases and double it; that's nearly the amount spent on addiction each year. Much of the money supporting the medical costs associated with drug addiction is absorbed by hospitals and taxpayers, with approximately 20 percent of Medicaid dollars and $1 in $4 Medicare dollars going to drug-addiction related expenses. The health care burden relating to drug abuse alone exceeds $180 billion annually.

Co-occurring mental disorders commonly precede or are the result of long term drug use and can increase costs associated with care. These costs are passed to the taxpayer and employer through higher insurance premiums and taxation. Coupled with a loss in productivity and lost wages, drug abuse represents an enormous financial burden on society and the economy.

Crime And Drug Addiction

Drug-related incarcerations make up more than 50 percent of federal prison populations and nearly 20 percent of state prison populations. Annual costs averaged across 50 states for state prison populations is greater than $32,000 per inmate, with federal stays averaging more than $26,000 per person, and the average drug-specific crime resulting in prison sentences of between three and nine years. Taxpayers shoulder the burden of $45 billion dollars for state prisons and $144 million for federal prisons annually.

The majority–approximately 80 percent–of incarcerated individuals has or is currently abusing illicit drugs or alcohol. Drug abuse is associated with substantial increases in rates of violent crime. Alcohol is a factor in 40 percent of the nearly 500,000 violent crime arrests made annually. Approximately a quarter of incarcerated individuals said their incarceration related directly to crimes committed to obtain money for drugs. On average, 5 percent of all homicides relate to drug use. Unfortunately, untreated, recidivism rates for drug use following prison release are as high as 95 percent.

On college campuses across the country, 95 percent of violent crimes reported, including sexual assaults, involve the use of alcohol. Violent crimes committed on college campuses can result in health care costs for the victims of these crimes, as well as lost revenue for universities.

How Drug Abuse Affects Society:

Increase in child custody losses
Increase in child abuse and neglect
Increase in addiction risks for children of drug-addicted parents
Increase in domestic disputes

Increased rates of homelessness and poverty
Substantial financial health care burden
Increased rates of co-occurring mental disorders
Increase in insurance premiums, taxes
Increased strain on co-workers
Increase in number of people incarcerated in state and federal prisons
Increase in rates of violent crimes on college campuses
Losses in revenue for businesses and universities

Drug addiction is a complex illness with far-reaching consequences for those who know, work with, and support the drug-addicted individual. Even if you don't know someone who is abusing drugs directly, you are likely impacted in other ways, whether through taxation, paying higher insurance premiums or college tuition, or in picking up hours at work. Drug addiction knows no boundaries.

Different types of drugs affect your body in different ways, and the effects associated with drugs can vary from person to person. How a drug effects an individual is dependent on a variety of factors including body size, general health, the amount and strength of the drug, and whether any other drugs are in the system at the same time. It is important to remember that illegal drugs are not controlled substances, and therefore the quality and strength may differ from one batch to another.

Drugs can have short-term and long-term effects. These effects can be physical and psychological, and can include dependency.

You may act differently, feel differently and think differently if you have taken drugs. And you may struggle to control your actions and thoughts.

You might begin to use drugs without thinking about any harm to your body. You might think drugs won't become a problem because you are only a casual user. The more you take a drug, the more likely you are to build up a tolerance to its effects. This can lead to the need to take larger doses to obtain the effects of the drug. For this reason, evidence suggests that after prolonged use, many drugs can cause dependence. Drug dependence can quickly begin to affect your psychological and physical health, and can also affect your work and social life.

It is important to remember that there is no safe level of drug use. Be careful when taking any kind of drug.

Different drugs, different effects

Drugs affect your body's central nervous system. They affect how you think, feel and behave. The three main types are depressants, hallucinogens and stimulants:

- Depressants slow or ‹depress› the function of the central nervous system. They slow the messages going to and from your brain. In small quantities depressants can cause a person to feel relaxed and less inhibited. In large amounts they may cause vomiting, unconsciousness and death. Depressants affect your concentration and coordination, and slow your ability to respond to situations. It is important to not operate heavy machinery while taking depressants. Alcohol, cannabis, GHB, opiates (heroin, morphine, codeine) and benzodiazepines (minor tranquillisers) are examples of depressants.

- Hallucinogens distort your sense of reality. You may see or hear things that are not really there, or see things in a distorted way. Other effects can include emotional and psychological euphoria, jaw clenching, panic, paranoia, gastric upset and nausea. Ketamine, LSD, PCP, ‹magic mushrooms› and cannabis are examples of hallucinogens.
- Stimulants speed or ‹stimulate› the central nervous system. They speed up messaging to and from the brain, making you feel more alert and confident. This can cause increased heart rate, blood pressure and body temperature, reduced appetite, agitation and sleeplessness. In large amounts stimulants may cause anxiety, panic, seizures, stomach cramps and paranoia. Caffeine, nicotine, amphetamines (speed and Ice), cocaine and ecstasy (MDMA) are examples of stimulants.

Risk factors for drug-related harm

The effects of a drug, and how long they last, depend on a number of factors:

- the type and strength of drugs that you use
- how the drug was made -- substances manufactured in home labs may contain bacteria, dangerous chemicals and other unsafe substances, and have an unknown strength. Even one dose may cause an overdose that leads to brain damage or death
- your physical characteristics (including height, weight, age, body fat and metabolism)
- the dose that you take
- how often and for how long you have been using drugs
- how you ingest the drug (by inhalation, by injection or orally). Compared with swallowing a drug, inhalation and injection are more likely to lead to overdose and dependence. If you are injecting drugs, sharing injecting equipment will increase your risk of contracting serious diseases such as hepatitis and HIV. It will also increase your risk of serious infection
- your mental health, mood and environment (that is, whether you are in a secure, happy place or an unsafe place) can affect the experience you have when taking drugs. If you have a mental health condition, drugs may exacerbate or complicate the symptoms of that condition
- whether you mix drugs, including alcohol. In particular, alcohol use may lead to high risk behaviour (such as drink driving) which can result in the serious injury or death of yourself or others

Physical harms from drug use

Drug use can affect short- and long-term health outcomes. Some of these health outcomes can be serious, and possibly irreversible.

Drug use can lead to risky or out of character behaviour. When affected by drugs:

- You are more likely to have an accident (at home, in a car, or wherever you are).
- You may be vulnerable to sexual assault or you may engage in unprotected sex. Either of these could lead to pregnancy and sexually transmitted infection.
- You could commit a sexual assault or other violent act.
- You may find it hard to sleep, think, reason, remember and solve problems.

Drug use can also result in long-term health outcomes that include:

- harm to organs and systems in your body, such as your throat, stomach, lungs, liver, pancreas, heart, brain, nervous system
- cancer (such as lung cancer from inhaling drugs)
- infectious disease, from shared injecting equipment and increased incidence of risk-taking behaviors
- harm to your baby, if you are pregnant
- acne, or skin lesions if the drug you are taking causes you to pick or scratch at your skin
- needle marks and collapsed veins, if you inject regularly
- baldness
- male pattern hair growth in women, such as facial hair
- jaw and teeth issues due to clenching and grinding your teeth; or bad breath, teeth cavities and gum disease
- mood swings and erratic behavior
- addiction
- psychosis (losing touch with reality)
- accidental overdose
- higher risk of mental illness, depression, suicide and death.

Effects of common drugs

Cannabis (hash, pot, dope, weed, grass, skunk, marijuana):

- may cause relaxation and altered perception
- can lead to increased heart rate and low blood pressure
- can make you feel relaxed and happy, but can also cause lethargy, anxiety, paranoia, and psychosis in extreme cases. A history or family history of mental illness may increase the possibility of more extreme psychotic reactions
- is linked to mental health problems such as schizophrenia and, when smoked, to lung diseases such as asthma, chronic bronchitis and lung, throat, mouth and tongue cancer
- affects how your brain works. Regular use can make it hard for you to

concentrate, learn and retain information

- reduces your fertility
- when mixed with tobacco, is likely to increase the risk of heart disease and lung cancer.

Cocaine (powder cocaine, coke, blow, Charlie, crack):

- gives you increased energy
- makes you feel happy, awake, confident and less inhibited, but has a nasty 'come down' that makes you feel depressed and unwell. (Using depressant drugs to help with the severity of come downs can increase the chances of the development of negative cycles of dependence.)
- can overstimulate the heart and nervous system and lead to a seizure, brain haemorrhage, stroke or heart attack (people have died from cocaine-induced heart failure)
- reduces your pain perception and may result in injury
- carries greater risk if mixed with alcohol or other stimulants, especially if you have high blood pressure or if you have an existing heart condition
- can harm your baby during pregnancy, and may cause miscarriage
- can increase the risk of mental health issues such a s anxiety, paranoia and psychosis
- if snorted, can cause damage to the lining of the nasal passage and nose
- if injected, can cause vein collapse and increased risk of HIV and hepatitis infection.

Mephedrone (meow meow, m-cat, plant food, bubble, meph):

- can induce feelings of happiness, euphoria and confidence, but can also cause anxiety and paranoia
- causes vomiting, sweating and headaches in some users
- can overstimulate your heart and nervous system
- can cause periods of insomnia
- can lead to fits and agitated and hallucinatory states
- if used in large amounts, can cause tingling of the hands and feet, seizure and respiratory failure
- has been linked to a number of deaths
- if injected, can cause vein collapse and increases the risk of HIV and hepatitis infection.

Ecstasy (MDMA, pills, E, eckies):

- can make you feel alert, warm and chatty
- can make sounds and colours seem more intense
- may cause anxiety, confusion, paranoia and even psychosis
- is linked (in cases of long-term use) to memory loss, depression and anxiety

- can lead to overheating and dehydration
- tends to stop your body producing enough urine, so your body retains fluid.

Speed (amphetamine, billy, whizz):

- can make you feel alert, confident and energetic
- can reduce appetite
- may make you agitated and aggressive
- may cause confusion, paranoia and even psychosis
- can make you very depressed and lethargic for hours or days, when used a lot
- can cause high blood pressure and heart attacks
- is more risky if mixed with alcohol, or if you have blood pressure or heart problems
- puts you at risk of overdose, vein and tissue damage, and infectious disease (such as hepatitis C and HIV), if you inject speed.

Ice (crystal meth, shabu, crystal, glass, shard, P):

- may create feelings of pleasure and confidence
- can make you feel alert and energetic
- can cause you to repeat simple things like itching and scratching
- can cause enlarged or dilated pupils and a dry mouth
- may make you grind your teeth
- can cause excessive sweat
- can increase your heart rate and breathing
- may reduce your appetite
- may increase your sex drive
- puts you at risk of infectious diseases (such as hepatitis B, hepatitis C and HIV) if you inject it
- can damage your nasal passages and cause nose bleeds if you snort it.

Effects of a 'come down'

A 'come down' is your body's reaction to the substances that you have taken, after the initial reaction. In other words, it is the after effect.

How long it lasts, and how bad it is, depends on the type of drug (stimulant or depressant) and your age, sex and tolerance.

Common after effects are flatness, depression and exhaustion. Or you may feel:

- shaky, dizzy, sweaty
- headachey
- nauseous
- fatigued
- not hungry
- sleepy or unable to sleep.

3

Narcotic Drugs

The term narcotic from ancient Greek narkō, "to make numb") originally referred medically to any psychoactivecompound with sleep-inducing properties. In the United States, it has since become associated with opiates and opioids, commonly morphine and heroin, as well as derivatives of many of the compounds found within raw opium latex. The primary three are morphine, codeine, and thebaine (while thebaine itself is only very mildly psychoactive, it is a crucial precursor in the vast majority of semi-synthetic opioids, such as oxycodone).

Legally speaking, the term "narcotic" is imprecisely defined and typically has negative connotations. When used in a legal context in the U.S., a narcotic drug is one that is totally prohibited, such as heroin, or one that is used in violation of governmental regulation.

In the medical community, the term is more precisely defined and generally does not carry the same negative connotations.

Statutory classification of a drug as a narcotic often increases the penalties for violation of drug control statutes. For example, although federal law classifies both cocaine and amphetamines as «Schedule II» drugs, the penalty for possession of cocaine is greater than the penalty for possession of amphetamines because cocaine, unlike amphetamines, is classified as a narcotic.

Opioid

Opioids are substances that act on opioid receptors to produce morphine-like effects. Medically they are primarily used for pain relief, including anesthesia. Other medical uses include suppression of diarrhea, replacement therapy for opioid use disorder, reversing opioid overdose, suppressing cough, suppressing opioid-induced constipation, as well as for executions in the United States. Extremely potent opioids such as carfentanil are only approved for veterinary use. Opioids are also frequently used non-medically for their euphoric effects or to prevent withdrawal.

Side effects of opioids may include itchiness, sedation, nausea, respiratory depression, constipation, and euphoria. Long-term use can cause tolerance, meaning that increased doses are required to achieve the same effect, and physical dependence, meaning that abruptly discontinuing the drug leads to unpleasant withdrawal symptoms. The euphoria attracts recreational use and frequent, escalating recreational use of opioids typically results in addiction. An overdose or concurrent use with other depressant drugs like benzodiazepines commonly results in death from respiratory depression.

Opioids act by binding to opioid receptors, which are found principally in the central and peripheral nervous system and the gastrointestinal tract. These receptors mediate both the psychoactive and the somatic effects of opioids. Opioid drugs include partial agonists, like the anti-diarrhea drug loperamide and antagonists like naloxegol for opioid-induced constipation, which do not cross the blood-brain barrier, but can displace other opioids from binding to those receptors.

Because opioids are addictive and may result in fatal overdose, most are controlled substances. In 2013, between 28 and 38 million people used opioids illicitly (0.6% to 0.8% of the global population between the ages of 15 and 65). In 2011, an estimated 4 million people in the United States used opioids recreationally or were dependent on them. As of 2015, increased rates of recreational use and addiction are attributed to over-prescription of opioid medications and inexpensive illicit heroin. Conversely, fears about over-prescribing, exaggerated side effects and addiction from opioids are similarly blamed for under-treatment of pain.

Terminology

Opioids include opiates, an older term that refers to such drugs derived from opium, including morphine itself. Other opioids are semi-synthetic and synthetic drugs such as hydrocodone, oxycodone and fentanyl; antagonist drugs such as naloxone; and endogenous peptides such as the endorphins. The terms opiate and narcotic are sometimes encountered as synonyms for opioid. Opiate is properly limited to the natural alkaloids found in the resin of the opium poppy although some include semi-synthetic derivatives.Narcotic, derived from words meaning 'numbness' or 'sleep', as an American legal term, refers to cocaine and opioids, and their source materials; it is also loosely applied to any illegal or controlled psychoactive drug. In some jurisdictions all controlled drugs are legally classified as narcotics. The term can have pejorative connotations and its use is generally discouraged where that is the case.

Medical uses

Pain

The weak opioid codeine, in low doses and combined with one or more other drugs, is commonly available without a prescription and can be used to treat mild pain. Other opioids are usually reserved for the relief of moderate to severe pain.

Acute pain

Opioids are effective for the treatment of acute pain (such as pain following surgery). For immediate relief of moderate to severe acute pain opioids are frequently the treatment of choice due to their rapid onset, efficacy and reduced risk of dependence. However a new report showed a clear risk of prolonged opioid use when opioid analgesics are initiated for an acute pain management following surgery or trauma. They have also been found to be important in palliative care to help with the severe, chronic, disabling pain that may occur in some terminal conditions such as cancer, and degenerative conditions such as rheumatoid arthritis. In many cases opioids are a successful long-term care strategy for those with chronic cancer pain.

Chronic non-cancer pain

Guidelines have suggested that the risk of opioids is likely greater than their benefits when used for most non-cancer chronic conditions including headaches, back pain, and fibromyalgia. Thus they should be used cautiously in chronic non-cancer pain. If used the benefits and harms should be reassessed at least every three months.

In treating chronic pain, opioids are an option to be tried after other less risky pain relievers have been considered, including paracetamol/ acetaminophen or NSAIDs like ibuprofen or naproxen. Some types of chronic pain, including the pain caused by fibromyalgia or migraine, are preferentially treated with drugs other than opioids. The efficacy of using opioids to lessen chronic neuropathic pain is uncertain.

Opioids are contraindicated as a first-line treatment for headache because they impair alertness, bring risk of dependence, and increase the risk that episodic headaches will become chronic. Opioids can also cause heightened sensitivity to headache pain. When other treatments fail or are unavailable, opioids may be appropriate for treating headache if the patient can be monitored to prevent the development of chronic headache.

Opioids are being used more frequently in the management of non-malignant chronic pain. This practice has now led to a new and growing problem with addiction and misuse of opioids. Because of various negative effects the use of opioids for long-term management of chronic pain is not indicated unless other less risky pain relievers have been found ineffective. Chronic pain which occurs only periodically, such as that from nerve pain, migraines, and fibromyalgia, frequently is better treated with medications other than opioids. Paracetamol and nonsteroidal anti-inflammatory drugs including ibuprofen and naproxen are considered safer alternatives. They are frequently used combined with opioids, such as paracetamol combined with oxycodone (Percocet) and ibuprofen combined with hydrocodone (Vicoprofen), which boosts the pain relief but is also intended to deter recreational use.

Cough

Codeine was once viewed as the «gold standard» in cough suppressants, but this position is now questioned. Some recent placebo-controlled trials have found that it may be no better than a placebo for some causes including acute cough in children. Thus, it is not recommended for children. Additionally, there is no evidence that hydrocodone is useful in children. Similarly, a 2012 Dutch guideline regarding the treatment of acute cough does not recommend its use. (The opioid analogue dextromethorphan, long claimed to be as effective a cough suppressant as codeine, has similarly demonstrated little benefit in several recent studies.)

Low dose morphine may help chronic cough but its use is limited by side effects.

Diarrhea and constipation

In cases of diarrhea-predominate irritable bowel syndrome, opioids may be used to suppress diarrhea. Loperamide is a peripherally selective opioid available without a prescriptionused to suppress diarrhea.

The ability to suppress diarrhea also produces constipation when opioids are used beyond several weeks. Naloxegol, a peripherally-selective opioid antagonist is now available to treat opioid induced constipation.

Shortness of breath

Opioids may help with shortness of breath particularly in advanced diseases such as cancer and COPD among others.

Adverse effects

In older adults, opioid use is associated with increased adverse effects such as "sedation, nausea, vomiting, constipation, urinary retention, and falls". As a result, older adults taking opioids are at greater risk for injury. Opioids do not cause any specific organ toxicity, unlike many other drugs, such as aspirin and paracetamol. They are not associated with upper gastrointestinal bleeding and kidney toxicity.

Research suggests that when methadone is used long-term it can build up unpredictably in the body and lead to potentially deadly slowed breathing. Used medically, approaching toxicity goes unrecognized because the pain medication effect ends long before the drug›s elimination half-life. According to the USCDC, methadone was involved in 31% of opioid related deaths in the US between 1999-2010 and 40% as the sole drug involved, far higher than other opioids. Studies of long term opioids have found that may stop them and minor side effects were common. Addiction occurred in about 0.3%. In the United States in 2016 opioid overdose resulted in the death of 1.7 in 10,000 people.

Reinforcement disorders

Tolerance

Tolerance is a process characterized by neuroadaptations that result in reduced drug effects. While receptor upregulation may often play an important role other mechanisms are also known. Tolerance is more pronounced for some effects than for others; tolerance occurs slowly to the effects on mood, itching, urinary retention, and respiratory depression, but occurs more quickly to the analgesia and other physical side effects. However, tolerance does not develop to constipation or miosis (the constriction of the pupil of the eye to less than or equal to two millimeters). This idea has been challenged, however, with some authors arguing that tolerance does develop to miosis.

Tolerance to opioids is attenuated by a number of substances, including:

- calcium channel blockers
- intrathecal magnesium and zinc
- NMDA antagonists, such as dextromethorphan, ketamine, and memantine.
- cholecystokinin antagonists, such as proglumide
- Newer agents such as the phosphodiesterase inhibitor ibudilast have also been researched for this application.

Tolerance is a physiologic process where the body adjusts to a medication that is frequently present, usually requiring higher doses of the same medication over time to achieve the same effect. It is a common occurrence in individuals taking high doses of opioids for extended periods, but does not predict any relationship to misuse or addiction.

Physical dependence

Physical dependence is the physiological adaptation of the body to the presence of a substance, in this case opioid medication. It is defined by the development of withdrawal symptoms when the substance is discontinued, when the dose is reduced abruptly or, specifically in the case of opioids, when an antagonist (e.g., naloxone) or an agonist-antagonist (e.g., pentazocine) is administered. Physical dependence is a normal and expected aspect of certain medications and does not necessarily imply that the patient is addicted.

The withdrawal symptoms for opiates may include severe dysphoria, craving for another opiate dose, irritability, sweating, nausea, rhinorrea, tremor, vomiting and myalgia. Slowly reducing the intake of opioids over days and weeks can reduce or eliminate the withdrawal symptoms. The speed and severity of withdrawal depends on the half-life of the opioid; heroin and morphine withdrawal occur more quickly than methadone withdrawal. The acute withdrawal phase is often followed by a protracted phase of depression and insomnia that can last for months. The symptoms of opioid withdrawal can be treated with other medications, such as clonidine. Physical dependence does not predict drug misuse or true addiction, and is closely related to the same mechanism as tolerance. While there is anecdotal claims of benefit with ibogaine, data to support its use in substance dependence is poor.

Addiction

Drug addiction is a complex set of behaviors typically associated with misuse of certain drugs, developing over time and with higher drug dosages.

Addiction includes psychological compulsion, to the extent that the sufferer persists in actions leading to dangerous or unhealthy outcomes. Opioid addiction includes insufflation or injection, rather than taking opioids orally as prescribed for medical reasons.

In European nations such as Austria, Bulgaria, and Slovakia, slow release oral morphine formulations are used in opiate substitution therapy (OST) for patients who do not well tolerate the side effects of buprenorphine or methadone. In other European countries including the UK, this is also legally used for OST although on a varying scale of acceptance.

Tamper-release formulations of time-controlled preparations of medications are intended to curb abuse and addiction rates while trying to still provide legitimate pain relief and ease of use to pain patients. Questions remain, however, about the efficacy and safety of these types of preparations. Further tamper resistant medications are currently under consideration with trials for market approval by the FDA.

The amount of evidence available only permits making a weak conclusion, but it suggests that a physician properly managing opioid use in patients with no history of substance dependence or substance abuse can give long-term pain relief with little risk of developing addiction, abuse, or other serious side effects.

Problems with opioids include the following:

- Some people find that opioids do not relieve all of their pain.
- Some people find that opioids side effects cause problems which outweigh the therapy's benefit
- Some people build tolerance to opioids over time. This requires them to increase their drug dosage to maintain the benefit, and that in turn also increases the unwanted side effects.
- Long-term opioid use can cause opioid-induced hyperalgesia, which is a condition in which the patient has increased sensitivity to pain.

All of the opioids can cause side effects. Common adverse reactions in patients taking opioids for pain relief include nausea and vomiting, drowsiness, itching, dry mouth, dizziness, and constipation.

Nausea and vomiting

Tolerance to nausea occurs within 7–10 days, during which antiemetics (e.g. low dose haloperidol once at night) are very effective Due to severe side effects such as tardive dyskinesia, haloperidol is now rarely used. A related drug, prochlorperazine is more often used, although it has similar risks. Stronger antiemetics such as ondansetron or tropisetron are sometimes used when nausea is severe or continuous and disturbing, despite their greater cost. A less expensive alternative is dopamine antagonists such as domperidone and metoclopramide. Domperidone does not cross the blood–brain barrier and produce adverse central antidopaminergic effects, but blocks opioid emetic action in the chemoreceptor trigger zone. (The drug is not available in the U.S.) Some antihistamines with anticholinergic properties (e.g. orphenadrine or diphenhydramine) may also be effective. The first-generation antihistamine hydroxyzine is very commonly used, with the added advantages of not causing movement disorders, and also possessing analgesic-sparing properties. Δ-tetrahydrocannabinol relieves nausea and vomiting; it also produces analgesia that may allow lower doses of opioids with reduced nausea and vomiting.

- 5-HT antagonists (e.g. ondansetron)
- Dopamine antagonists (e.g. domperidone)
- Anti-cholinergic antihistamines (e.g. diphenhydramine)
- Δ-tetrahydrocannabinol (e.g. dronabinol)

Vomiting is due to gastric stasis (large volume vomiting, brief nausea relieved by vomiting, oesophageal reflux, epigastric fullness, early satiation), besides direct action on the chemoreceptor trigger zone of the area postrema, the vomiting centre of the brain. Vomiting can thus be prevented by prokinetic agents (e.g. domperidone or metoclopramide). If vomiting has already started, these drugs need to be administered by a non-oral route (e.g. subcutaneous for metoclopramide, rectally for domperidone).

- Prokinetic agents (e.g. domperidone)
- Anti-cholinergic agents (e.g. orphenadrine)

Drowsiness

Tolerance to drowsiness usually develops over 5–7 days, but if troublesome, switching to an alternative opioid often helps. Certain opioids such as fentanyl, morphine and diamorphine (heroin) tend to be particularly sedating, while others such as oxycodone, tilidine and meperidine (pethidine) tend to produce comparatively less sedation, but individual patients responses can vary markedly and some degree of trial and error may be needed to find the most suitable drug for a particular patient. Otherwise, treatment with CNSstimulants is generally effective.

- Stimulants (e.g. caffeine, modafinil, amphetamine, methylphenidate)

Itching

Itching tends not to be a severe problem when opioids are used for pain relief, but antihistamines are useful for counteracting itching when it occurs. Non-sedating antihistamines such as fexofenadine are often preferred as they avoid increasing opioid induced drowsiness. However, some sedating antihistamines such as orphenadrine can produce a synergistic pain relieving effect permitting smaller doses of opioids be used. Consequently, several opioid/antihistamine combination products have been marketed, such as Meprozine (meperidine/promethazine) and Diconal (dipipanone/cyclizine), and these may also reduce opioid induced nausea.

- Antihistamines (e.g. fexofenadine)

Constipation

Opioid-induced constipation (OIC) develops in 90 to 95% of people taking opioids long-term. Since tolerance to this problem does not develop readily, most people on long-term opioids need to take a laxative or enemas. While all opioids cause constipation, there are some differences between drugs, with studies suggesting tramadol, tapentadol, methadone and fentanyl may cause relatively less constipation, while with codeine, morphine, oxycodone or hydromorphone constipation may be comparatively more severe. Opioid rotation is commonly used to try and minimise the impact of constipation in long-term users.

Treatment

Treatment of OIC is successional and dependent on severity. The first mode of treatment is non-pharmacological, and includes lifestyle modifications like increasing dietary fiber, fluid intake (around 1.5 L (51 US fl oz) per day), and physical activity. If non-pharmacological measures are ineffective, laxatives, including stool softeners (e.g., docusate), bulk-forming laxatives (e.g., fiber supplements), stimulant laxatives (e.g., bisacodyl, senna), and/or enemas, may be used. A common laxative regimen for OIC is the combination of docusate and bisacodyl. Osmotic laxatives, including lactulose, polyethylene glycol, and milk of magnesia (magnesium hydroxide), as well as mineral oil (a lubricant laxative), are also commonly used for OIC.

If laxatives are insufficiently effective (which is often the case), opioid formulations or regimens that include a peripherally-selective opioid antagonist, such as methylnaltrexone bromide, naloxegol, alvimopan, or naloxone (as in oxycodone/naloxone), may be tried A 2008 Cochrane review found that the evidence was tentative for alvimopan, naloxone, or methylnaltrexone bromide

Respiratory depression

Respiratory depression is the most serious adverse reaction associated with opioid use, but it usually is seen with the use of a single, intravenous dose in an opioid-naïve patient. In patients taking opioids regularly for pain relief, tolerance to respiratory depression occurs rapidly, so that it is not a clinical problem. Several drugs have been developed which can partially block respiratory depression, although the only respiratory stimulant currently approved for this purpose is doxapram, which has only limited efficacy in this application. Newer drugs such as BIMU-8 and CX-546 may be much more effective. Respiratory stimulants: carotid chemoreceptor agonists (e.g. doxapram), 5-HT agonists (e.g. BIMU8), □-opioid agonists (e.g. BW373U86) and AMPAkines (e.g. CX717) can all reduce respiratory depression caused by opioids without affecting analgesia, but most of these drugs are only moderately effective or have side effects which preclude use in humans. 5-HT agonists such as 8-OH-DPAT and repinotan also counteract opioid-induced respiratory depression, but at the same time reduce analgesia, which limits their usefulness for this application.

Opioid antagonists (e.g. naloxone, nalmefene, diprenorphine)

Opioid-induced hyperalgesia

Opioid-induced hyperalgesia – where individuals using opioids to relieve pain paradoxically experience more pain as a result of that medication – has been observed in some people. This phenomenon, although uncommon, is seen in some people receiving palliative care, most often when dose is increased rapidly. If encountered, rotation between several different opioid pain medications may decrease the development of increased pain. Opioid induced hyperalgesia more commonly occurs with chronic use or brief high doses but some research suggests that it may also occur with very low doses.

Side effects such as hyperalgesia and allodynia, sometimes accompanied by a worsening of neuropathic pain, may be consequences of long-term treatment with opioid analgesics, especially when increasing tolerance has resulted in loss of efficacy and consequent progressive dose escalation over time. This appears to largely be a result of actions of opioid drugs at targets other than the three classic opioid receptors, including the nociceptin receptor, sigma receptor and Toll-like receptor 4, and can be counteracted in animal models by antagonists at these targets such as J-113,397, BD-1047 or (+)-naloxone respectively. No drugs are currently approved specifically for counteracting opioid-induced hyperalgesia in humans and in severe cases the only solution may be to discontinue use of opioid analgesics and replace them with non-opioid analgesic drugs. However, since individual sensitivity to the development of this side effect is highly dose dependent and may vary depending which opioid analgesic is used, many patients can avoid this side effect simply through dose reduction of the opioid drug (usually accompanied by the addition of a supplemental non-opioid analgesic), rotating between different opioid drugs, or by switching to a milder opioid with a mixed mode of action that also counteracts neuropathic pain, particularly tramadol or tapentadol NMDA receptor antagonists such as ketamine

- SNRIs such as milnacipran
- Anticonvulsants such as gabapentin or pregabalin

Other adverse effects

Low sex hormone levels

Clinical studies have consistently associated medical and recreational opioid use with hypogonadism (low sex hormone levels) in different sexes. The effect is dose-dependent. Most studies suggest that the majority (perhaps as much as 90%) of chronic opioid users suffer from hypogonadism. Opioids can also interfere with menstruation in women by limiting the production of luteinizing hormone (LH). Opioid-induced hypogonadism likely causes the strong association of opioid use with osteoporosis and bone fracture, due to deficiency in estradiol. It also may increase pain and thereby interfere with the intended clinical effect of opioid treatment. Opioid-induced hypogonadism is likely caused by their agonism of opioid receptors in the hypothalamus and the pituitary gland One study found that the depressed testosterone levels of heroin addicts returned to normal within one month of abstinence, suggesting that the effect is readily reversible and is not permanent. As of 2013, the effect of low-dose or acute opioid use on the endocrine system is unclear Long-term use of opioids can effect the other hormonal systems as well.

Disruption of work

Use of opioids may be a risk factor for failing to return to work.

Persons performing any safety-sensitive task should not use opioids. Health care providers should not recommend that workers who drive or use heavy equipment including cranes or forklifts treat chronic or acute pain with opioids. Workplaces which manage workers who perform safety-sensitive operations should assign workers to less sensitive duties for so long as those workers are treated by their physician with opioids.

People who take opioids long term have increased likelihood of being unemployed. Taking opioids may further disrupt the patient›s life and the adverse effects of opioids themselves can become a significant barrier to patients having an active life, gaining employment, and sustaining a career.

In addition, lack of employment may be a predictor of aberrant use of prescription opioids.

Increased accident-proneness

Opioid use may increase accident-proneness. Opioids may increase risk of traffic accidents and accidental falls.

Rare side effects

Infrequent adverse reactions in patients taking opioids for pain relief include: dose-related respiratory depression (especially with more potent opioids), confusion, hallucinations, delirium, urticaria, hypothermia, bradycardia/tachycardia, orthostatic hypotension, dizziness, headache, urinary retention, ureteric or biliary spasm, muscle rigidity, myoclonus (with high doses), and flushing (due to histamine release, except fentanyl and remifentanil). Both therapeutic and chronic use of opioids can compromise the function of the immune system. Opioids decrease the proliferation of macrophage progenitor cells and lymphocytes, and affect cell differentiation (Roy & Loh, 1996). Opioids may also inhibit leukocytemigration. However the relevance of this in the context of pain relief is not known.

Interactions

Physicians treating patients using opioids in combination with other drugs keep continual documentation that further treatment is indicated and remain aware of opportunities to adjust treatment if the patient's condition changes to merit less risky therapy.

With other depressant drugs

The concurrent use of opioids with other depressant drugs such as benzodiazepines or ethanol increases the rates of adverse events and overdose. As with an overdose of opioid alone, the combination of an opioid and another depressant may precipitate respiratory depression often leading to death. These risks are lessened with close monitoring by a physician, who may conduct ongoing screening for changes in patient behavior and treatment compliance.

Opioid antagonist

Opioid effects (adverse or otherwise) can be reversed with an opioid antagonist such as naloxone or naltrexone.These competitive antagonists bind to the opioid receptors with higher affinity than agonists but do not activate the receptors. This displaces the agonist, attenuating or reversing the agonist effects. However, the elimination half-life of naloxone can be shorter than that of the opioid itself, so repeat dosing or continuous infusion may be required, or a longer acting antagonist such as nalmefene may be used. In patients taking opioids regularly it is essential that the opioid is only partially reversed to avoid a severe and distressing reaction of waking in excruciating pain. This is achieved by not giving a full dose but giving this in small doses until the respiratory rate has improved. An infusion is then started to keep the reversal at that level, while maintaining pain relief. Opioid antagonists remain the standard treatment for respiratory depression following opioid overdose, with naloxone being by far the most commonly used, although the longer acting antagonist nalmefene may be used for treating overdoses of long-acting opioids such as methadone, and diprenorphine is used for reversing the effects of extremely potent opioids used in veterinary medicine such as etorphine and carfentanil. However, since opioid antagonists also block the beneficial effects of opioid analgesics, they are generally useful only for treating overdose, with use of opioid antagonists alongside opioid analgesics to reduce side effects, requiring careful dose titration and often being poorly effective at doses low enough to allow analgesia to be maintained.

Pharmacology

Opioids bind to specific opioid receptors in the nervous system and other tissues. There are three principal classes of opioid receptors, μ, (mu, kappa, and delta), although up to seventeen have been reported, and include theand (Epsilon, Iota, Lambda and Zeta) receptors. Conversely, (Sigma) receptors are no longer considered to be opioid receptors because their activation is not reversed by the opioid inverse-agonist naloxone, they do not exhibit high-affinity binding for classical opioids, and they are stereoselective for dextro-rotatory isomers while the other opioid receptors are stereo-selective for levo-rotatory isomers. In addition, there are three subtypes of μ-receptor: μ and μ, and the newly discovered μ. Another receptor of clinical importance is the opioid-receptor-like receptor 1 (ORL1), which is involved in pain responses as well as having a major role in the development of tolerance to μ-opioid agonists used as analgesics. These are all G-protein coupled receptors acting on GABAergic neurotransmission.

The pharmacodynamic response to an opioid depends upon the receptor to which it binds, its affinity for that receptor, and whether the opioid is an agonist or an antagonist. For example, the supraspinalanalgesic properties of the opioid agonist morphine are mediated by activation of the μ receptor; respiratory depression and physical dependence by the μ receptor; and sedation and spinal analgesia by the receptor. Each group of opioid receptors elicits a distinct set of neurological responses, with the receptor subtypes (such as μ and μ for example) providing even more [measurably] specific responses. Unique to each opioid is its distinct binding affinity to the various classes of opioid receptors (e.g. the μ and opioid receptors are activated at different magnitudes according to the specific receptor binding affinities of the opioid). For example, the opiate alkaloid morphine exhibits high-affinity binding to the μ-opioid receptor, while ketazocine exhibits high affinity to receptors. It is this combinatorial mechanism that allows for such a wide class of opioids and molecular designs to exist, each with its own unique effect profile. Their individual molecular structure is also responsible for their different duration of action, whereby metabolic breakdown (such as N-dealkylation) is responsible for opioid metabolism.

Functional selectivity

A new strategy of drug development takes receptor signal transduction into consideration. This strategy strives to increase the activation of desirable signalling pathways while reducing the impact on undesirable pathways. This differential strategy has been given several names, including functional selectivity and biased agonism. The first opioid that was intentionally designed as a biased agonist and placed into clinical evaluation is the drug oliceridine. It displays analgesic activity and reduced adverse effects.

Opioid comparison

Extensive research has been conducted to determine equivalence ratios comparing the relative potency of opioids. Given a dose of an opioid, an equianalgesic table is used to find the equivalent dosage of another. Such tables are used in opioid rotation practices, and to describe an opioid by comparison to morphine, the reference opioid. Equianalgesic tables typically list drug half-lives, and sometimes equianalgesic doses of the same drug by means of administration, such as morphine: oral and intravenous.

Binding profiles

In the 1990s, opioid prescribing increased significantly. Once used almost exclusively for the treatment of acute pain or pain due to cancer, opioids are now prescribed liberally for people experiencing chronic pain. This has been accompanied by rising rates of accidental addiction and accidental overdoses leading to death. According to the International Narcotics Control Board, the United States and Canada lead the per capita consumption of prescription opioids. The number of opioid prescriptions per capita in the United States and Canada is double the consumption in the European Union, Australia, and New Zealand. Certain populations have been affected by the opioid addiction crisis more than others, including First World communities and low-income populations. Public health specialists say that this may result from unavailability or high cost of alternative methods for addressing chronic pain.

Naturally occurring opioids

Opioids are among the world's oldest known drugs. The earliest known evidence of Papaver somniferum in a human archaeological site dates to the Neolithic period around 5,700-5,500 BC. Its seeds have been found at Cueva de los Murciélagos in the Iberian Peninsula and La Marmotta in the Italian Peninsula.

Use of the opium poppy for medical, recreational, and religious purposes can be traced to the 4th century BC, when ideograms on Sumerians clay tablets mention the use of «Hul Gil», a «plant of joy». Opium was known to the Egyptians, and is mentioned in the Ebers Papyrus as an ingredient in a mixture for the soothing of children, and for the treatment of breast abscesses.

Opium was also known to the Greeks. It was valued by Hippocrates (c.460 – c.370 BC) and his students for its sleep-inducing properties, and used for the treatment of pain. The Latin saying «Sedare dolorem opus divinum est», trans. «Alleviating pain is the work of the divine», has been variously ascribed to Hippocrates and to Galen of Pergamum. The medical use of opium is later discussed by Pedanius Dioscorides (c. 40 – 90 AD), a Greek physician serving in the Roman army, in his five-volume work, De Materia Medica.

During the Islamic Golden Age, the use of opium was discussed in detail by Avicenna (c.980 – June 1037 AD) in The Canon of Medicine. The book's five volumes include information on opium's preparation, an array of physical effects, its use to treat a variety of illness, contraindications for its use, its potential danger as a poison and its potential for addiction. Avicenna discouraged opium's use except as a last resort, preferring to address the causes of pain rather than trying to minimize it with analgesics. Many of Avicenna's observations have been supported by modern medical research.

Exactly when opium became known in India and China is uncertain, but opium was mentioned in the Chinese medical work K'ai-pao-pen-tsdo (973 AD) By 1590 AD, opium poppies were a staple spring crop in the Subahs of Agra, Oudh and Allahabad in what is now Uttar Pradesh.

The physician Paracelsus (ca.1493–1541) is often credited with reintroducing opium into medical use in Western Europe, during the German Renaissance. He extolled opium's benefits for medical use. He also claimed to have an "arcanum", a pill which he called laudanum, that was superior to all others, particularly when death was to be cheated. ("Ich hab' ein Arcanum — heiss' ich Laudanum, ist über das Alles, wo es zum Tode reichen will.") Later writers have asserted that Paracelsus› recipe for laudanum contained opium, but its composition remains unknown.

Laudanum

The term laudanum was used generically for a useful medicine until the 17th century. After Thomas Sydenham introduced the first liquid tincture of opium, «laudanum» came to mean a mixture of both opium and alcohol. Sydenham›s 1669 recipe for laudanum mixed opium with wine, saffron, clove and cinnamon. Sydenham›s laudanum was used widely in both Europe and the Americas until the 20th century. Other popular medicines, based on opium, included Paregoric, a much milder liquid preparation for children; Black-drop, a stronger preparation; and Dover's powder.

The opium trade

Opium became a major colonial commodity, moving legally and illegally through trade networks involving India, the Portuguese, the Dutch, the British and China, among others.The British East India Company saw the opium trade as an investment opportunity in 1683 AD. In 1773 the Governor of Bengal established a monopoly on the production of Bengal opium, on behalf of the East India Company. The cultivation and manufacture of Indian opium was further centralized and controlled through a series of acts, between 1797 and 1949. The British balanced an economic deficit from the importation of Chinese tea by selling Indian opium which was smuggled into China in defiance of Chinese government bans. This led to the First (1839–1842) and Second Opium Wars (1856–1860) between China and Britain.

Morphine

In the 19th century, two major scientific advances were made that had far-reaching effects. Around 1804, German pharmacist Friedrich Sertürner isolated morphine from opium. He described its crystallization, structure, and pharmacological properties in a well-received paper in 1817 Morphine was the first alkaloid to be isolated from any medicinal plant, the beginning of modern scientific drug discovery. The second advance, nearly fifty years later, was the refinement of the hypodermic needle by Alexander Wood and others. Development of a glass syringe with a subcutaneous needle made it possible to easily administer controlled measurable doses of a primary active compound

Morphine was initially hailed as a wonder drug for its ability to ease pain. It could help people sleep, and had other useful side effects, including control of coughing and diarrhea. It was widely prescribed by doctors, and dispensed without restriction by pharmacists. During the American Civil War, opium and laudanum were used extensively to treat soldiers. It was also prescribed frequently for women, for menstrual pain and diseases of a «nervous character». At first it was assumed (wrongly) that this new method of application would not be addictive.

Codeine

Codeine was discovered in 1832 by Pierre Jean Robiquet. Robiquet was reviewing a method for morphine extraction, described by Scottish chemist William Gregory (1803-1838). Processing the residue left from Gregory›s procedure, Robiquet isolated a crystalline substance from the other active components of opium. He wrote of his discovery: «Here is a new substance found in opium ... We know that morphine, which so far has been thought to be the only active principle of opium, does not account for all the effects and for a long time the physiologists are claiming that there is a gap that has to be filled.» His discovery of the alkaloid led to the development of a generation of antitussive and antidiarrheal medicines based on codeine.

Semisynthetic and synthetic opioids

Synthetic opioids were invented, and biological mechanisms for their actions discovered, in the 20th century. Scientists have searched for non-addictive forms of opioids, but have created stronger ones instead. In England Charles Romley Alder Wright developed hundreds of opiate compounds in his search for a nonaddictive opium derivative. In 1874 he became the first person to synthesize diamorphine (heroin), using a process called acetylation which involved boiling morphine with acetic anhydride for several hours.

Heroin received little attention until it was independently synthesized by Felix Hoffmann (1868–1946), working for Heinrich Dreser (1860–1924) at Bayer Laboratories. Dreser brought the new drug to market as an analgesic and a cough treatment for tuberculosis, bronchitis, and asthma in 1898. Bayer ceased production in 1913, after heroin›s addictive potential was recognized Several semi-synthetic opioids were developed in Germany in the 1910s. The first, oxymorphone, was synthesized from thebaine, an opioid alkaloid in opium poppies, in 1914.Next, Martin Freund and Edmund Speyer developed oxycodone, also from thebaine, at the University of Frankfurt in 1916. In 1920, hydrocodone was prepared by Carl Mannichand Helene Löwenheim, deriving it from codeine. In 1924, hydromorphone was synthesized by adding hydrogen to morphine. Etorphine was synthesized in 1960, from the oripavinein opium poppy straw. Buprenorphine was discovered in 1972.

The first fully synthetic opioid was meperidine (later demerol), found serendipitously by German chemist Otto Eisleb (or Eislib) at IG Farben in 1932. Meperidine was the first opiate to have a structure unrelated to morphine, but with opiate-like properties. Its analgesis effects were discovered by Otto Schaumann in 1939. Gustav Ehrhart and Max Bockmühl, also at IG Farben, built on the work of Eisleb and Schaumann. They developed "Hoechst 10820" (later methadone) around 1937. In 1959 the Belgian physician Paul Janssen developed fentanyl, a synthetic drug with 30 to 50 times the potency of heroin. Nearly 150 synthetic opioids are now known.Endorphins

Endorphins (contracted from «endogenous morphine") are endogenous opioid neuropeptides and peptide hormones in humans and other animals. They are produced by the central nervous system and the pituitary gland. The term "endorphins" implies a pharmacological activity (analogous to the activity of the corticosteroid category of biochemicals) as opposed to a specific chemical formulation. It consists of two parts: endo- and -orphin; these are short forms of the words endogenous and morphine, intended to mean "a morphine-like substance originating from within the body". The class of endorphins includes three compounds endorphin (alpha endorphins), □-endorphin (beta endorphins), and endorphin (gamma endorphins)—which preferentially bind to μ-opioid receptors. The principal function of endorphins is to inhibit the communication of pain signals; they may also produce a feeling of euphoria very similar to that produced by other opioids.

History

Opioid neuropeptides were first discovered in 1974 by two independent groups of investigators:

- John Hughes and Hans Kosterlitz of Scotland isolated – from the brain of a pig – what some called «enkephalins" (from the Greek cerebrum).
- Around the same time, in a calf brain, Rabi Simantov and Solomon H. Snyder of the United States found what Eric Simon (who independently discovered opioid receptors in vertebral brains) later termed «endorphin» by an abbreviation of «endogenous morphine», meaning «morphine produced naturally in the body». Studies have demonstrated that human and diverse animal tissues are capable of producing morphine, which is not a peptide. They have been continually researched for their pain relieving properties and role in the feeling of pleasure.

Synthesis

The three types of endorphins that exist are made through the fragmentation of precursor proteins. The original protein is called proopiomelanocortin (POMC). This protein is fragmented into many different smaller proteins including beta-lipotropin (LPH). LPH, a pituitary hormone with little opiate activity, is then continually fragmented into different peptides giving rise to Endorphin, Endorphin, Endorphin and many other peptides.

Types

The class of endorphins includes three endogenous opioid peptides:

- Endorphin – The smallest fragment in the family and is composed of 16 amino acids. They are the same as the first 16 amino acids as the endorphin. The sequenced the protein has been shown to be: Tyr-Gly-Gly-Phe-Met-Thr-Ser-Glu-Lys-Ser-Gln-Thr-Pro-Leu-Val-Thr-OH.
- Endorphin – The longest fragment in the family and is composed of 31 amino acids. The sequence has been shown to be: Tyr-Gly-Gly-Phe-Met-Thr-Ser-Glu-Lys-Ser-Gln-Thr-Pro-Leu-Val-Thr-Leu-Phe-Lys-Asn-Ala-Ile-Ile-Lys-Asn-Ala-Tyr-Lys-Lys-Gly-Glu. .
- Endorphin – The second longest fragment and is composed of 17 amino acids. It also matches the first 17 amino Acids of -endorphin. The sequence has been shown to be: Tyr-Gly-Gly-Phe-Met-Thr-Ser-Glu-Lys-Ser-Gln-Thr-Pro-Leu-Val-Thr-Leu-OH.

Mechanism of action

Endorphins are naturally produced in response to pain. This phenomenon happens in both the Central Nervous System (CNS) and the Peripheral Nervous System (PNS). In the PNS, endorphins, primarily -endorphin, are released from the pituitary gland and bind to μ-receptors. The binding of these two components inhibits the pain signal of the periphery nerves by blocking the neurotransmitter substance P. The mechanism in the CNS is similar but works by blocking a different neurotransmitter. When the endorphin binds to the μ-receptor, it inhibits the release of the neurotransmitter gamma-aminobutyric acid (GABA) which, in turn, increases the production and release of dopamine, the neurotransmitter associated with pleasure.

Their production can also be triggered by various human activities. Vigorous aerobic exercise can stimulate the release of □-endorphin which contributes to a phenomenon known as a "runner's high."

Laughter may also stimulate endorphin production; a 2011 study showed that attendees at a comedy club showed increased resistance to pain. Endorphins are also released during various activities including eating food, sex, orgasm, listening to music and eating chocolate.

Properties

Endorphins play a major role in the body's response to inhibiting pain but endorphins have also been looked at for their role in pleasure. There has been a lot of research in the euphoric state that is produced after the release of endorphins in cases such as runner's high, orgasms, and eating appetizing food. Endorphins have also been looked into as a way to aid in the treatment of anxiety and depression through exercising.

On the other hand, endorphins may also be involved in exercise addiction. The release of endorphins a person gets while exercising will produce a feeling of euphoria. With consistent exercise, the brain may down-regulate the production of endorphins in periods of rest and a person will need to continue to exercise more intensely in order to receive the same feeling.

As a result, health care organizations and public health groups, such as Physicians for Responsible Opioid Prescribing, have called for decreases in the prescription of opioids. In 2016, the Centers for Disease Control and Prevention (CDC) issued a new set of guidelines for the prescription of opioids «for chronic pain outside of active cancer treatment, palliative care, and end-of-life care».

Society and culture

Definition

The term "opioid" originated in the 1950s. It combines «opium» + «-oid» meaning «opiate-like» («opiates» being morphine and similar drugs derived from opium). The first scientific publication to use it, in 1963, included a footnote stating, "In this paper, the term, 'opioid', is used in the sense originally proposed by George H. Acheson (personal communication) to refer to any chemical compound with morphine-like activities". By the late 1960s, research found that opiate effects are mediated by activation of specific molecular receptors in the nervous system, which were termed «opioid receptors». The definition of «opioid» was later refined to refer to substances that have morphine-like activities that are mediated by the activation of opioid receptors. One modern pharmacology textbook states: «the term opioid applies to all agonists and antagonists with morphine-like activity, and also the naturally occurring and synthetic opioid peptides». Another pharmacology reference eliminates the morphine-like requirement: «Opioid, a more modern term, is used to designate all substances, both natural and synthetic, that bind to opioid receptors (including antagonists)». Some sources define the term opioid to exclude opiates, and others use opiatecomprehensively instead of opioid, but opioid used inclusively is considered modern, preferred and is in wide use.

Efforts to reduce abuse in the US

In 2011, the Obama administration released a white paper describing the administration's plan to deal with the opioid crisis. The administration's concerns about addiction and accidental overdosing have been echoed by numerous other medical and government advisory groups around the world. As of 2015, prescription drug monitoring programs exist in every state, except for Missouri. These programs allow pharmacists and prescribers to access patients' prescription histories in order to identify suspicious use. However, a survey of US physicians published in 2015 found that only 53% of doctors used these programs, while 22% were not aware that the programs were available to them. The Centers for Disease Control and Prevention was tasked with establishing and publishing a new guideline, and was heavily lobbied. In 2016, the United States Centers for Disease Control and Prevention published its Guideline for Prescribing Opioids for Chronic Pain, recommending that opioids only be used when benefits for pain and function are expected to outweigh risks, and then used at the lowest effective dosage, with avoidance of concurrent opioid and benzodiazepine use whenever possible. Research suggests that the prescription of high doses of opioids related to chronic opioid therapy (COT) can at times be prevented through state legislative guidelines and efforts by health plans that devote resources and establish shared expectations for reducing higher doses. Research has also suggested that automated algorithms may be able to identify patients who need more intensive screening and/ or intervention for non-medical opioid use; however, there is no standard for determining non-medical opioid use, and few algorithms have yet to be applied to real world settings.

Global shortages

Morphine and other poppy-based medicines have been identified by the World Health Organization as essential in the treatment of severe pain. As of 2002, seven countries (USA, UK, Italy, Australia, France, Spain and Japan) use 77% of the world›s morphine supplies, leaving many emerging countries lacking in pain relief medication. The current system of supply of raw poppy materials to make poppy-based medicines is regulated by the International Narcotics Control Board under the provision of the 1961 Single Convention on Narcotic Drugs. The amount of raw poppy materials that each country can demand annually based on these provisions must correspond to an estimate of the country's needs taken from the national consumption within the preceding two years. In many countries, underprescription of morphine is rampant because of the high prices and the lack of training in the prescription of poppy-based drugs. The World Health Organization is now working with administrations from various countries to train healthworkers and to develop national regulations regarding drug prescription to facilitate a greater prescription of poppy-based medicines.

Another idea to increase morphine availability is proposed by the Senlis Council, who suggest, through their proposal for Afghan Morphine, that Afghanistan could provide cheap pain relief solutions to emerging countries as part of a second-tier system of supply that would complement the current INCB regulated system by maintaining the balance and closed system that it establishes while providing finished product morphine to those suffering from severe pain and unable to access poppy-based drugs under the current system.

Recreational use

Opioids can produce strong feelings of euphoria and are frequently used recreationally. Traditionally associated with illicit opioids such as heroin, prescription opioids are misused recreationally.

Drug misuse and non-medical use include the use of drugs for reasons or at doses other than prescribed. Opioid misuse can also include providing medications to persons for whom it was not prescribed. Such diversion may be treated as crimes, punishable by imprisonment in many countries. In 2014, almost 2 million Americans abused or were dependent on prescription opioids.

Classification

There are a number of broad classes of opioidsNatural opiates: alkaloids contained in the resin of the opium poppy, primarily morphine, codeine, and thebaine, but not papaverine and noscapine which have a different mechanism of action; The following could be considered natural opiates: The leaves from Mitragyna speciosa (also known as kratom) contain a few naturally-occurring opioids, active via Mu- and Delta receptors. Salvinorin A, found naturally in the Salvia divinorum plant, is a kappa-opioid receptor agonist Esters of morphine opiates: slightly chemically altered but more natural than the semi-synthetics, as most are morphine prodrugs, diacetylmorphine (morphine diacetate; heroin), nicomorphine (morphine dinicotinate), dipropanoylmorphine (morphine dipropionate), desomorphine, acetylpropionylmorphine, dibenzoylmorphine, diacetyldihydromorphine;

- Semi-synthetic opioids: created from either the natural opiates or morphine esters, such as hydromorphone, hydrocodone, oxycodone, oxymorphone, ethylmorphine and buprenorphine;
- Fully synthetic opioids: such as fentanyl, pethidine, levorphanol, methadone, tramadol, tapentadol, and dextropropoxyphene;
- Endogenous opioid peptides, produced naturally in the body, such as endorphins, enkephalins, dynorphins, and endomorphins. Morphine, and some other opioids, which are produced in small amounts in the body, are included in this category.

Tramadol and tapentadol, which act as monoamine uptake inhibitors also act as mild and potent agonists (respectively) of the μ-opioid receptor.

Both drugs produce analgesiaeven when naloxone, an opioid antagonist, is administered.

Some minor opium alkaloids and various substances with opioid action are also found elsewhere, including molecules present in kratom, Corydalis, and Salvia divinorum plants and some species of poppy aside from Papaver somniferum. There are also strains which produce copious amounts of thebaine, an important raw material for making many semi-synthetic and synthetic opioids. Of all of the more than 120 poppy species, only two produce morphine.

Amongst analgesics there are a small number of agents which act on the central nervous system but not on the opioid receptor system and therefore have none of the other (narcotic) qualities of opioids although they may produce euphoria by relieving pain—a euphoria that, because of the way it is produced, does not form the basis of habituation, physical dependence, or addiction. Foremost amongst these are nefopam, orphenadrine, and perhaps phenyltoloxamine or some other antihistamines. Tricyclic antidepressantshave painkilling effect as well, but they're thought to do so by indirectly activating the endogenous opioid system. Paracetamol is predominantly a centrally acting analgesic (non-narcotic) which mediates its effect by action on descending serotoninergic (5-hydroxy triptaminergic) pathways, to increase 5-HT release (which inhibits release of pain mediators). It also decreases cyclo-oxygenase activity. It has recently been discovered that most or all of the therapeutic efficacy of paracetamol is due to a metabolite, AM404, which enhances the release of serotonin and inhibits the uptake of anandamide Other analgesics work peripherally (i.e., not on the brain or spinal cord). Research is starting to show that morphine and related drugs may indeed have peripheral effects as well, such as morphine gel working on burns. Recent investigations discovered opioid receptors on peripheral sensory neurons. A significant fraction (up to 60%) of opioid analgesia can be mediated by such peripheral opioid receptors, particularly in inflammatory conditions such as arthritis, traumatic or surgical pain. Inflammatory pain is also blunted by endogenous opioid peptides activating peripheral opioid receptors.

It was discovered in 1953 that humans and some animals naturally produce minute amounts of morphine, codeine, and possibly some of their simpler derivatives like heroin and dihydromorphine, in addition to endogenous opioid peptides. Some bacteria are capable of producing some semi-synthetic opioids such as hydromorphone and hydrocodone when living in a solution containing morphine or codeine respectively.

Many of the alkaloids and other derivatives of the opium poppy are not opioids or narcotics; the best example is the smooth-muscle relaxant papaverine. Noscapine is a marginal case as it does have CNS effects but not necessarily similar to morphine, and it is probably in a category all its own.

Dextromethorphan (the stereoisomer of levomethorphan, a semi-synthetic opioid agonist) and its metabolite dextrorphan have no opioid analgesic effect at all despite their structural similarity to other opioids; instead they are potent NMDA antagonists and sigma 1 and 2-receptor agonists and are used in many over-the-counter cough suppressants.

Salvinorin A is a unique selective, powerful □-opioid receptor agonist. It is not properly considered an opioid nevertheless, because:

- chemically, it is not an alkaloid; and
- it has no typical opioid properties: absolutely no anxiolytic or cough-suppressant effects. It is instead a powerful hallucinogen.

Endogenous opioids

Opioid-peptides that are produced in the body include:

- Endorphins
- Enkephalins
- Dynorphins
- Endomorphins

Endorphin is expressed in Pro-opiomelanocortin (POMC) cells in the arcuate nucleus, in the brainstem and in immune cells, and acts through μ-opioid receptors. endorphin has many effects, including on sexual behavior and appetite. endorphin is also secreted into the circulation from pituitary corticotropes and melanotropes. neo-endorphin is also expressed in POMC cells in the arcuate nucleus.

met-enkephalin is widely distributed in the CNS and in immune cells; [met]-enkephalin is a product of the proenkephalin gene, and acts through μ and opioid receptors. leu-enkephalin, also a product of the proenkephalin gene, acts through opioid receptors.

Dynorphin acts through opioid receptors, and is widely distributed in the CNS, including in the spinal cord and hypothalamus, including in particular the arcuate nucleus and in both oxytocin and vasopressin neurons in the supraoptic nucleus.

Endomorphin acts through μ-opioid receptors, and is more potent than other endogenous opioids at these receptors.

United Nations

Single Convention on Narcotic Drugs, 1961

The adoption of this Convention is regarded as a milestone in the history of international drug ban. The Single Convention codified all existing multilateral treaties on drug control and extended the existing control systems to include the cultivation of plants that were grown as the raw material of narcotic drugs. The principal objectives of the Convention are to limit the possession, use, trade, distribution, import, export, manufacture and production of drugs exclusively to medical and scientific purposes, and to address drug trafficking through international cooperation to deter and discourage drug traffickers. The Convention also established the International Narcotics Control Board, merging the Permanent Central Board and the Drug Supervisory Board.

The 1961 Convention seeks to control more than 116 drugs that it classifies as narcotic. These include:

- plant-based products such as opium and its derivatives morphine, codeine and heroin (the primary category of drug listed in the Convention);
- synthetic narcotics such as methadone and pethidine; and
- cannabis, coca and cocaine.

The Convention divides drugs into four groups, or schedules, in order to enforce a greater or lesser degree of control for the various substances and compounds. Opium smoking and eating, coca leaf chewing, cannabis resin smoking and the non-medical use of cannabis are prohibited. The 1972 Protocol to this Convention calls for increased efforts to prevent illicit production of, traffic in and use of narcotics as defined by the Convention, while highlighting the need to provide treatment and rehabilitation services to drug abusers.

INCB Yellow List

This document contains the current list of narcotic drugs under international control and additional information to assist governments in filling in the International Narcotics Control Board questionnaires related to narcotic drugs, namely, form A, form B and form C.

In medicine, a chemical agent that induces stupor, coma, or insensibility to pain (also called narcotic analgesic).

In the context of international drug control, "narcotic drug" means any drug defined as such under the 1961 Convention.

World Health Organization

Studies on the definition of counterfeit medicines in WHO member states

The nature of legal definitions: the unambiguity requirementIn order to avoid room for difference in interpretation, lawmakers (codificators) sometimes deviate from etymological (definiendum plus definientia) definitions. In doing so, they approach the term from the law enforcement point of view. The best example is the definition of narcotics in the United Nations Conventions. Narcotics are substances and preparations that induce drowsiness, sleep, stupor, insensibility, etc., and that these effects (and their rate) are complicated to prove, e.g. during litigation. Thus, the legal definition of a narcotic is whether or not it is listed on the Schedules of the Convention. If it is on some of the Schedules, it is narcotic.

Lexicon of alcohol and drug terms published by the World Health Organization

The term usually refers to opiates or opioids, which are called narcotic analgesics. In common parlance and legal usage, it is often used imprecisely to mean illicit drugs, irrespective of their pharmacology. For example, narcotics control legislation in Canada, USA, and certain other countries includes cocaine and cannabis as well as opioids (see also conventions, international drug).

Because of this variation in usage, the term is best replaced by one with a more specific meaning (e.g. opioid).United Nations Commission on Narcotic Drugs

The United Nations Commission on Narcotic Drugs is one of the functional commissions of the United Nations Economic and Social Council (ECOSOC) and is the central drug policy-making body within the United Nations system. The Commission has important functions under the drug control treaties in force today; most notably, it can amend the Schedules of controlled substances under the Single Convention on Narcotic Drugs and the Convention on Psychotropic Substances.

The Commission on Narcotic Drugs was established by the ECOSOC in 1946, with Canadian Charles Henry Ludovic Sharman as its first chair. Its predecessor, the Advisory Committee on the Traffic in Opium and Other Dangerous Drugs, was established by the first Assembly of the League of Nations on 15 December 1920. The Advisory Committee held its first meeting from 2-5 May 1921, and continued its activities until 1940.

Powers

The drug control treaties divide power between the Commission and the International Narcotics Control Board. The Commission has power to influence drug control policy by advising other bodies and deciding how various substances will be controlled. However, enforcement power is reserved to the Board.

Under Article 8 of the Single Convention on Narcotic Drugs, the Commission's powers are to:

- Amend the Schedules;
- Call the attention of the International Narcotics Control Board to any matters which may be relevant to the functions of the Board;
- Make recommendations for the implementation of the aims and provisions of the Single Convention, including programmes of scientific research and the exchange of information of a scientific or technical nature; and
- Draw the attention of non-parties to decisions and recommendations which it adopts under the Single Convention, with a view to their considering taking action in accordance therewith.

Under Article 17 of the Convention on Psychotropic Substances, the Commission has power to amend the Schedules by a two-thirds vote and "may consider all matters pertaining to the aims of this Convention and to the implementation of its provisions, and may make recommendations relating thereto."

The United Nations General Assembly has power to modify the Commission›s decisions, with the exception of scheduling decisions.

Role in drug scheduling

The drug control treaties divide drugs into four Schedules with varying levels of control. Article 3 of the Single Convention and Article 2 of the

Convention on Psychotropic Substances set out the scheduling procedure, giving the Commission the power to decide which Schedule a drug or other substance shall be placed into. However, the Economic and Social Council has power to alter or reverse the Commission›s scheduling decisions. In addition, each Schedule has certain findings that the World Health Organization must make with regard to a drug or substance before it be placed in that Schedule. The relationship between the WHO and the Commission is described as follows by the Commentary on the Single Convention on Narcotic Drugs:

The Commission on Narcotic Drugs decides whether a substance is to be placed under international control. It can take a positive decision only in accordance with the recommendation of the World Health Organization. It can include the substance only in that Schedule which is recommended by the Organization. If the World Health Organization recommends Schedule I, the Commission cannot decide to add the substance to Schedule II, or vice versa. The Commission must either accept the Schedule recommended by the World Health Organization or abstain from extending control at all. It may, however, decide to place a drug only in Schedule I and not in Schedule IV if the World Health Organization has recommended simultaneously inclusion in both these Schedules. In no case can the Commission decide to extend control to a substance if the World Health Organization has not recommended to do it.

Article 12 of the United Nations Convention Against Illicit Traffic in Narcotic Drugs and Psychotropic Substances grants the Commission power to decide whether a precursor substance used illicit drug manufacture should be controlled, and if so, which category of controlled precursor substances—Table I or Table II—it should be placed into. The Board›s findings on scientific matters in reference to the substance are binding on the Commission, however. And, as with drug scheduling under the other two treaties, the Convention allows the Economic and Social Council to review and overturn the Commission's decisions in reference to precursor substance control.

Membership and decision making

The Commission consists of 53 states, serving four-year terms, with the following distribution of seats among regions:

- Eleven for African States;
- Eleven for Asian States;
- Ten for Latin American and Caribbean States;
- Six for Eastern European States;
- Fourteen for Western European and other States;
- One seat to rotate between the Asian, and the Latin American and Caribbean States every four years.

Economic and Social Council resolutions 845 (XXXII), and 1147 (XLI) provide that members are elected:

- From among the States Members of the United Nations and members of the specialized agencies and the Parties to the Single Convention on Narcotic Drugs, 1961;

- With due regard to the adequate representation of countries that are important producers of opium or coca leaves, of countries that are important in the field of the manufacture of narcotic drugs, and of countries in which drug addiction or the illicit traffic in narcotic drugs constitutes an important problem;
- Taking into account the principle of equitable geographical distribution.

The Commission is an intergovernmental body made up of states rather than individuals. Decisions are usually taken by consensus, with the exception of decisions on scheduling of drugs, which are taken pursuant to the voting procedures foreseen in its rules of procedure. State representatives engage in this decision making process in accordance with their own policies and laws. For instance, 21 U.S.C. § 811(d)(2)(B) of the U.S. Controlled Substances Act provides that the recommendations of the Secretary of Health and Human Services in reference to drug scheduling shall be binding on the U.S. representative.

Criticism

Being composed of government and ministerial representatives with diplomatic mission in Vienna, the Commission on Narcotic Drugs is regarded more of a political commission as opposed to a group of experts, which is why many discussions and negotiations are not based on in-depth knowledge on drug policy issues. In addition, decisions taken within the CND are primarily outcomes of time-consuming political negotiations which need to result in a consensus, allowing policy perspectives to be pushed aside by political interests of certain stakeholders.

Another aspect of criticism of the CND is related to the bureaucratic nature of the commission's working process. While the CND focuses on the issue of drugs - a multidisciplinary topic which also concerns human rights, health and development - the CND rarely establishes coordination with other relevant UN agencies such as the Joint United Nations Programme on HIV/AIDS (UNAIDS), the Human Rights Council, the Office of the High Commissioner for Human Rights (OHCHR), the World Health Organization, or the United Nations Development Programme.

Equianalgesic

An equianalgesic chart is a conversion chart that lists equivalent doses of analgesics (drugs used to relieve pain). Equianalgesic charts are used for calculation of an equivalent dose (a dose which would offer an equal amount of analgesia) between different analgesics. Tables of this general type are also available for NSAIDs, benzodiazepines, depressants, stimulants, anticholinergics and others as well.

Equianalgesic tables are available in different formats, such as pocket-sized cards for ease of reference. A frequently-seen format has the drug names in the left column, the route of administration in the center columns and any notes in the right column.

Purpose

There are several reasons for switching a patient to a different pain medication. These include practical considerations such as lower cost or unavailability of a drug at the patient's preferred pharmacy, or medical reasons such as lack of effectiveness of the current drug or to minimize adverse effects. Some patients request to be switched to a different narcotic due to stigma associated with a particular drug (e.g. a patient refusing methadone due to its association with opioid addiction treatment). Equianalgesic charts are also used when calculating an equivalent dosage of the same drug, but with a different route of administration.

Precautions

An equianalgesic chart can be a useful tool, but the user must take care to correct for all relevant variables such as route of administration, cross tolerance, half-life and the bioavailability of a drug. For example, the narcotic levorphanol is 4–8 times stronger than morphine, but also has a much longer half-life. Simply switching the patient from 40 mg of morphine to 10 mg of levorphanol would be dangerous due to dose accumulation, and hence frequency of administration should also be taken into account.

There are other concerns about equianalgesic charts. Many charts derive their data from studies conducted on opioid-naïve patients. Patients with chronic (rather than acute) pain may respond to analgesia differently. Repeated administration of a medication is also different from single dosing, as many drugs have active metabolites that can build up in the body. Patient variables such as sex, age, and organ function may also influence the effect of the drug on the system. These variables are rarely included in equianalgesic charts.

Opioid equivalency table

Opioids are a class of compounds that elicit analgesic (pain killing) effects in humans and animals by binding to the μ-opioid receptor within the central nervous system. The following table lists opioid and non-opioid analgesic drugs and their relative potencies. Values for the potencies represent opioids taken orally unless another route of administration is provided. As such, their bioavailabilities differ, and they may be more potent when taken intravenously. Methadone is different from most opioids considering its potency can vary depending on how long it is taken. Acute use, 1–3 days, yields a potency about 1.5× stronger than that of morphine and chronic use (7 days+) yields a potency about 2.5 to 5× that of morphine due to methadone being stored in fat tissue, thus giving higher serum levels with longer use. Similarly, the effect of tramadol increases after consecutive dosing due to the accumulation of its active metabolite and an increase of the oral bioavailability in chronic use; this effect becomes less significant again with even longer use as tolerance develops.

Narcoterrorism

Narcoterrorism is a term coined by former President Fernando Belaúnde Terry of Peru in 1983 when describing terrorist-type attacks against his nation's anti-narcotics police. In its original context, narcoterrorism is understood to mean the attempts of narcotics traffickers to influence the policies of a government or a society through violence and intimidation, and to hinder the enforcement of anti-drug laws by the systematic threat or use of such violence. Pablo Escobar's violence in his dealings with the Colombian government is probably one of the best known and best documented examples of narcoterrorism.

The term has become a subject of controversy, largely due to its use in discussing violent opposition to the US government's War on Drugs.

The term is being increasingly used for known terrorist organizations that engage in drug trafficking activity to fund their operations and gain recruits and expertise. Such organizations include FARC, ELN, AUC in Colombia, PCP-SL in Peru, Hamas and the Taliban.

A 2013 Congressional Research Service report noted that in 2003, the Drug Enforcement Administration (DEA) reported that 14 of 36 (39%) of the groups designated by the U.S. as foreign terrorist organizations «were involved ‹to some degree› in illicit narcotics activity» while in fiscal year 2010, the U.S. Department of Justice (DOJ) «reported that 29 of the top 63 international drug syndicates, identified as such on the consolidated priority organization target (CPOT) list, were associated with terrorists.»

In 2000 the U.S. began funding, continued under the U.S. Bush administration, of Plan Colombia, intending to eradicate drug crops and to act against drug lords accused of engaging in narcoterrorism, including among them the leaders of the marxist FARC and the AUC paramilitary forces. The U.S. government is funding large-scale drug eradication campaigns and supporting Colombian military operations, seeking the extradition of commanders.

Although al-Qaeda is often said to finance its activities through drug trafficking, the 9/11 Commission Report notes that «while the drug trade was a source of income for the Taliban, it did not serve the same purpose for al Qaeda, and there is no reliable evidence that bin Laden was involved in or made his money through drug trafficking.» The organization gains most of its finances through donations, particularly those by «wealthy Saudi individuals».

Anti-Narcotics Force

The Anti-Narcotics Force is a Federal Executive bureau of the Government of Pakistan, tasked with combating the narcotics smuggling and use within Pakistan. ANF works under umbrella of Pakistan Army and Ministry of Narcotcs Control. Due to misconception on Section 4 of ANF ACT 1997, the force's head consisted the active-duty general officer of Pakistan Army. Although the law prescribes that any competent person may be appointed as Director General. Currently a two star Army Officer, Major general Arif Malik HI(M) is deputed as Director General. The ANF also has sole responsibility for co-ordinating and pursuing Pakistan narcotics investigations abroad.

The superintendence of the Force is vest with the Federal Government whereas, administration of the Force is vested with the Director-General who shall exercise in respect of the Force all powers of an Inspector-General of Police under the Police Act, 1861 (V of 1861), and all other powers under the Act. In case of any officers and members from the Armed Forces, the Director-General shall have all powers conferred by or under the Pakistan Army Act, 1952 (XXXIX of 1952), the Pakistan Air Force Act, 1953 (VI op 1953), and the Pakistan Navy Ordinance, 1961 (XXXVI of 1961), respectively as an officer empowered to convene a General Court Martial. The Force consists of approximately 3100 agents across the country.

ANF Setup

Anti Narcotics Force Headquarters is situated at Rawalpindi controlling its outfits through 5x Regional Headquarters i.e. North at Rawalpindi, KP at Peshawar, Punjab at Lahore, Sindh at Karachi and Balochistan at Quetta. Regional Headquarters are controlling their area of domain through their various Police Stations. There are 9x Directorates at HQ ANF:

- Logistics Directorate
- Enforcement Directorate (A, B, and I Branches)
- Law Directorate
- Assets and Financial Investigation Directorate
- Planning & Development Directorate
- International Cooperation Directorate
- Information Technology Directorate
- Drug Demand Reduction Directorate
- General Staff
- Aviation Branch

Association of other Institutions regarding Anti Narcotics and Anti Smuggling

To protect Pakistan's National Security, the Anti Narcotics Force under the insight of Ministry of Narcotics Control, is works in co-ordination with other Law Enforcement Agencies of Pakistan. Such as:

- Pakistan Coast Guards
- Pakistan Customs
- Provincial Excise
- Frontier Corps (KPK and Balochistan)
- Frontier Constabulary
- Pakistan Rangers (Punjab and Sindh)
- Political Levies and Khasadar Force
- Provincial Police (KPK, Punjab, Sindh, GB, AJK and Balochistan)

History

Pakistan Narcotics Board (PNB) was set up in 1957, in the Revenue Division in order to meet Pakistan›s obligations under the International Opium

Convention of 1925. PNB comprised representatives from the Provincial Governments and some Federal Ministries/Divisions.

Pakistan Narcotics Control Board (PNCB) was established in 1973 with five Regional Directorates, in response to UN Convention on Narcotics Control, with the mandate to combat narcotics in the Country. PNCB functioned as an attached department of Ministry of Interior till 1989 with strength of 883 all ranks. Narcotics Control Division (NCD) was established in 1989 and the Board became its attached department.

Anti Narcotics Task Force (ANTF) comprising 388 all ranks from Pakistan Army was established in December 1991 as an attached department of NCD.

Anti Narcotics Force (ANF) was raised on 21 February 1995 by merging PNCB and ANTF.

Narcotics Control Division (NCD) was declared Ministry of Narcotics Control in 2001 but it was reverted to NCD under Ministry of Interior and Narcotics Control (MOI&NC) in 2013.

Ministry of Narcotics Control (MNC) Ministry of Narcotics Control was established in August 2017.

ANF Intelligence and Investigation

There are distinct stages for Investigating a case.

Stages

Assets of the convicts in narcotics cases are confiscated in favour of Federal Government through following stages usually:

- Tracing: Finding out the true sources, disposition, movement or ownership of assets and includes determining the movement or conversion of assets by any means.
- Freezing: Prohibiting by an order made by the Special Court or an officer authorised under CNS Act 1997 the transfer, conversion, disposal or movement of any assets and includes the holding, controlling, assuming custody or managing any assets in pursuance of such order and, in the case of assets which are perishable the disposal thereof
- Forfeiture: Forfeiting of asset /property in favour of Federal Government.
- Realization: On finalisation of forfeiture of assets and execution petition, the assets are realised in favour of Federal Government.

Laws

Assets Investigation is conducted under relevant sections / provisions provided by the following laws:

- Control of Narcotics Substance Act, 1997
- Anti Narcotics Force Act, 1997
- Criminal Procedure Court 1898
- Anti Money Laundering Act, 2010

- Prevention of Smuggling Act, 1977

The Operations

According to activities of smugglers and areas which facilitate their interest, the operations of the Anti Narcotics force can be divided into following two categories:

- Anti Narcotics, Arms and Ammunition
- Anti Explosive Chemicals
- Anti Money Laundering

Narcotics Interdiction Committee

To make the co-ordinating role of the Federal Government effective and to ensure that narcotics interdiction by various law enforcement agencies proceeds under well-synchronized efforts, a Narcotics Interdiction Committee (NIC) has been set up with the following composition:

ANF's Charter of Duty

Supply Reduction

Limiting the smuggling trafficking and distribution of Narcotics. Coordinating eradication of opium poppy. Ensuring no heroin lab becomes functional. Inquire/Investigate assets of drug barons. Pursuing Legal cases relentlessly.

Demand Reduction

Reducing the demand of illicit drugs through preventive education, treatment and rehabilitation as well as harm reduction programmes.

Coordination Liaison at National and International Level

Enhancing international co-operation in the fight against drugs and liaison with the United Nations Office on Drugs and Crime, International Narcotics Control Board, International Police, Narcotics Affairs Section (US Embassy), Drugs Enforcement Agency, Foreign Anti Narcotics Community, Drug Liaison Officers etc.

International Initiatives

To make joint efforts for the control of drug trafficking, the agency in collaboration with Government of Pakistan has signed MoUs with 32 countries and Letters of Intent with 2 x countries. Moreover, 15 x new MoUs and revision for 5 x existing MoUs are also under process. Additionally, specific treaties have been signed with 29 x countries for extradition of convicts on certain offences including drug trafficking. Details of these agreements are as under:

World Anti-Narcotics Day

UNODC observes 26 June as the "INTERNATIONAL DAY AGAINST DRUG ABUSE AND ILLICIT TRAFFICKING", established by the UN General Assembly in 1987. This observance manifests to further escalate UN's resolve in creating a drug free society by reducing both demand as well as supply of illicit drugs and increasing awareness among general masses regarding drugs abuse. Each Year UNODC selects themes for International Drug Day and launches campaigns to raise public appreciation regarding the global drug issue and its effects on complete humanity

The magnitude of drug menace not only undermines global public health, socio-economic synopsis and international stability, it has also become an issue of National Security for Pakistan. Pakistan itself is a poppy free country, but its population became a victim of regional opiate production. We are facing the brunt of trafficking of opiates and cannabis from the West, precursors from the East and Amphetamine Type Stimulants from elsewhere.

Each year International Drug Day is celebrated by Anti Narcotics Force. ANF celebrate Drug Day in a wholesome manner so as to generate a strong message for the international community and domestic masses for general awareness and society's participation by introducing a variety of drug demand awareness activities in addition to drug burning ceremonies.

Model Addiction and Treatment Centres

ANF is also playing a lead role in mass awareness and community participation programs to educate the people against drug abuse as Drug Demand Reduction has always been an important segment of our Strategy. ANF besides many awareness ventures runs 5 Model Addiction and Treatment Centres (MATRCs) at Rawalpindi, Peshawar, Quetta, Sukkur and Karachi and since their raising over twelve thousand patients have been treated.

Under the policy guidelines provided by NCD and with the co-operation of our allied countries, civil society and the media, ANF is doing the best it can and has had significant successes in all three regimes of operation i.e. Drug Supply Reduction, Drug Demand Reduction and International Cooperation. Men and women of ANF are fully committed to protecting our compatriots from the peril at cost of risk to their own lives. Dangerous interactions

Risks

Poly drug use often carries with it more risk than use of a single drug, due to an increase in side effects, and drug synergy. The potentiating effect of one drug on another is sometimes considerable and here the licit drugs and medicines – such as alcohol, nicotine and antidepressants – have to be considered in conjunction with the controlled psychoactive substances. The risk level will depend on the dosage level of both substances. If the drugs taken are illegal, they have a chance of being mixed (also known as «cutting») with other substances which dealers are reported to do to increase the perceived quantity when selling to others to increase their returns. This is particularly common with powdered drugs such as cocaine or MDMA which can be mixed with relative ease by adding another white powdery substance to the drug. This cumulative effect can lead to further unintended harm to health dependent on what is being covertly added. Concerns also exist about a number of pharmacological pairings: alcohol and cocaine increase cardiovascular toxicity; alcohol or depressant drugs, when taken with opioids, lead to an increased risk of overdose; and opioids or cocaine taken with ecstasy or amphetamines also result in additional acute toxicity. Benzodiazepines can cause death when mixed with other CNS depressants such as opioids, alcohol, or barbiturates.

4
Drug Abuse

Substance abuse, also known as drug abuse, is a patterned use of a drug in which the user consumes the substance in amounts or with methods which are harmful to themselves or others, and is a form of substance-related disorder. Widely differing definitions of drug abuse are used in public health, medical and criminal justice contexts. In some cases criminal or anti-social behaviour occurs when the person is under the influence of a drug, and long term personality changes in individuals may occur as well. In addition to possible physical, social, and psychological harm, use of some drugs may also lead to criminal penalties, although these vary widely depending on the local jurisdiction.

Drugs most often associated with this term include: alcohol, cannabis, barbiturates, benzodiazepines, cocaine, methaqualone, opioids and some substituted amphetamines like methamphetamine and MDMA. The exact cause of substance abuse is not clear, with the two predominant theories being: either a genetic disposition which is learned from others, or a habit which if addiction develops, manifests itself as a chronic debilitating disease.

In 2010 about 5% of people (230 million) used an illicit substance. Of these 27 million have high-risk drug use otherwise known as recurrent drug use causing harm to their health, psychological problems, or social problems that put them at risk of those dangers. In 2015 substance use disorders resulted in 307,400 deaths, up from 165,000 deaths in 1990. Of these, the highest numbers are from alcohol use disorders at 137,500, opioid use disorders at 122,100 deaths, amphetamine use disordersat 12,200 deaths, and cocaine use disorders at 11,100.

Drug Possession

Drug possession is the crime of willfully possessing illegal substances, such as marijuana, cocaine, methamphetamine, or heroin. Drug possession accounts for over 80 percent of all drug-related arrests in the United States, according to the Department of Justice. Additionally, almost half of those arrests are for marijuana possession. In part because of law enforcement campaigns targeting these crimes, arrests for drug possession have almost doubled within the last two decades.

What is Possession?

Possession of a drug or another illegal controlled substance occurs only when a defendant is knowingly in possession of the substance. This requires two things. First, the defendant must have known that he or she was carrying the drug or substance at issue. For instance, if a man borrows his friend's car and, when stopped by police, it is discovered that there are drugs concealed in the car, the man may not be charged with drug possession if he can show he had no idea the car contained drugs. Second, the defendant must have known, or reasonably should have known, that the substance he or she was carrying is actually illegal. Thus, if a husband hands his wife some medication that she believes he has a prescription for, when in fact he obtained the drug illegally, she would probably not be charged with possession because she believed the drug was legal. In reality, a defense that someone did not know the substance was illegal is often difficult to prove, for individuals are assumed to have a reasonable knowledge and understanding about drugs and substances in their possession.

Possession applies equally to both actual and constructive possession of an illegal substance. Actual possession applies to those individuals who are physically in control of the drugs at the time of discovery, such as someone who has drugs in his or her pocket. Constructive possession means that the individual has control over and access to the drugs, even if he or she may not be holding onto them at the time of arrest. For instance, a man who keeps drugs in a cabinet in his home is still liable for drug possession.

The crime of drug possession also extends to items beyond the drugs themselves, including precursor chemicals used to make drugs and drug paraphernalia. Drug paraphernalia typically includes items like syringes, pipes, or bongs. Since these items may also be used for legal purposes, such as dispensing of legal medication or smoking tobacco, prosecution for possession of drug paraphernalia typically requires additional evidence to connect the item to drug use, such as residue left on a drug pipe.

Punishment for Drug Possession

Drug possession is criminalized under both state and federal laws, and it is typically broken down into two categories: simple possession and possession with intent to distribute. While simple possession is often a misdemeanor, possession with intent to distribute typically carries much harsher sentences. Laws often distinguish between the two based on the amount of drugs in a person's possession at the time of arrest, for large quantities of a drug suggest the person intends to share it or sell it to others. However, other evidence of distribution may also be obtained, such as scales, plastic baggies, business cards, or statements from witnesses who received drugs from the defendant.

Defendants charged with simple possession are typically subject only to fines and possible probation or rehabilitation programs. Those charged with possession with intent to distribute may face fines up to $100,000 or more and possible incarceration of up to 10 years, depending on the type of drug and the amount in possession.

Sentencing for drug possession crimes has been under scrutiny in recent years for the high number of offenders sent to prison and rising prison populations. For this reason, some states have created alternative drug courts to deal with defendants charged with felony drug crimes. Drug courts focus on rehabilitation of the defendant, as opposed to incarceration, and typically require the defendant to participate in year-long drug rehabilitation programs, as well as random drug testing. Recent statistics on the efficacy of drug courts are very promising. According to the National Association of Drug Court Professionals, almost three-quarters of drug court graduates remain arrest-free for at least two years after completing drug court, with most remaining arrest-free for far longer. Comparatively, the Department of Justice reports that almost two-thirds of those incarcerated for drug crimes are rearrested within three years of their release from jail.

Many people don't understand why or how other people become addicted to drugs. They may mistakenly think that those who use drugs lack moral principles or willpower and that they could stop their drug use simply by choosing to. In reality, drug addiction is a complex disease, and quitting usually takes more than good intentions or a strong will. Drugs change the brain in ways that make quitting hard, even for those who want to. Fortunately, researchers know more than ever about how drugs affect the brain and have found treatments that can help people recover from drug addiction and lead productive lives.

What Is drug addiction?

Addiction is a chronic disease characterized by drug seeking and use that is compulsive, or difficult to control, despite harmful consequences. The initial decision to take drugs is voluntary for most people, but repeated drug use can lead to brain changes that challenge an addicted person's self-control and interfere with their ability to resist intense urges to take drugs. These brain changes can be persistent, which is why drug addiction is considered a "relapsing" disease—people in recovery from drug use disorders are at increased risk for returning to drug use even after years of not taking the drug.

It's common for a person to relapse, but relapse doesn't mean that treatment doesn't work. As with other chronic health conditions, treatment should be ongoing and should be adjusted based on how the patient responds. Treatment plans need to be reviewed often and modified to fit the patient's changing needs.

What happens to the brain when a person takes drugs?

Most drugs affect the brain's "reward circuit," causing euphoria as well as flooding it with the chemical messenger dopamine. A properly functioning reward system motivates a person to repeat behaviors needed to thrive, such as eating and spending time with loved ones. Surges of dopamine in the reward circuit cause the reinforcement of pleasurable but unhealthy behaviors like taking drugs, leading people to repeat the behavior again and again.

As a person continues to use drugs, the brain adapts by reducing the ability of cells in the reward circuit to respond to it. This reduces the high that the person feels compared to the high they felt when first taking the drug—an effect known as tolerance. They might take more of the drug to try and achieve the same high. These brain adaptations often lead to the person becoming less and less able to derive pleasure from other things they once enjoyed, like food, sex, or social activities.

Long-term use also causes changes in other brain chemical systems and circuits as well, affecting functions that include:

- learning
- judgment
- decision-making
- stress
- memory
- behavior

Despite being aware of these harmful outcomes, many people who use drugs continue to take them, which is the nature of addiction.

Why do some people become addicted to drugs while others don't?

No one factor can predict if a person will become addicted to drugs. A combination of factors influences risk for addiction. The more risk factors a person has, the greater the chance that taking drugs can lead to addiction. For example:

- Biology. The genes that people are born with account for about half of a person's risk for addiction. Gender, ethnicity, and the presence of other mental disorders may also influence risk for drug use and addiction.
- Environment. A person's environment includes many different influences, from family and friends to economic status and general quality of life. Factors such as peer pressure, physical and sexual abuse, early exposure to drugs, stress, and parental guidance can greatly affect a person's likelihood of drug use and addiction.
- Development. Genetic and environmental factors interact with critical developmental stages in a person's life to affect addiction risk. Although taking drugs at any age can lead to addiction, the earlier that drug use begins, the more likely it will progress to addiction. This is particularly problematic for teens. Because areas in their brains that control decision-making, judgment, and self-control are still developing, teens may be especially prone to risky behaviors, including trying drugs.

Can drug addiction be cured or prevented?

As with most other chronic diseases, such as diabetes, asthma, or heart disease, treatment for drug addiction generally isn't a cure. However, addiction is treatable and can be successfully managed. People who are recovering from an addiction will be at risk for relapse for years and possibly for their whole lives. Research shows that combining addiction treatment medicines with behavioral therapy ensures the best chance of success for most patients. Treatment approaches tailored to each patient's drug use patterns and any co-occurring medical, mental, and social problems can lead to continued recovery

More good news is that drug use and addiction are preventable. Results from NIDA-funded research have shown that prevention programs involving families, schools, communities, and the media are effective for preventing or reducing drug use and addiction. Although personal events and cultural factors affect drug use trends, when young people view drug use as harmful, they tend to decrease their drug taking. Therefore, education and outreach are key in helping people understand the possible risks of drug use. Teachers, parents, and health care providers have crucial roles in educating young people and preventing drug use and addiction.

- Drug addiction is a chronic disease characterized by drug seeking and use that is compulsive, or difficult to control, despite harmful consequences.
- Brain changes that occur over time with drug use challenge an addicted person's self-control and interfere with their ability to resist intense urges to take drugs. This is why drug addiction is also a relapsing disease.
- Relapse is the return to drug use after an attempt to stop. Relapse indicates the need for more or different treatment.
- Most drugs affect the brain's reward circuit by flooding it with the chemical messenger dopamine. Surges of dopamine in the reward circuit cause the reinforcement of pleasurable but unhealthy activities, leading people to repeat the behavior again and again.
- Over time, the brain adjusts to the excess dopamine, which reduces the high that the person feels compared to the high they felt when first taking the drug—an effect known as tolerance. They might take more of the drug, trying to achieve the same dopamine high.
- No single factor can predict whether a person will become addicted to drugs. A combination of genetic, environmental, and developmental factors influences risk for addiction. The more risk factors a person has, the greater the chance that taking drugs can lead to addiction.
- Drug addiction is treatable and can be successfully managed.
- More good news is that drug use and addiction are preventable. Teachers, parents, and health care providers have crucial roles in educating young people and preventing drug use and addiction.

People use drugs for many reasons: they want to feel good, stop feeling bad, or perform better in school or at work, or they are curious because others are doing it and they want to fit in. The last reason is very common among teens.

Drugs excite the parts of the brain that make you feel good. But after you take a drug for a while, the feel-good parts of your brain get used to it. Then you need to take more of the drug to get the same good feeling. Soon, your brain and body must have the drug to just feel normal. You feel sick, awful, anxious, and irritable without the drug. You no longer have the good feelings that you had when you first used the drug. This is true if you use illegal drugs or if you misuse prescription drugs. Misuse includes taking a drug differently than how your doctor tells you to (taking more or crushing pills to "shoot up" or snort), taking someone else's prescription, or taking it just to get "high."

Drug use can start as a way to escape—but it can quickly make your life worse. Besides just not feeling well, different drugs can affect your brain and body in many different ways. Here are a few:

- Alcohol: You might have trouble making decisions, solving problems, remembering,
- and learning.
- Marijuana: You might forget things you just learned or have trouble focusing.
- Prescription pain relievers (opioids) or sedatives:Your heart rate and breathing
- may slow to dangerous levels, leading to coma or death.
- Heroin: Similar to opioid pain relievers, your heart rate and breathing may slow
- to dangerous levels, leading to coma or death.
- Prescription stimulants (e.g., ADHD medications):Your body temperature could
- get dangerously high, or you may have an irregular heartbeat, heart failure, or seizures.
- Cocaine and methamphetamine: You may get violent, have panic attacks or feel
- paranoid, or have a heart attack.
- MDMA (Ecstasy or Molly): You may feel confused for a long time after you take it
- and have problems with attention, memory, and sleep.
- LSD: Your emotions may change quickly, and you might not be able to recognize
- reality; frightening flashbacks can happen long after use.
- Inhalants: Your heart, kidneys, lungs, and brain may get damaged; even a healthy
- person can suffer heart failure and death within minutes of sniffing a lot of an inhalant.

Many drugs can also make driving a car unsafe. Marijuana can slow reaction time, make you judge time and distance poorly, and decrease coordination (how you move your body). Cocaine and methamphetamine can make a driver aggressive and reckless. Certain kinds of sedatives, called benzodiazepines, can make you dizzy or drowsy. These effects can lead to crashes that can cause injuries and even death.

People from all walks of life can experience problems with their drug use, regardless of age, race, background, or the reason they started using drugs in the first place. Some people experiment with recreational drugs out of curiosity, to have a good time, because friends are doing it, or to ease problems such as stress, anxiety, or depression. However, it's not just illegal drugs, such as cocaine or heroin, that can lead to abuse and addiction. Prescription medications such as painkillers, sleeping pills, and tranquilizers can cause similar problems. In fact, next to marijuana, prescription painkillers are the most abused drugs in the U.S. and more people die from overdosing powerful opioid painkillers each day than from traffic accidents and gun deaths combined. And addiction to opioid painkillers can be so powerful it has become the major risk factor for heroin abuse.

Of course, drug use—either illegal or prescription—doesn't automatically lead to abuse. Some people are able to use recreational or prescription drugs without experiencing negative effects, while others find that substance use takes a serious toll on their health and well-being. Similarly, there is no specific point at which drug use moves from casual to problematic. Drug abuse and addiction is less about the type or amount of the substance consumed or the frequency of your drug use, and more about the consequences of that drug use. If your drug use is causing problems in your life—at work, school, home, or in your relationships—you likely have a drug abuse or addiction problem.

If you're worried about your own or a loved one's drug use, learning how drug abuse and addiction develops—and why it can have such a powerful hold—will give you a better understanding of how to best deal with the problem and regain control of your life. Recognizing that you have a problem is the first step on the road to recovery, one that takes tremendous courage and strength. Facing your problem without minimizing the issue or making excuses can feel frightening and overwhelming, but recovery is within reach. If you're ready to seek help, you can overcome your addiction and build a satisfying, drug-free life for yourself.

Risk factors for drug addiction

While anyone can develop problems from using drugs, vulnerability to substance addiction differs from person to person. While your genes, mental health, family and social environment all play a role, risk factors that increase your vulnerability include:

- Family history of addiction
- Abuse, neglect, or other traumatic experiences
- Mental disorders such as depression and anxiety
- Early use of drugs
- Method of administration—smoking or injecting a drug may increase its addictive potential

Myths and facts about drug abuse and addiction

Myth 1: Overcoming addiction is simply a matter of willpower. You can stop using drugs if you really want.

Fact: Prolonged exposure to drugs alters the brain in ways that result in powerful cravings and a compulsion to use. These brain changes make it extremely difficult to quit by sheer force of will.

Five common myths
Myth 2: Using drugs like opioid painkillers are safe since they're so commonly prescribed by doctors. Fact: Short-term medical use of opioid painkillers can help to manage severe pain after an accident or surgery, for example. However, regular or longer-term use of opioids can lead to addiction. Misuse of these drugs or
Myth 3: Addiction is a disease; there's nothing that can be done about it. Fact: Most experts agree that addiction is a disease that affects the brain, but that doesn't mean anyone is helpless. The brain changes associated with addiction can be treated and reversed through therapy, medication, exercise, and other treatments.
Myth 4: Addicts have to hit rock bottom before they can get better. Fact: Recovery can begin at any point in the addiction process—and the earlier, the better. The longer drug abuse continues, the stronger the addiction becomes and the harder it is to treat. Don't wait to intervene until the addict has lost everything.
Myth 5: You can't force someone into treatment; they have to want help. Fact: Treatment doesn't have to be voluntary to be successful. People who are pressured into treatment by their family, employer, or the legal system are just as likely to benefit as those who choose to enter treatment on their own. As they sober up and their thinking clears, many formerly resistant addicts decide they want to change.
Myth 6: Treatment didn't work before, so there's no point trying again. Fact: Recovery from drug addiction is a long process that often involves setbacks. Relapse doesn't mean that treatment has failed or that sobriety is a lost cause. Rather, it's a signal to get back on track, either by going back to treatment or adjusting the treatment approach.

How drug abuse and addiction develops

There's a fine line between regular drug use and drug abuse and addiction. Very few drug abusers or addicts are able to recognize when they've crossed that line. While frequency or the amount of drugs consumed do not necessarily constitute drug abuse or addiction, they can often be indicators of drug-related problems.

If the drug fulfills a valuable need, you may find yourself increasingly relying on it. You may take illegal drugs to calm or energize yourself or make you more confident. You may start abusing prescription drugs to relieve pain, cope with panic attacks, or improve concentration at school or work. If you are using drugs to fill a void in your life, you're more at risk of crossing the line from casual drug use to drug abuse and addiction. To maintain a healthy balance in your life, you need to have positive experiences and feel good about your life without any drug use.

Drug abuse may start as a way to socially connect. People often try drugs for the first time in social situations with friends and acquaintances. A strong desire to fit in to the group can make it feel like doing the drugs with them is the only option.

Problems can sometimes sneak up on you, as your drug use gradually increases over time. Smoking a joint with friends over the weekend, or taking ecstasy at a rave, or painkillers when your back aches, for example, can change from using drugs a couple of days a week to using them every day. Gradually, getting and using the drug becomes more and more important to you.

As drug abuse takes hold, you may miss or frequently be late for work or school, your job performance may progressively deteriorate, and you may start to neglect social or family responsibilities. Your ability to stop using is eventually compromised. What began as a voluntary choice has turned into a physical and psychological need.

Eventually drug abuse can consume your life, stopping social and intellectual development. This only reinforces feelings of isolation.

Drug addiction and the brain

While each drug produces different physical effects, all abused substances share one thing in common: repeated use can alter the way the brain functions. This includes commonly abused prescription medications as well as recreational drugs.

Taking the drug causes a rush of the hormone dopamine in your brain, which triggers feelings of pleasure. Your brain remembers these feelings and wants them repeated.

When you become addicted, the substance takes on the same significance as other survival behaviors, such as eating and drinking.

Changes in your brain interfere with your ability to think clearly, exercise good judgment, control your behavior, and feel normal without drugs.

No matter which drug you're addicted to, the uncontrollable craving to use grows more important than anything else, including family, friends, career, and even your own health and happiness.

The urge to use is so strong that your mind finds many ways to deny or rationalize the addiction. You may drastically underestimate the quantity of drugs you're taking, how much it impacts your life, and the level of control you have over your drug use.

With the right treatment and support, you can counteract the disruptive effects of drug use and regain control of your life. The first obstacle is to recognize and admit you have a problem, or listen to loved ones who are often better able to see the negative effects drug use is having on your life.

Signs and symptoms of drug abuse and addiction

Although different drugs have different physical effects, the symptoms of addiction are similar. If you recognize yourself in the following signs and symptoms of substance abuse and addiction, talk to someone about your drug use.

Common signs and symptoms of drug abuse

Neglecting responsibilities at school, work, or home (e.g. flunking classes, skipping work, neglecting your children).

Using drugs under dangerous conditions or taking risks while high, such as driving while on drugs, using dirty needles, or having unprotected sex.

Experiencing legal trouble, such as arrests for disorderly conduct, driving under the influence, or stealing to support a drug habit.

Problems in your relationships, such as fights with your partner or family members, an unhappy boss, or the loss of friends.

Common signs and symptoms of drug addiction

You've built up a drug tolerance. You need to use more of the drug to experience the same effects you used to attain with smaller amounts.

You use to avoid or relieve withdrawal symptoms. If you go too long without drugs, you experience symptoms such as nausea, restlessness, insomnia, depression, sweating, shaking, and anxiety.

Loss of control over your drug use. You often do drugs or use more than you planned, even though you told yourself you wouldn't. You may want to stop using, but you feel powerless.

Your life revolves around drug use. You spend a lot of time using and thinking about drugs, figuring out how to get them, or recovering from the drug's effects.

You've abandoned activities you used to enjoy, such as hobbies, sports, and socializing, because of your drug use.

You continue to use drugs, despite knowing it's hurting you. It's causing major problems in your life—blackouts, financial issues, infections, mood swings, depression, paranoia—but you use anyway.

Drug abusers often try to conceal their symptoms and downplay their problem. If you're worried that a friend or loved one might be abusing

drugs, look for the following warning signs:

Physical warning signs

- Bloodshot eyes, pupils larger or smaller than usual
- Changes in appetite or sleep patterns
- Sudden weight loss or weight gain
- Deterioration of physical appearance, personal grooming habits
- Unusual smells on breath, body, or clothing
- Tremors, slurred speech, or impaired coordination

Behavioral warning signs

- Drop in attendance and performance at work or school
- Unexplained financial problems; borrowing or stealing
- Engaging in secretive or suspicious behaviors
- Sudden change in friends, favorite hangouts, and hobbies
- Frequently getting into trouble (fights, accidents, illegal activities)

Psychological warning signs

- Unexplained change in personality or attitude
- Sudden mood swings, irritability, or angry outbursts
- Periods of unusual hyperactivity, agitation, or giddiness
- Lack of motivation; appears lethargic or "spaced out"
- Appears fearful, anxious, or paranoid

Warning signs of commonly abused drugs

Marijuana: Glassy, red eyes; loud talking, inappropriate laughter followed by sleepiness; loss of interest, motivation; weight gain or loss.

Stimulants (including amphetamines, cocaine, crystal meth): Dilated pupils; hyperactivity; euphoria; irritability; anxiety; excessive talking followed by depression or excessive sleeping at odd times; may go long periods of time without eating or sleeping; weight loss; dry mouth and nose.

Inhalants (glues, aerosols, vapors): Watery eyes; impaired vision, memory and thought; secretions from the nose or rashes around the nose and mouth; headaches and nausea; appearance of intoxication; drowsiness; poor muscle control; changes in appetite; anxiety; irritability; lots of cans/aerosols in the trash.

Hallucinogens (LSD, PCP): Dilated pupils; bizarre and irrational behavior including paranoia, aggression, hallucinations; mood swings; detachment from people; absorption with self or other objects, slurred speech; confusion.

Heroin: Contracted pupils; no response of pupils to light; needle marks; sleeping at unusual times; sweating; vomiting; coughing, sniffling; twitching; loss of appetite.

Warning signs of prescription drug abuse and addiction

In recent years, prescription drug abuse has become an escalating problem, most commonly involving opioid painkillers, anti-anxiety medications, sedatives, and stimulants. Many people start taking these drugs to cope with a specific medical problem—taking painkillers following injury or surgery, for example. However, over time, increased doses are needed to achieve the same level of pain relief and some users can become physically dependent, experiencing withdrawal symptoms if they try to quit. One of the earliest warning signs of a developing problem is going through the medication at a faster-than-expected rate. In other cases, people start abusing medication not prescribed for them in order to experience a high, relieve tension, increase alertness, or improve concentration.

To avoid developing problems with a prescription medication, it's important to take it only as directed, use the lowest dose for the shortest period possible, and to talk to your doctor about other methods of treating the problem. Being aware of any signs of dependency can help identify prescription drug problems at an early stage and help to prevent them progressing into an addiction.

Warning signs of commonly abused prescription drugs

Opioid painkillers (including OxyContin, Vicodin, Norco): Drooping eyes, constricted pupils even in dim light, sudden itching or flushing, slurred speech; drowsiness, lack of energy; inability to concentrate, lack of motivation, decline in performance at work or school; neglecting friendships and social activities.

Anti-anxiety medications, sedatives, and hypnotics (including Xanax, Valium, Ambien): Contracted pupils; drunk-like, slurred speech, difficulty concentrating, clumsiness; poor judgment, drowsiness, slowed breathing.

Stimulants (including Ritalin, Concerta, Adderall, Dexedrine): Dilated pupils, reduced appetite; agitation, anxiety, irregular heartbeat, high body temperature; insomnia, paranoia.

If you suspect that a friend or family member has a drug problem, here are a few things you can do:

Speak up. Talk to the person about your concerns, and offer your help and support without being judgmental. The earlier addiction is treated, the better. Don't wait for your loved one to hit bottom! List specific examples of your loved one's behavior that have you worried and urge them to seek help.

Take care of yourself. Stay safe. Don't put yourself in dangerous situations. Don't get so caught up in someone else's drug problem that you neglect your own needs. Make sure you have people you can talk to and lean on for support.

Avoid self-blame. You can support a person with a substance abuse problem and encourage treatment, but you can't force an addict to change. You can't control your loved one's decisions. Letting the person accept responsibility for their actions is an essential step along the way to recovery.

Warning signs of teen drug abuse

As with adults, teenage drug abuse isn't limited to illegal drugs. In fact, teens are more likely to abuse prescription and over-the-counter drugs, including painkillers, stimulants, sedatives, and tranquilizers. In many cases, these drugs are much easier for teens to procure, yet they can have dangerous, even lethal, side effects.

While experimenting with any kind of drug doesn't automatically lead to drug abuse, early use is a risk factor for developing more serious drug abuse and addiction down the road. Risk of drug abuse also increases greatly during times of transition, such as changing schools, moving, or divorce. The challenge for parents is to distinguish between the normal, often volatile, ups and downs of the teen years and the red flags of substance abuse. These include:

Having bloodshot eyes or dilated pupils; using eye drops to try to mask these signs

Skipping class; declining grades; suddenly getting into trouble at school

Missing medications, prescriptions, money or valuables

Acting uncharacteristically isolated, withdrawn, angry, or depressed

Sudden mood changes or repeated health complaints, constant fatigue

Dropping one group of friends for another; being secretive about the new peer group

Loss of interest in old hobbies; lying about new interests and activities

Demanding more privacy; locking doors; avoiding eye contact; sneaking around

7 steps parents can take to curb teen drug use

- Talk openly about the dangers of both illegal and prescription drug use with your kids. Providing a safe and open environment to talk about these issues can make a real difference in the likelihood that they'll use or abuse drugs.
- Lay down rules and consequences. Your teen should understand that using drugs comes with specific consequences. But don't make hollow threats or set rules that you cannot enforce—and make sure your spouse agrees and is prepared to enforce the rules. Remind your teen that taking someone else's prescription or sharing theirs with others is illegal.
- Monitor your teen's activity. Know where your teen goes and who they hang out with. It's also important to routinely check potential hiding places for drugs—in backpacks, between books on a shelf, in DVD cases or make-up cases. Monitor your teen's use of the Internet to check for illegal online purchases.
- Keep prescription medicines in a safe place, avoid stockpiling them, and dispose of any unused prescription medicines. Monitor your prescription refills carefully.
- Encourage other interests and social activities. Expose your teen to healthy hobbies and activities, such as team sports and after-school clubs.
- Talk to your child about underlying issues. Drug use can be the result of other problems. Is your teen having trouble fitting in? Has there been a recent major change, like a move or divorce causing stress?

- Get help. Teenagers often rebel against their parents but if they hear the same information from a different authority figure, they may be more inclined to listen. Try a sports coach, family doctor, therapist, or drug counselor.

Next step: Getting help for drug abuse or addiction

Addiction is a complex problem that affects every aspect of your life. Overcoming addiction requires reaching out for support and making changes to the way you live, deal with problems, and relate to others. Recovery is within your reach but don't try to go it alone; it's very easy to get discouraged and rationalize "just one more." Whether you choose to go to rehab, rely on self-help programs, get therapy, or take a self-directed treatment approach, support is essential. Read:

Drug addiction is when you can't stop taking the drug even if you want to. The urge is too strong to control, even if you know the drug is causing harm. The addiction can become more important than the need to eat or sleep. The urge to get and use the drug can fill every moment of your life. The addiction replaces all the things you used to enjoy. A person who is addicted might do almost anything—lie, steal, or hurt people—to keep taking the drug. This can lead to problems with your family and friends, and can even lead to arrest and jail. You can get addicted to illegal drugs as well as prescription drugs if you misuse them.

Drug addiction is a chronic disease. That means it stays with you for a long time, even if you stop using for a while. It doesn't go away like a cold. A person with an addiction can get treatment, but quitting for good can be very hard.

At first, taking drugs is usually your choice. But as you continue to take them, using self-control can become harder and harder; this is the biggest sign of addiction. Brain studies of people with addiction show physical changes in parts of the brain that are very important for judgment, making decisions, learning and memory, and controlling behavior. Scientists have shown that when this happens to the brain, it changes how the brain works and it explains the harmful behaviors of addiction that are so hard to control.

Sometimes people quit their drug use for a while because they're away from triggers that remind them about their drug use. Away from home, drugs might be less available. Once you go back to normal life, you're likely to start using again unless you take action to avoid your triggers. This return to drug use is called a relapse. People recovering from addiction often have one or more relapses along the way if they don't take steps to avoid their triggers.

A trigger is anything that makes you feel the urge to go back to using drugs. It can be a place, person, thing, smell, feeling, picture, or memory that reminds you of taking a drug and getting high. A trigger can be something stressful that you want to escape from. It can even be something that makes you feel happy. People fighting addiction need to stay away from the people and triggers that can make them start using drugs again, just like people with breathing problems need to avoid smoke and dust.

People who have stayed sober for a while, either because they were in jail or in treatment, should know that they are at a high risk of overdose if they relapse and take the same amount of drug they used to. Their cravings may not have decreased, but their tolerance has, meaning their body can't handle high doses of the drug anymore. Without immediate treatment, overdose often leads to death. This is why you often hear about people dying of an overdose soon after leaving rehab.

- Trouble at home. If your home is an unhappy place, or was when you were growing up, you might be more likely to have a drug problem. When kids aren›t well cared for, or there are lots of fights, or a parent is using drugs, the chance of addiction goes up.
- Mental health problems. People who have untreated mental health problems, such as depression or anxiety, or untreated attention deficit/hyperactivity disorder (ADHD) are more likely to become addicted. They might use drugs to try to feel better.
- Trouble in school, trouble at work, trouble with making friends. Failures at school or work, or trouble getting along with people, can make life hard. You might use drugs to get your mind off these problems.
- Hanging around other people who use drugs. Friends or family members who use drugs might get you into trouble with drugs as well.
- Starting drug use when you're young. When kids use drugs, it affects how their bodies and brains finish growing. Using drugs when you›re young increases your chances of becoming addicted when you›re an adult.
- Your biology. Everyone›s bodies react to drugs differently. Some people like the feeling the first time they try a drug and want more. Other people hate how it feels and never try it again. Scientists don't have a test yet that will predict how each person will react.

Can drug addiction be treated?

Yes. People who get treatment and stick with it can stop using drugs. They can change their lives so they don't go back to taking drugs. But they have to try hard and follow the treatment program for a long time. Recovery from addiction means you have to stop using drugs AND learn new ways of thinking, feeling, and dealing with problems. It's best not to use in the first place. If you do get addicted, it'll be a long You may also need treatment for problems that led to your drug use, such as depression, anxiety, or other mental health problems.

Classification

Public health definitions

Public health practitioners have attempted to look at substance use from a broader perspective than the individual, emphasizing the role of society, culture, and availability. Some health professionals choose to avoid the terms alcohol or drug «abuse» in favor of language they consider more objective, such as "substance and alcohol type problems" or "harmful/problematic use" of drugs. The Health Officers Council of British Columbia — in their 2005 policy discussion paper, A Public Health Approach to Drug Control in Canada — has adopted a public health model of psychoactive substance use that challenges the simplistic black-and-white construction of the binary (or complementary) antonyms «use» vs. «abuse». This model explicitly recognizes a spectrum of use, ranging from beneficial use to chronic dependence.

Medical definitions

'Drug abuse' is no longer a current medical diagnosis in either of the most used diagnostic tools in the world, the American Psychiatric Association's Diagnostic and Statistical Manual of Mental Disorders (DSM), and the World Health Organization's International Statistical Classification of Diseases (ICD).

Value judgment

This diagram depicts the correlations among the usage of 18 legal and illegal drugs: alcohol, amphetamines, amyl nitrite, benzodiazepine, cannabis, chocolate, cocaine, caffeine, crack, ecstasy, heroin, ketamine, legal highs, LSD, methadone, magic mushrooms (MMushrooms), nicotine and volatile substance abuse (VSA). Usage is defined as having used the drug at least once during years 2005–2015. The colored links between drugs indicate the correlations with $|r|>0.4$, where $|r|$ is the absolute valueof the Pearson correlation coefficient.

Philip Jenkins suggests that there are two issues with the term «drug abuse». First, what constitutes a «drug» is debatable. For instance, GHB, a naturally occurring substance in the central nervous system is considered a drug, and is illegal in many countries, while nicotine is not officially considered a drug in most countries.

Second, the word "abuse" implies a recognized standard of use for any substance. Drinking an occasional glass of wine is considered acceptable in most Western countries, while drinking several bottles is seen as an abuse. Strict temperance advocates, who may or may not be religiously motivated, would see drinking even one glass as an abuse. Some groups even condemn caffeine use in any quantity. Similarly, adopting the view that any (recreational) use of cannabis or substituted amphetamines constitutes drug abuse implies a decision made that the substance is harmful, even in minute quantities. In the U.S., drugs have been legally classified into five categories, schedule I, II, III, IV, or V in the Controlled Substances Act. The drugs are classified on their deemed potential for abuse. Usage of some drugs is strongly correlated. For example, the consumption of seven illicit drugs (amphetamines, cannabis, cocaine, ecstasy, legal highs, LSD, and magic mushrooms) is correlated and the Pearson correlation coefficient $r>0.4$ in every pair of them; consumption of cannabis is strongly correlated ($r>0.5$) with usage of nicotine (tobacco), heroin is correlated with cocaine ($r>0.4$) and methadone ($r>0.45$), and is strongly correlated with crack ($r>0.5$)

Drug misuse

Drug misuse is a term used commonly when prescription medication with sedative, anxiolytic, analgesic, or stimulantproperties are used for mood alteration or intoxication ignoring the fact that overdose of such medicines can sometimes have serious adverse effects. It sometimes involves drug diversion from the individual for whom it was prescribed.

Prescription misuse has been defined differently and rather inconsistently based on status of drug prescription, the uses without a prescription, intentional use to achieve intoxicating effects, route of administration, co-ingestion with alcohol, and the presence or absence of dependence symptoms. Chronic use of certain substances leads to a change in the central nervous system known as a 'tolerance' to the medicine such that more of the substance is needed in order to produce desired effects. With some substances, stopping or reducing use can cause withdrawal symptoms to occur, but this is highly dependent on the specific substance in question.

The rate of prescription drug use is fast overtaking illegal drug use in the United States. According to the National Institute of Drug Abuse, 7 million people were taking prescription drugs for nonmedical use in 2010. Among 12th graders, nonmedical prescription drug use is now second only to cannabis. In 2011, «Nearly 1 in 12 high school seniors reported nonmedical use of Vicodin; 1 in 20 reported such use of OxyContin.» Both of these drugs contain opioids. A 2017 survey of 12th graders in the United States, found misuse of oxycontin of 2.7 percent, compared to 5.5 percent at its peak in 2005. Misuse of the combination hydrocodone/paracetamol was at its lowest since a peak of 10.5 percent in 2003. This decrease may be related to public health initiatives and decreased availability.

Avenues of obtaining prescription drugs for misuse are varied: sharing between family and friends, illegally buying medications at school or work, and often "doctor shopping" to find multiple physicians to prescribe the same medication, without knowledge of other prescribers.

Increasingly, law enforcement is holding physicians responsible for prescribing controlled substances without fully establishing patient controls, such as a patient "drug contract". Concerned physicians are educating themselves on how to identify medication-seeking behavior in their patients, and are becoming familiar with "red flags" that would alert them to potential prescription drug abuse.

Signs and symptoms

Depending on the actual compound, drug abuse including alcohol may lead to health problems, social problems, morbidity, injuries, unprotected sex, violence, deaths, motor vehicle accidents, homicides, suicides, physical dependence or psychological addiction.

There is a high rate of suicide in alcoholics and other drug abusers. The reasons believed to cause the increased risk of suicide include the long-term abuse of alcohol and other drugs causing physiological distortion of brain chemistry as well as the social isolation. Another factor is the acute intoxicating effects of the drugs may make suicide more likely to occur. Suicide is also very common in adolescent alcohol abusers, with 1 in 4 suicides in adolescents being related to alcohol abuse. In the US, approximately 30% of suicides are related to alcohol abuse. Alcohol abuse is also associated with increased risks of committing criminal offences including child abuse, domestic violence, rapes, burglaries and assaults.

Drug abuse, including alcohol and prescription drugs, can induce symptomatology which resembles mental illness. This can occur both in the intoxicated state and also during the withdrawal state. In some cases these substance induced psychiatric disorders can persist long after detoxification, such as prolonged psychosis or depression after amphetamine or cocaine abuse. A protracted withdrawal syndrome can also occur with symptoms persisting for months after cessation of use. Benzodiazepines are the most notable drug for inducing prolonged withdrawal effects with symptoms sometimes persisting for years after cessation of use. Both alcohol, barbiturate as well as benzodiazepine withdrawal can potentially be fatal. Abuse of hallucinogens can trigger delusional and other psychotic phenomena long after cessation of use.

Cannabis may trigger panic attacks during intoxication and with continued use, it may cause a state similar to dysthymia. Researchers have found that daily cannabis use and the use of high-potency cannabis are independently associated with a higher chance of developing schizophrenia and other psychotic disorders.

Severe anxiety and depression are commonly induced by sustained alcohol abuse, which in most cases abates with prolonged abstinence. Even sustained moderate alcohol use may increase anxiety and depression levels in some individuals. In most cases these drug induced psychiatric disorders fade away with prolonged abstinence.

Impulsivity

Impulsivity is characterized by actions based on sudden desires, whims, or inclinations rather than careful thought. Individuals with substance abuse have higher levels of impulsivity, and individuals who use multiple drugs tend to be more impulsive. A number of studies using the Iowa gambling task as a measure for impulsive behavior found that drug using populations made more risky choices compared to healthy controls. There is a hypothesis that the loss of impulse control may be due to impaired inhibitory control resulting from drug induced changes that take place in the frontal cortex. The neurodevelopmental and hormonal changes that happen during adolescence may modulate impulse control that could possibly lead to the experimentation with drugs and may lead to the road of addiction. Impulsivity is thought to be a facet trait in the neuroticism personality domain (overindulgence/negative urgency) which is prospectively associated with the development of substance abuse.

Screening and assessment

There are several different screening tools that have been validated for use with adolescents such as the CRAFFT Screening Test and in adults the CAGE questionnaire.

Some recommendations for screening tools for substance misuse in pregnancy include that they take less than 10 minutes, should be used routinely, include an educational component. Tools suitable for pregnant women include i.a. 4Ps, T-ACE, TWEAK, TQDH (Ten-Question Drinking History), and AUDIT.

Treatment

Psychological

From the applied behavior analysis literature, behavioral psychology, and from randomized clinical trials, several evidenced based interventions have emerged: behavioral marital therapy, motivational Interviewing, community reinforcement approach, exposure therapy, contingency management They help suppress cravings and mental anxiety, improve focus on treatment and new learning behavioral skills, ease withdrawal symptoms and reduce the chances of relapse.

In children and adolescents, cognitive behavioral therapy (CBT) and family therapy currently has the most research evidence for the treatment of substance abuse problems. Well-established studies also include ecological family-based treatment and group CBT. These treatments can be administered in a variety of different formats, each of which has varying levels of research support Research has shown that what makes group CBT most effective is that it promotes the development of social skills, developmentally appropriate emotional regulatory skills and other interpersonal skills. A few integrated treatment models, which combines parts from various types of treatment, have also been seen as both well-established or probably effective. A study on maternal alcohol and drug use has shown that integrated treatment programs have produced significant results, resulting in higher negative results on toxicology screens. Additionally, brief school-based interventions have been found to be effective in reducing adolescent alcohol and cannabis use and abuse. Motivational interviewing can also be effective in treating substance use disorder in adolescents.

Alcoholics Anonymous and Narcotics Anonymous are one of the most widely known self-help organizations in which members support each other not to use alcohol. Social skillsare significantly impaired in people suffering from alcoholism due to the neurotoxic effects of alcohol on the brain, especially the prefrontal cortex area of the brain. It has been suggested that social skills training adjunctive to inpatient treatment of alcohol dependence is probably efficacious, including managing the social environment.

Medication

A number of medications have been approved for the treatment of substance abuse. These include replacement therapies such as buprenorphine and methadone as well as antagonist medications like disulfiram and naltrexone in either short acting, or the newer long acting form. Several other medications, often ones originally used in other contexts, have also been shown to be effective including bupropion and modafinil. Methadone and buprenorphine are sometimes used to treat opiate addiction. These drugs are used as substitutes for other opioids and still cause withdrawal symptoms.

Antipsychotic medications have not been found to be useful. Acamprostate is a glutamatergic NMDA antagonist, which helps with alcohol withdrawal symptoms because alcohol withdrawal is associated with a hyperglutamatergic system.

Dual diagnosis

It is common for individuals with drugs use disorder to have other psychological problems. The terms "dual diagnosis" or "co-occurring disorders," refer to having a mental health and substance use disorder at the same time. According to the British Association for Psychopharmacology (BAP), "symptoms of psychiatric disorders such as depression, anxiety and psychosis are the rule rather than the exception in patients misusing drugs and/or alcohol."

Individuals who have a comorbid psychological disorder often have a poor prognosis if either disorder is untreated. Historically most individuals with dual diagnosis either received treatment only for one of their disorders or they didn't receive any treatment all. However, since the 1980s, there has been a push towards integrating mental health and addiction treatment. In this method, neither condition is considered primary and both are treated simultaneously by the same provider.

Epidemiology

The initiation of drug and alcohol use is most likely to occur during adolescence, and some experimentation with substances by older adolescents is common. For example, results from 2010 Monitoring the Future survey, a nationwide study on rates of substance use in the United States, show that 48.2% of 12th graders report having used an illicit drug at some point in their lives. In the 30 days prior to the survey, 41.2% of 12th graders had consumed alcohol and 19.2% of 12th graders had smoked tobacco cigarettes. In 2009 in the United States about 21% of high school students have taken prescription drugs without a prescription. And earlier in 2002, the World Health Organization estimated that around 140 million people were alcohol dependent and another 400 million with alcohol-related problems.

Studies have shown that the large majority of adolescents will phase out of drug use before it becomes problematic. Thus, although rates of overall use are high, the percentage of adolescents who meet criteria for substance abuse is significantly lower (close to 5%). According to BBC, «Worldwide, the UN estimates there are more than 50 million regular users of morphine diacetate (heroin), cocaine and synthetic drugs.»

More than 70,200 Americans died from drug overdoses in 2017. Among these, the sharpest increase occurred among deaths related to fentanyl and synthetic opioids (28,466 deaths). See charts below.

History

APA, AMA, and NCDA

In 1932, the American Psychiatric Association created a definition that used legality, social acceptability, and cultural familiarity as qualifying factors:

...as a general rule, we reserve the term drug abuse to apply to the illegal, nonmedical use of a limited number of substances, most of them drugs, which have properties of altering the mental state in ways that are considered by social norms and defined by statute to be inappropriate, undesirable, harmful, threatening, or, at minimum, culture-alien.

In 1966, the American Medical Association's Committee on Alcoholism and Addiction defined abuse of stimulants (amphetamines, primarily) in terms of 'medical supervision':

...'use' refers to the proper place of stimulants in medical practice; 'misuse' applies to the physician's role in initiating a potentially dangerous course of therapy; and 'abuse' refers to self-administration of these drugs without medical supervision and particularly in large doses that may lead to psychological dependency, tolerance and abnormal behavior.

In 1973, the National Commission on Marijuana and Drug Abuse stated:

...drug abuse may refer to any type of drug or chemical without regard to its pharmacologic actions. It is an eclectic concept having only one uniform connotation: societal disapproval. ... The Commission believes that the term drug abuse must be deleted from official pronouncements and public policy dialogue. The term has no functional utility and has become no more than an arbitrary codeword for that drug use which is presently considered wrong.

DSM

The first edition of the American Psychiatric Association's Diagnostic and Statistical Manual of Mental Disorders (published in 1952) grouped alcohol and drug abuse under Sociopathic Personality Disturbances, which were thought to be symptoms of deeper psychological disorders or moral weakness. The third edition, published in 1980, was the first to recognize substance abuse (including drug abuse) and substance dependence as conditions separate from substance abuse alone, bringing in social and cultural factors. The definition of dependence emphasised tolerance to drugs, and withdrawal from them as key components to diagnosis, whereas abuse was defined as «problematic use with social or occupational impairment» but without withdrawal or tolerance.

In 1987, the DSM-IIIR category "psychoactive substance abuse," which includes former concepts of drug abuse is defined as "a maladaptive pattern of use indicated by...continued use despite knowledge of having a persistent or recurrent social, occupational, psychological or physical problem that is caused or exacerbated by the use (or by) recurrent use in situations in which it is physically hazardous." It is a residual category, with dependence taking precedence when applicable. It was the first definition to give equal weight to behavioural and physiological factors in diagnosis. By 1988, the DSM-IV defines substance dependence as "a syndrome involving compulsive use, with or without tolerance and withdrawal"; whereas substance abuse is "problematic use without compulsive use, significant tolerance, or withdrawal." Substance abuse can be harmful to your health and may even be deadly in certain scenarios. By 1994, The fourth edition of the Diagnostic and Statistical Manual of Mental Disorders (DSM) issued by the American Psychiatric Association, the DSM-IV-TR, defines substance dependence as "when an individual persists in use of alcohol or other drugs despite problems related to use of the substance, substance dependence may be diagnosed.» followed by criteria for the diagnose

DSM-IV-TR defines substance abuse as:

- A. A maladaptive pattern of substance use leading to clinically significant impairment or distress, as manifested by one (or more) of the following, occurring within a 12-month period:
- Recurrent substance use resulting in a failure to fulfill major role obligations at work, school, or home (e.g., repeated absences or poor work performance related to substance use; substance-related absences, suspensions or expulsions from school; neglect of children or household)
- Recurrent substance use in situations in which it is physically hazardous (e.g., driving an automobile or operating a machine when impaired by substance use)
- Recurrent substance-related legal problems (e.g., arrests for substance-related disorderly conduct)
- Continued substance use despite having persistent or recurrent social or interpersonal problems caused or exacerbated by the effects of the substance (e.g., arguments with spouse about consequences of intoxication, physical fights)
- B. The symptoms have never met the criteria for Substance Dependence for this class of substance.

The fifth edition of the DSM (DSM-5), was released in 2013, and it revisited this terminology. The principal change was a transition from the abuse/dependence terminology. In the DSM-IV era, abuse was seen as an early form or less hazardous form of the disease characterized with the dependence criteria. However, the APA's 'dependence' term, as noted above, does not mean that physiologic dependence is present but rather means that a disease state is present, one that most would likely refer to as an addicted state. Many involved recognize that the terminology has often led to confusion, both within the medical community and with the general public. The American Psychiatric Association requested input as to how the terminology of this illness should be altered as it moves forward with DSM-5 discussion. In the

DSM-5, substance abuse and substance dependence have been merged into the category of substance use disorders and they now longer exist as individual concepts. While substance abuse and dependence were either present or not, substance use disorder has three levels of severity: mild, moderate and severe.

Society and culture

Legal approaches

Most governments have designed legislation to criminalize certain types of drug use. These drugs are often called «illegal drugs» but generally what is illegal is their unlicensedproduction, distribution, and possession. These drugs are also called "controlled substances". Even for simple possession, legal punishment can be quite severe (including the death penalty in some countries). Laws vary across countries, and even within them, and have fluctuated widely throughout history.

Attempts by government-sponsored drug control policy to interdict drug supply and eliminate drug abuse have been largely unsuccessful. In spite of the huge efforts by the U.S., drug supply and purity has reached an all-time high, with the vast majority of resources spent on interdiction and law enforcement instead of public health. In the United States, the number of nonviolent drug offenders in prison exceeds by 100,000 the total incarcerated population in the EU, despite the fact that the EU has 100 million more citizens.

Despite drug legislation (or perhaps because of it), large, organized criminal drug cartels operate worldwide. Advocates of decriminalization argue that drug prohibition makes drug dealing a lucrative business, leading to much of the associated criminal activity.

Cost

Policymakers try to understand the relative costs of drug-related interventions. An appropriate drug policy relies on the assessment of drug-related public expenditure based on a classification system where costs are properly identified.

Labelled drug-related expenditures are defined as the direct planned spending that reflects the voluntary engagement of the state in the field of illicit drugs. Direct public expenditures explicitly labeled as drug-related can be easily traced back by exhaustively reviewing official accountancy documents such as national budgets and year-end reports. Unlabelled expenditure refers to unplanned spending and is estimated through modeling techniques, based on a top-down budgetary procedure. Starting from overall aggregated expenditures, this procedure estimates the proportion causally attributable to substance abuse (Unlabelled Drug-related Expenditure = Overall Expenditure × Attributable Proportion). For example, to estimate the prison drug-related expenditures in a given country, two elements would be necessary: the overall prison expenditures in the country for a given period, and the attributable proportion of inmates due to drug-related issues. The product of the two will give a rough estimate that can be compared across different countries.

Europe

As part of the reporting exercise corresponding to 2005, the European Monitoring Centre for Drugs and Drug Addiction's network of national focal points set up in the 27 European Union (EU) Member States, Norway, and the candidates countries to the EU, were requested to identify labeled drug-related public expenditure, at the country level.

This was reported by 10 countries categorized according to the functions of government, amounting to a total of EUR 2.17 billion. Overall, the highest proportion of this total came within the government functions of Health (66%) (e.g. medical services), and Public Order and Safety (POS) (20%) (e.g. police services, law courts, prisons). By country, the average share of GDP was 0.023% for Health, and 0.013% for POS. However, these shares varied considerably across countries, ranging from 0.00033% in Slovakia, up to 0.053% of GDP in Ireland in the case of Health, and from 0.003% in Portugal, to 0.02% in the UK, in the case of POS; almost a 161-fold difference between the highest and the lowest countries for Health, and a 6-fold difference for POS. Why do Ireland and the UK spend so much in Health and POS, or Slovakia and Portugal so little, in GDP terms?

To respond to this question and to make a comprehensive assessment of drug-related public expenditure across countries, this study compared Health and POS spending and GDP in the 10 reporting countries. Results found suggest GDP to be a major determinant of the Health and POS drug-related public expenditures of a country. Labelled drug-related public expenditure showed a positive association with the GDP across the countries considered: $r = 0.81$ in the case of Health, and $r = 0.91$ for POS. The percentage change in Health and POS expenditures due to a one percent increase in GDP (the income elasticity of demand) was estimated to be 1.78% and 1.23% respectively.

Being highly income elastic, Health and POS expenditures can be considered luxury goods; as a nation becomes wealthier it openly spends proportionately more on drug-related health and public order and safety interventions.

UK

The UK Home Office estimated that the social and economic cost of drug abuse to the UK economy in terms of crime, absenteeism and sickness is in excess of £20 billion a year. However, the UK Home Office does not estimate what portion of those crimes are unintended consequences of drug prohibition (crimes to sustain expensive drug consumption, risky production and dangerous distribution), nor what is the cost of enforcement. Those aspects are necessary for a full analysis of the economics of prohibition.

United States

These figures represent overall economic costs, which can be divided in three major components: health costs, productivity losses and non-health direct expenditures.

Health-related costs were projected to total $16 billion in 2002.

Productivity losses were estimated at $128.6 billion. In contrast to the other costs of drug abuse (which involve direct expenditures for goods and services), this value reflects a loss of potential resources: work in the labor market and in household production that was never performed, but could reasonably be expected to have been performed absent the impact of drug abuse.

Included are estimated productivity losses due to premature death ($24.6 billion), drug abuse-related illness ($33.4 billion), incarceration ($39.0 billion), crime careers ($27.6 billion) and productivity losses of victims of crime ($1.8 billion).

The non-health direct expenditures primarily concern costs associated with the criminal justice system and crime victim costs, but also include a modest level of expenses for administration of the social welfare system. The total for 2002 was estimated at $36.4 billion. The largest detailed component of these costs is for state and federal corrections at $14.2 billion, which is primarily for the operation of prisons. Another $9.8 billion was spent on state and local police protection, followed by $6.2 billion for federal supply reduction initiatives.

According to a report from the Agency for Healthcare Research and Quality (AHRQ), Medicaid was billed for a significantly higher number of hospitals stays for Opioid drug overuse than Medicare or private insurance in 1993. By 2012, the differences were diminished. Over the same time, Medicare had the most rapid growth in number of hospital stays.

Special populations

Immigrants and refugees

Immigrant and refugees have often been under great stress, physical trauma and depression and anxiety due to separation from loved ones often characterize the pre-migration and transit phases, followed by «cultural dissonance,» language barriers, racism, discrimination, economic adversity, overcrowding, social isolation, and loss of status and difficulty obtaining work and fears of deportation are common. Refugees frequently experience concerns about the health and safety of loved ones left behind and uncertainty regarding the possibility of returning to their country of origin. For some, substance abuse functions as a coping mechanism to attempt to deal with these stressors.

Immigrants and refugees may bring the substance use and abuse patterns and behaviors of their country of origin, or adopt the attitudes, behaviors, and norms regarding substance use and abuse that exist within the dominant culture into which they are entering

Street children

Street children in many developing countries are a high risk group for substance misuse, in particular solvent abuse. Drawing on research in Kenya,

Cottrell-Boyce argues that "drug use amongst street children is primarily functional – dulling the senses against the hardships of life on the street – but can also provide a link to the support structure of the 'street family' peer group as a potent symbol of shared experience."

Musicians

In order to maintain high-quality performance, some musicians take chemical substances. Some musicians take drugs or alcohol to deal with the stress of performing. As a group they have a higher rate of substance abuse. The most common chemical substance which is abused by pop musicians is cocaine, because of its neurological effects. Stimulants like cocaine increase alertness and cause feelings of euphoria, and can therefore make the performer feel as though they in some ways 'own the stage'. One way in which substance abuse is harmful for a performer (musicians especially) is if the substance being abused is aspirated. The lungs are an important organ used by singers, and addiction to cigarettes may seriously harm the quality of their performance. Smoking causes harm to alveoli, which are responsible for absorbing oxygen.

Veterans

Substance abuse can be another contributing factor that affects physical and mental health of veterans. Substance abuse may also damage personal relationships families and lead to financial difficulty. There is evidence to suggest that substance abuse disproportionately affects the homeless veteran population. A 2015 Florida study compared causes of homelessness between veterans and non veteran populations in a self reporting questionnaire. The results from the study found that 17.8% of the homeless veteran participants attributed their homelessness to alcohol and drug related problems compared to just 3.7% of the non-veteran homeless group.

A 2003 study found that homelessness was associated with access to support from family/friends and services. However, this relationship was not true when comparing homeless participants who had a current substance-use disorders. The U.S. Department of Veterans Affairs provide a summary of treatment options for veterans with substance use disorder. For treatments that do not involve medication, they offer a therapeutic options that focused on finding outside support groups and "looking at how substance use problems may relate to other problems such as PTSD and depression".

Addictive personality

An addictive personality refers to a particular set of personality traits that make an individual predisposed to developing addictions. This hypothesis states that there may be common personality traits observable in people suffering from addiction. Alan R. Lang of Florida State University, author of an addiction study prepared for the United States National Academy of Sciences, said, "If we can better identify the personality factors, they can help us devise better treatment and can open up new strategies to intervene and break the patterns of addiction."

Description

The following factors are believed to influence addiction susceptibility.

Psychological factors

Alan R Lang's research found that, while there is no single set of traits that is definitive of an "addictive personality", several "significant personality factors" exist, including:

- Impulsivity
- Sensation seeking
- Nonconformity combined with weak commitment to socially valued goals for achievement
- Social alienation and tolerance for deviance
- Heightened stress coupled with lack of coping skills.

Some claim the existence of "addictive beliefs" in people more likely to develop addictions, such as "I cannot make an impact on my world" or "I am not good enough", which may lead to developing traits associated with addiction, such as depression and emotional insecurity. People who strongly believe that they control their own lives and are mostly self-reliant in learning information (rather than relying on others) are less likely to become addicted. However, it is unclear whether these traits are causes, results or merely associated coincidentally. For example, depression due to physical disease can cause feelings of hopelessness that are mitigated after successful treatment of the underlying condition, and addiction can increase dependence on others.

Genetic, physical and environmental factors

Specific genetic variants predispose to drug addiction—it's one of the behavioral disorders most strongly correlated with genetic makeup. Exposure to sustained stress in childhood, such as physical or sexual abuse, especially accompanied by unpredictable parental behavior also correlate with addiction.

Interaction of biopsychosocial factors

Individual traits can share common underlying factors or interact. For example, depression, poor self-control, and compulsive behavior are linked to neurotransmitter abnormalities, i.e., biological mechanisms. Likewise, there is a gene/environment connection in that individuals with particular personality traits may self-select into different environments, e.g., they may seek out work environments where addictive substances are more readily available.

Signs and symptoms

People who suffer from an addictive personality spend excessive time on a behavior or with an item, not as a hobby but because they feel they have to. Addiction can be defined when the engagement in the activity or experience affects the person's quality of life in some way. In this way, many people who maintain an addictive personality isolate themselves from social situations in order to mask their addiction.

People that face this issue are currently defined to have a brain disease as promoted by the National Institute on Drug Abuse and other authorities. People who experience addictive personality disorders typically act on impulses and cannot deal with delayed gratification. At the same time, people with this type of personality tend to believe that they do not fit into societal norms and therefore, acting on impulses, deviate from conformity to rebel. People with addictive personalities are very sensitive to emotional stress. They have trouble handling situations that they deem frustrating, even if the event is for a very short duration. The combination of low self-esteem, impulsivity and low tolerance for stress causes these individuals to have frequent mood swings and often suffer from some sort of depression. A coping mechanism to deal with their conflicting personality becomes their addiction and the addiction acts as something that the person can control when they find it difficult to control their personality traits.

People with addictive personalities typically switch from one addiction to the next. These individuals may show impulsive behavior such as excessive caffeine consumption, Internet use, eating chocolate or other sugar-laden foods, television watching, or even running.

Extraversion, self-monitoring, and loneliness are also common characteristics found in those who suffer from addiction. Individuals who score high on self-monitoring are more prone to developing an addiction. High self-monitors are sensitive to social situations; they act how they think others expect them to act. They wish to fit in, hence they are very easily influenced by others. Likewise, those who have low self-esteem also seek peer approval; therefore, they participate in "attractive" activities such as smoking or drinking to try to fit in.

People with addictive personalities find it difficult to manage their stress levels. In fact, lack of stress tolerance is a telltale sign of the disorder. They find it difficult to face stressful situations and fight hard to get out of such conditions. Long-term goals prove difficult to achieve because people with addictive personalities usually focus on the stress that comes with getting through the short-term goals. Such personalities will often switch to other enjoyable activities the moment that they are deprived of enjoyment in their previous addiction.

Addictive individuals feel highly insecure when it comes to relationships. They may often find it difficult to make commitments in relationships or trust their beloved because of the difficulty they find in achieving long-term goals. They constantly seek approval of others and as a result, these misunderstandings may contribute to the destruction of relationships. People suffering from addictive personality disorder usually undergo depression and anxiety, managing their emotions by developing addiction to alcohol, other types of drugs, or other pleasurable activities.

An addict is more prone to depression, anxiety, and anger. Both the addict›s environment, genetics and biological tendency contribute to their addiction.

People with very severe personality disorders are more likely to become addicts. Addictive substances usually stop primary and secondary neuroses, meaning people with personality disorders like the relief from their pain.

Personality traits and addiction

Addiction is defined by scholars as "a reliance on a substance or behavior that the individual has little power to resist." Substance-based addictions are those based upon the release of dopamine in the brain, upon which the range of sensations produced by the euphoric event in the brain changes the brain's immediate behavior, causing more susceptibility for future addictions. Behavior-based addictions, on the other hand, are those that are not linked to neurological behavior as much and are thus thought to be linked to personality traits; it is this type of addiction that combines a behavior with a mental state and the repeated routine is therefore associated with the mental state.

Alan R. Lang, a psychology professor at Florida State University, wrote in a study that the continuing search for the personality traits that play a part in the development of addictions are important for the broader fight against addiction. Identifying the different personality traits will help in the long term when it comes to the treatment of addiction, the strategies to intervene, and how to break the pattern of addiction. With addictive tragedies becoming prevalent in communities around the United States, scientists are asking questions about the aspects of psychological makeup and how they contribute to addiction. They also want to know if there are common threads that are in all addictions, from hard drugs to cigarettes and from gambling to overeating. Through the information that already exists on the personality›s role in addictions, with a lot of emphasis on drugs and alcohol, a study from the National Academy of Sciences says that there is no single set of psychological characteristics that pertain to all addictions. The study did show, however, that there are common elements between all addictions.

Common forms of addictive behavior

Substance addiction

One form of addiction is substance addiction. This is different from substance abuse in that abuse of a substance is not really definable while substance addiction is a behavioral addiction where there is an overwhelming involvement with the use and buying of drugs or alcohol. It is a mental dependence or addiction to a substance but not a physical addiction, although it can lead to a physical addiction in the end.

Gambling

Another common addiction that may attract those with addictive personalities is gambling. When an addict behaves mindlessly and irresponsibly while gambling, it can grow to be a bigger problem. A gambler with an addictive personality goes through three stages. The first is the «winning phase» in which the person can still control his or her own behavior. Second comes the «losing phase» where the individual starts to gamble alone, borrowing cash and gambling large sums of money, compiling debt which he or she may not be able to pay off. Finally, the «desperation phase» of the addictive behavior gambler is when the person takes further risks, may engage in illegal loans and activities and even experience depression or attempt suicide.

Eating disorders

Addictive personality behaviors even include eating disorders, such as anorexia, bulimia and compulsive overeating. There are many external factors that also contribute to disordered eating behavior, but for some it can develop into a pathology quite similar to addiction. Those with anorexia nervosa channel their success into this one goal: losing weight. Once a person starts dieting, it is very difficult for him or her to quit. This is similarly true for those suffering from bulimia. A person is said to have bulimia when he or she binges on large amounts of food and then prevents digestion by purging (laxatives, vomiting, water pills, etc.). With compulsive eating, the person has a compulsive urge or craving to eat and will eat even when not hungry. This addictive behavior often results in obesity.

Compulsive buying

Addictive personality can also manifest as compulsive buying disorder. Compulsive buying is different from hoarding or normal purchasing behavior in that it is about the process of buying, not the process of acquisition: goods are bought purely for the sake of buying, and the items themselves get put away and are rarely ever used. People who buy this way describe the act as giving them a high or a buzz. Compulsive buying becomes a disorder when it entails negative effects on the person's life; these can include financial debt, psychological issues, and interpersonal and marital conflict.

Compulsive buying disorder is frequently comorbid; that is, compulsive buyers have another, concurrent or underlying disorder. Many are experiencing depression and buy things to make themselves feel better—to them, the act is much the same as taking a drug. One study found that 20% have an eating disorder as well. Further disorders that go hand-in-hand with it include mood and anxiety disorders. And like people with other addictions, people with compulsive buying problems tend to get confused by their feelings and to poorly tolerate aversive psychological states such as bad moods. Compulsive buying may lead to psychological problems because the afflicted become dependent on the high it gives them. It puts them in a positive mood at the moment, but later they feel guilt and anxiety over their purchases.

Currently the only treatment for compulsive buying is cognitive behavioral therapy. One way prevention can be achieved is through education: one study found that adolescents who have taken a class or course on finance and financial planning were less likely to buy impulsively.

Cell phone use

Another form of addictive personality is problematic cell phone use. A recent study indicates that people who are addicted to their cell phones share common traits with those who suffer from an addictive personality. Characteristics such as self-monitoring, low self-esteem, and peer approval-motivation are commonly found in those who are addicted to their cell phones as well as those who suffer from any other addiction such as alcoholism. Despite personality characteristics leading to addictive tendencies, cell phones themselves can partly be blamed for causing addiction. Improvements in cell phones such as GPS, music players, cameras, web browsing, and e-mail can make them an indispensable instrument to an individual. Technological advancements reinforce the over-attachment people have to their cell phones, thus contributing to addictive personality.

Internet and computer use

A more recent addiction that is being looked into is Internet addiction (also known as pathological Internet use). This addiction has become more prevalent in younger generations as computer technologies advance. When people suffer from internet addiction they are unable to control their use of the Internet. This can lead to psychological, social, school and work difficulties. Those addicted to the internet may be drawn to social networking sites, online games or other sites. Symptoms of this addiction include the following: mood changes, excessive time spent online, perceived social control while online, and withdrawal when away from the computer.

Tanning

Another form of behavior that is still being investigated is obsessive sun tanning as a behavioral addiction. In a recent study, researchers have proved that many frequent tanners demonstrate signs and symptoms adapted from substance abuse or dependence criteria. Many people who admit to being frequent tanners say they tan to look good, feel good, and to relax. People who partake in excessive tanning are usually completely aware of the health risks associated with it, just like addicted smokers are completely aware of the health risks of smoking. The health hazards are even more severe for high-risk age groups such as teenagers and young adults. Due to the fact that the health risks do not deter tanners from their habit, they are exhibiting self-destructive behavior that resembles the characteristics of those who suffer from substance abuse.

Frequent tanners have said a primary reason why they participate in artificial tanning is to experience the "feel good" feeling tanning salons have to offer. Researchers have found that ultraviolet (UV) radiation from tanning beds offers mood-enhancing effects that act as a treatment for seasonal affective disorder (SAD). SAD is when a person exhibits minor depression during seasonal changes, such as during the winter months. Ultraviolet radiation has been proven to increase the level of melatonin in the body. Melatonin plays a key role in sleep patterns and is suggested to reduce anxiety levels. Thus, those who go tanning experience a sense of relaxation afterwards. This sensation is what possibly drives tanners to continue tanning regardless of the health risks. More research needs to be done, but many researchers are beginning to add tanning to the list of addictive processes.

Exercise

Exercise provides physical benefits, but performed persistently to unreasonable excess, becomes hazardous, in addition to leading to interpersonal difficulties: such persons are considered exercise-dependent. Vigorous and steady exercise releases endorphins and endocannabinoids, naturally produced chemicals that are mimicked by opioids and tetrahydrocannabinol (THC, the active principle of marijuana) respectively. They are together responsible for the "Runner's High". THC binds to the brains CB1 (Cannabinoid Receptor Type 1) receptors: knockout mice that are CB1-deficient show reduced wheel-running.

Exercise addicts undergo emotional withdrawals in the absence of exercise. Performed reasonably, however, exercise is used therapeutically as an adjunct to treat mild-to-moderate depression and opioid addiction/withdrawal, because of its mood-boosting effects and because the released endorphins substitute for opioids.

Relation to leadership

When people are seeking a leader they look for qualities like honesty, intelligence, creativity, and charisma, but a leader also needs to be driven and be willing to challenge certain ideas and practices. The fact is that the psychological profile of a great leader is a compulsive risk-taker. It has been realized that what is sought in leaders is often the same kind of personality found in addicts, whether they are addicted to alcohol, other drugs, or sex. The reason that this connection exists is because pleasure is a motivator that is central to learning. Dopamine can be artificially created by substances that carry a risk for addiction, like cocaine, heroin, nicotine and alcohol. People with risk-taking and obsessive personality traits, which are often found in addicts, can be useful in becoming a leader. For many leaders, it is not the case that they are able to do well in spite of their addiction; rather, the same brain wiring and chemistry that make them addicts serve them well in becoming a good leader.

Treatment

When treating addictive personalities, the primary or presenting addiction needs to be treated first. Only once the behavior is under control can the person truly begin to do any of the therapeutic work necessary for recovery Common forms of treatment for addictive personalities include cognitive behavioral therapy, as well as other behavioral approaches. These treatments help patients by providing healthy coping skills training, relapse prevention, behavior interventions, family and group therapy, facilitated self-change approaches, and aversion therapy. Behavioral approaches include using positive reinforcement and behavioral modeling. Along with these, other options that help with treating those who suffer with addictive personality include social support, help with goal direction, rewards, enhancing self-efficacy and help teaching coping skills.

Another important skill to learn in treatment, which can be overlooked, is self-soothing. People with addictive personalities use their addictions as coping mechanisms when in stressful situations. However, since their addictions do not actually soothe them, so much as they provide momentary relief from anxiety or uncomfortable emotions, these individuals feel the need to use their addiction more often. Thus, self-soothing and other mindfulness-based interventions can be used for treatment because they provide healthier coping mechanisms once the addictive behavior has been removed. These strategies relate to the use of dialectical behavior therapy, another useful technique. DBT provides ways to tolerate distress and regulate emotions, both of which are challenging to someone with an addictive personality. DBT may not be the most effective treatment for all substance abusers, but there is evidence that it is helpful for most alcoholics and addicts, as well as in eating disorders, and those with co-occurring conditions.

Another form of treatment that has been considered for people with addictive personalities who tend towards substance abuse is medication. A medication called Disulfiram was created in 1947. This pill was used for alcoholics and would cause adverse effects if combined with alcohol. This medication is still used today but two others have been made to help treat alcohol dependence (Acamprosate and Naltrexone). Along with alcohol addictions, Naltrexone is also used for opioid addiction. Although these medications have proven results in decreasing heavy drinking, doctors still have to consider the patients› health and the risky side effects when prescribing these medications.

Controversy

There is an ongoing debate about the question of whether an addictive personality really exists. There are two sides of this argument, each with many levels and variations. One side believes that there are certain traits and dimensions of personality that, if existent in a person, cause the person to be more prone to developing addictions throughout their life. The other side argues that addiction is in chemistry, as in how the brain's synapses respond to neurotransmitters and is therefore not affected by personality. A major argument in favor of defining and labeling an addictive personality has to do with the human ability to make decisions and the notion of free will. This argument suggests human beings are aware of their actions and what the consequences of their own actions are and many choose against certain things because of this. This can be seen in that people are not forced to drink excessively or smoke every day, but it is within the reach of their own free will that some may choose to do so. Therefore, those with addictive personalities are high in neuroticism and hence choose to engage in riskier behaviors. The theory of addictive personalities agrees that there are two types of people: risk-takers and risk-averse. Risk-takers enjoy challenges, new experiences and want instant gratification. These people enjoy the excitement of danger and trying new things. On the other hand, risk-averse are those who are by nature cautious in what they do and the activities they involve themselves in. It is the personality traits of individuals that combine to create either a risk-taker or risk-averse person.

Some people believe that claiming that there is such thing as an addictive personality belittles the types and significance of many tough addictions. Others also argue that by placing a label on the type of people that have addictions, this stereotypes people and denies that addiction can happen to anyone. Some people who agree with this argument believe that claiming an addictive personality may be used as an excuse by some who do not use drugs, and are hence not addicted, to explain why they are not addicted to drugs and other people are.

Other arguments against this theory of addictive personalities is that it is very deterministic. By labeling someone with an addictive personality, one may think that there is no way to change the outcome and that he or she will inevitably develop addictions. Also, this label may cause many to believe that there is no way to change this or treat addictions, which, according to many researchers and doctors, is untrue.Combined drug intoxication

Combined drug intoxication (CDI), also known as multiple drug intake(MDI) or lethal intoxication, is an unnatural cause of human death. CDI is often confused with drug overdose, but it is a different phenomenon. It is distinct because it is due to the simultaneous use of multiple drugs, whether the drugs are prescription, over-the-counter, recreational, or some other combination. Alcohol can exacerbate the symptoms and may directly contribute to increased severity of symptoms. The reasons for toxicity vary depending on the mixture of drugs. Usually, most victims die after using two or more drugs in combination that suppress breathing, and the low blood oxygen level causes brain death.

The CDI/MDI phenomenon seems to be becoming more common in recent years. In December 2007, according to Dr. John Mendelson, a pharmacologist at the California Pacific Medical Center Research Institute, deaths by combined drug intoxication were relatively "rare" ("one in several million"), though they appeared then to be "on the rise". In July 2008, the Associated Press and CNN reported on a medical study showing that over two decades, from 1983 to 2004, such deaths have soared. It has also become a prevalent risk for older patients.

Risk factors

People who engage in polypharmacy and other hypochondriac behaviors are at an elevated risk of death from CDI. Other dangers of combining drugs include «brain damage, heart problems, seizures, stomach bleeding, liver damage/ liver failure, heatstroke, coma, suppressed breathing, and respiratory failure», along with many other complications. Disorders like depression and anxiety can also stem from polydrug use. Elderly people are at the highest risk of CDI, because of having many age-related health problems requiring many medications combined with age-impaired judgment, leading to confusion in taking medications. Elderly patients are often prescribed more than one drug within the same drug class, and doctors may treat the side effects of prescribed drugs with even more drugs, which can overwhelm the patient.

Prevention

In general, the simultaneous use of multiple drugs should be carefully monitored by a qualified individual such as board certified and licensed medical doctor, either an MD or DOClose association between prescribing physicians and pharmacies, along with the computerization of prescriptions and patients' medical histories, aim to avoid the occurrence of dangerous drug interactions. Lists of contraindications for a drug are usually provided with it, either in monographs, package inserts (accompanying prescribed medications), or in warning labels (for OTC drugs). CDI/MDI might also be avoided by physicians requiring their patients to return any unused prescriptions. Patients should ask their doctors and pharmacists if there are any interactions between the drugs they are taking.

5

Drug Trafficking

Introduction

Drug trafficking is a global illicit trade involving the cultivation, manufacture, distribution and sale of substances which are subject to drug prohibition laws. UNODC is continuously monitoring and researching global illicit drug markets in order to gain a more comprehensive understanding of their dynamics. Drug trafficking is a key part of this research. Further information can be found in the yearly World Drug Report. Drug trafficking, also known as drug distribution, is the crime of selling, transporting, or illegally importing unlawful controlled substances, such as heroin, cocaine, marijuana, or other illegal drugs. Drug trafficking also applies to the illegal selling or transportation of prescription drugs, which has become an increasing problem in recent years. According to the Department of Justice, the sale and manufacture of drugs accounts for almost one-fifth of all drug-related arrests.

The crime of drug trafficking is similar to drug possession, since it requires that the perpetrator knowingly possesses an illegal controlled substance. Thus, an individual cannot engage in drug trafficking while being unaware that he or she is in possession of a drug, or if he or she reasonably but mistakenly believes that the substance is legal. However, drug trafficking also requires that a prosecutor show that the perpetrator was involved in the sale, transport, or importation of such drugs, or intended to sell or deliver the drugs. This additional requirement elevates the status of the crime and makes it a felony.

Since possession and trafficking can look the same at first glance, prosecution for drug trafficking typically requires producing additional circumstantial evidence to indicate that a defendant is in possession of drugs not only for personal use but for commercial purposes. This may include the presence of a scale at the time of arrest, or other materials like plastic baggies or business cards. A prosecutor may also show that the defendant was in possession of a large amount of cash, or kept business records detailing his or her sales and purchases. Finally, the government may rely on the testimony of other witnesses who bought or sold drugs to the defendant, or were aware of his or her drug trafficking operation.

Penalties for Drug Trafficking

Drug trafficking is a very serious crime and is punished more harshly than drug possession. It is criminalized under both federal and state laws, and it is often prosecuted as a federal crime when a defendant moves drugs across state lines. Drug trafficking charges can be applied to small-scale street dealers or large drug cartels, and punishments will typically vary depending on the scale of the defendant's operation and the type of drugs being trafficked. Thus, for instance, a defendant may face anywhere from 3-10 years of imprisonment and fines of over $100,000 for marijuana trafficking, but he or she may face up to 25 years in prison and fines of half a million dollars if convicted of trafficking in heroin. These sentences may be even higher if certain factors, called "enhancements," are present. One example of an enhancement is selling drugs in a school zone.

A conviction for drug trafficking also makes a criminal susceptible to additional punishments, particularly in the context of an international operation. This can include the forfeiture of all assets related to the drug trafficking business, such as bank accounts, cars, or properties used in the crime. Seizure of assets is often required if the defendant is sentenced to more than one year in jail. Additionally, since drug trafficking is a felony, it may also make defendants susceptible to immigration consequences, including possible deportation after a prison sentence is served.

At current levels, world heroin consumption (340 tons) and seizures represent an annual flow of 430-450 tons of heroin into the global heroin market. Of that total, opium from Myanmar and the Lao People's Democratic Republic yields some 50 tons, while the rest, some 380 tons of heroin and morphine, is produced exclusively from Afghan opium. While approximately 5 tons are consumed and seized in Afghanistan, the remaining bulk of 375 tons is trafficked worldwide via routes flowing into and through the countries neighbouring Afghanistan.

The Balkan and northern routes are the main heroin trafficking corridors linking Afghanistan to the huge markets of the Russian Federation and Western Europe. The Balkan route traverses the Islamic Republic of Iran (often via Pakistan), Turkey, Greece and Bulgaria across South-East Europe to the Western European market, with an annual market value of some $20 billion. The northern route runs mainly through Tajikistan and Kyrgyzstan (or Uzbekistan or Turkmenistan) to Kazakhstan and the Russian Federation. The size of that market is estimated to total $13 billion per year.

Global heroin flows from Asian points of origin

In 2008, global heroin seizures reached a record level of 73.7 metric tons. Most of the heroin was seized in the Near and Middle East and South-West Asia

(39 per cent of the global total), South-East Europe (24 per cent) and Western and Central Europe (10 per cent). The global increase in heroin seizures over the period 2006-2008 was driven mainly by continued burgeoning seizures in the Islamic Republic of Iran and Turkey. In 2008, those two countries accounted for more than half of global heroin seizures and registered, for the third consecutive year, the highest and second highest seizures worldwide, respectively.

In 2007 and 2008, cocaine was used by some 16 to 17 million people worldwide, similar to the number of global opiate users. North America accounted for more than 40 per cent of global cocaine consumption (the total was estimated at around 470 tons), while the 27 European Union and four European Free Trade Association countries accounted for more than a quarter of total consumption. These two regions account for more than 80 per cent of the total value of the global cocaine market, which was estimated at $88 billion in 2008.

For the North American market, cocaine is typically transported from Colombia to Mexico or Central America by sea and then onwards by land to the United States and Canada. Cocaine is trafficked to Europe mostly by sea, often in container shipments. Colombia remains the main source of the cocaine found in Europe, but direct shipments from Peru and the Plurinational State of Bolivia are far more common than in the United States market.

Drug distribution or trafficking laws penalize the selling, transportation, and illegal import of unlawful controlled substances, such as marijuana, cocaine, heroin, methamphetamines, and other illegal drugs. The punishment for drug trafficking can vary widely depending on several factors including the type and quantity of drugs involved, the type of drugs, geographic area of distribution, and whether children were targeted. Sentences for drug distribution and trafficking can generally range from 3-5 years to life in prison, but can be substantially higher when larger quantities are involved.

Drug trafficking/distribution is a felony, and is a more serious crime than drug possession. If you're found in possession of drugs, you could be charged with trafficking if police believe you intended to sell them. If you're found with a large quantity of drugs or cash at the time of your arrest, it is likely you'll be facing drug distribution charges.

Drug distribution or trafficking also applies to the illegal distribution of prescription drugs, such as pain killers or sleeping pills. The illegal distribution of prescription drugs often involves hydrocodone products and pharmaceutical opiates.

Drug Trafficking & Controlled Substances

When a state or federal government classifies a substance as "controlled," it generally means that the use and distribution of the substance is governed by law. Controlled substances are often classified at different levels or "schedules" under federal and state statutes. For instance, marijuana is listed as a "Schedule I controlled substance," cocaine is listed under Schedule II, anabolic steroids under Schedule III, under the federal Controlled Substances Act. The Act lists the drugs that fall under each Schedule.

- Schedule I means the drug is highly addictive; has no accepted medical use; and is not safe even under medical supervision.
- Schedule II means the drug is highly addictive; has medical uses; may lead to severe drug dependence.
- Schedule III means the drug has a low potential for abuse; has accepted medical uses; and moderate risk of dependence.
- Schedule IV and V both have low potential for drug abuse; have accepted medical uses; and have limited potential for dependence.

Trafficking Charges

Both federal and state laws come into play on drug trafficking cases. If a person is caught trafficking a controlled substance across state lines, federal law will apply, but if the drug trafficking is entirely within one state, that state's laws will apply.

There is a multitude of federal drug laws on the books, plus each state also has its own set of drug laws. Many state laws are modeled after the federal laws and provide minimum sentencing standards for offenders. Lawmakers generally pass these laws to deter the major drug cartels, but more often it is the lower level dealers that get prosecuted. Indeed, the controversy around drug trafficking laws is that a petty drug dealer can often face a longer sentence than violent criminals.

Federal Drug Trafficking Charges

The Federal government prohibits any person from manufacturing, distributing, dispensing, or possessing controlled substances. A person found in violation is subject to sentencing based on the quantity of the prohibited substance. The details about prison sentences and fines for controlled substances are found in federal statutes. As an example, here are a few of the applicable penalties:

- 10 years to life in prison for 1 kilogram of heroin; 5 kilograms of cocaine; or 1000 kilograms of marijuana;
- 5 to 40 years for 100 grams of heroin; or 500 grams of cocaine; or
- Not more than 5 years for 50 kilograms of marijuana.

The prison sentences increase for higher amounts controlled substances. There are also penalty enhancements if death or serious bodily injury results and for prior convictions. In addition, prison term enhancements can apply to convictions for drug trafficking if the person is considered the leader or if a firearm is involved. Note that the firearm sentences are not concurrent with the sentence for drug trafficking. This means that the convicted person would serve the prison term for the drug offense and then serve the additional term for the firearm afterwards.

State Drug Trafficking Charges

Just like federal law, all states prohibit the manufacture, distribution, or possession of controlled substances. Typically, state prison sentences are less than a federal prison sentence, but not always. Further, states control smaller amounts than the federal government. For instance, Arizona assumes that possession of 1 gram of heroin, 9 grams of cocaine or 2 pounds of marijuana by a person is for distribution.

Legalized Marijuana

The legalization of marijuana by some states has thrown a monkey wrench into the drug trafficking laws. Marijuana is still illegal as far as the federal government is concerned and their enforcement has not changed even in states that have legalized it on a state level. It is important to note that trafficking over certain amounts of marijuana is still illegal even where marijuana is legal. For instance, it is a felony in Colorado to transport as little as 4 ounces with the jail time and fines increasing with higher quantities.

Get Legal Help with Your Drug Trafficking Case

Drug trafficking charges could result in jail time, seized assets, and a ruined reputation. For this reason, it's in your best interest to contact a local drug crime attorney to discuss your case and learn about your options moving forward.

Proximity to the largest producers of heroin and hashish-the Golden Triangle and Golden Crescent (Afghanistan-Pakistan-Iran) -has made India's border vulnerable to drug trafficking. Indigenous production of low grade heroin as well as various psychotropic and prescription drugs and their growing demand in the neighbouring countries and international market have added a new dimension to the problem of drug trafficking. Trends and patterns of drug trafficking in the country demonstrate that there is a gradual shift from traditional/natural drugs towards synthetic drugs that are being trafficked. Trafficking of drugs takes place overwhelmingly through land borders followed by sea and air routes. Given the vulnerability of the borders to drug trafficking, India has tried to tackle the problem through the strategy of drug supply and demand reduction, which involves enacting laws, co-operating with voluntary organisations, securing its borders and coasts by increasing surveillance, as well as seeking the active cooperation of its neighbours and the international community.

Main global cocaine flows, 2008

Following a significant increase over the period 2002-2005, global cocaine seizure totals have recently followed a stable trend, amounting to 712 tons in 2007 and 711 tons in 2008. Seizures continued to be concentrated in the Americas and Europe. However, the transition from 2007 to 2008 brought about a geographical shift in seizures towards the source countries for cocaine. Seizures in South America accounted for 59 per cent of the global total for 2008, compared with 45 per cent in 2007.

Legal drug trade

Legal drug trade, as with other goods object of commerce, in opposition to smuggling or illegal drug trade, most psychotropic substances' commerce is under control and taxationby world governments, regardless of the relative perceived danger of the goods that are the object of legislation.

Legal commerce in drugs can be categorized according to the purpose of consumption (therapeutic vs recreational), type of drug involved and phase of the trading process, i.e.: production, distribution or consumption.

Therapeutic use

Production

Drugs useful for treating diseases are the object of pharmaceutical research and medical practice, and produced by the pharmaceutical industry, which in theory should be above United Nations legislation prohibiting use or sole possession of the drugs termed illegal for other purposes.

Distribution

Pharmaceutical companies, through authorized dealers, guarantee the distribution of their products to their customers. Since antiquity, there have been stores specialized in drug selling. Today, they are called pharmacies or, straightforwardly, drugstores. Certain drugs officially considered trade-able without medical supervision are also sold in non-specialized stores, such as supermarkets.

Consumption

Therapeutic drug consumption can take place in an outpatient setting, or during hospitalization.

Recreational use

Production

Alcoholic beverages, containing psychoactive ethyl alcohol, are produced legally throughout the world. Their production supports a commercial alcohol industry. Consumption of alcohol is subject to regulation in most countries, namely by means of age restrictions.

Tobacco, a recreational drug containing nicotine, is produced legally in countries such as Cuba, China, and the United States. This also supports a tobacco industry and the production of a variety of tobacco products, which, like alcoholic beverages, are subject to age restrictions in most countries.

Caffeine, a stimulant drug, is extracted from plants including the coffee plant and the tea bush. It is the most widely consumed psychoactive substance in the world, remaining unregulated and generally recognized as safe by the U.S. Food and Drug Administration.

Distribution

There are authorized dealers which provide consumers with legal intoxicants, every industry developing a network of distribution to connect with its clients. Drug publicity by producers and distributors aims at increasing consumption.

Consumption

Legal drugs for recreation are taken by people in private and in public, including places devoted to drug selling for consumption in situ, such as bars and certain restaurants.

Cultural biases

The above-mentioned substances represent the most important products legally produced for the purposes of mind-altering effects. Some critics argue that cannabis and opioids occupy the social position of alcohol and tobacco in some non-western countries, where alcohol and its users could be treated in a way resembling the harassment and prosecution of illegal drug users in western countries, in cultural defiance of the UN's worldwide prohibition. They are also the most important public health concern, as a result of prohibition of certain other drugs.

Illegal drug trade

The illegal drug trade or drug trafficking is a global black market dedicated to the cultivation, manufacture, distribution and sale of drugs that are subject to drug prohibition laws. Most jurisdictions prohibit trade, except under license, of many types of drugs through the use of drug prohibition laws.

The United Nations Office on Drugs and Crime's World Drug Report 2005 estimates the size of the global illicit drug market at US$321.6 billion in 2003 alone. With a world GDP of US$36 trillion in the same year, the illegal drug trade may be estimated as nearly 1% of total global trade. Consumption of illegal drugs is widespread globally and remains very difficult for local authorities to thwart its popularity.

History

Chinese authorities issued edicts against opium smoking in 1729, 1796 and 1800. The West prohibited addictive drugs throughout the late 19th and early 20th centuries.

In the early 19th century, an illegal drug trade in China emerged. As a result, by 1838 the number of Chinese opium-addicts had grown to between four and twelve million. The Chinese government responded by enforcing a ban on the import of opium; this led to the First Opium War (1839-1842) between the United Kingdom and Qing-dynasty China. The United Kingdom won and forced China to allow British merchants to sell Indian-grown opium. Trading in opium was lucrative, and smoking opium had become common in the 19th century, so British merchants increased trade with the Chinese. The Second Opium War broke out in 1856, with the British joined this time by the French. After the two Opium Wars, the British Crown, via the treaties of Nanking (1842), and Tianjin (1858), obligated the Chinese government to pay large sums of money for opium they had seized and destroyed, which were referred to as «reparations».

In 1868, as a result of the increased use of opium, the UK restricted the sale of opium in Britain by implementing the 1868 Pharmacy Act. In the United States, control of opium remained under the control of individual US states until the introduction of the Harrison Act in 1914, after 12 international powers signed the International Opium Convention in 1912.

Between 1920 and 1933 the Eighteenth Amendment to the United States Constitution banned alcohol in the United States. Prohibition proved almost impossible to enforce and resulted in the rise of organized crime, including the modern American Mafia, which identified enormous business opportunities in the manufacturing, smuggling and sale of illicit liquor.

The beginning of the 21st century saw drug use increase in North America and Europe, with a particularly increased demand for marijuana and cocaine. As a result, international organized crime syndicates such as the Sinaloa Cartel and 'Ndrangheta have increased cooperation among each other in order to facilitate trans-Atlantic drug-trafficking. Use of another illicit drug, hashish, has also increased in Europe.

Drug trafficking is widely regarded by lawmakers as a serious offense around the world. Penalties often depend on the type of drug (and its classification in the country into which it is being trafficked), the quantity trafficked, where the drugs are sold and how they are distributed. If the drugs are sold to underage people, then the penalties for trafficking may be harsher than in other circumstances.

Drug smuggling carries severe penalties in many countries. Sentencing may include lengthy periods of incarceration, flogging and even the death penalty (in Singapore, Malaysia, Indonesia and elsewhere). In December 2005, Van Tuong Nguyen, a 25-year-old Australian drug smuggler, was hanged in Singapore after being convicted in March 2004. In 2010, two people were sentenced to death in Malaysia for trafficking 1 kilogram (2.2 lb) of cannabis into the country. Execution is mostly used as a deterrent, and many have called upon much more effective measures to be taken by countries to tackle drug trafficking; for example, targeting specific criminal organisations (which are often also active in the smuggling of other goods (i.e. wildlife) and even people In a lot of cases, links between politicians and the criminal organisations have been proven to exist.

Societal effects

The countries of drug production and transit are some of the most affected by the drug trade, though countries receiving the illegally imported substances are also adversely affected. For example, Ecuador has absorbed up to 300,000 refugees from Colombia who are running from guerrillas, paramilitaries and drug lords. While some applied for asylum, others are still illegal immigrants. The drugs that pass from Colombia through Ecuador to other parts of South America create economic and social problems.

Honduras, through which an estimated 79% of cocaine passes on its way to the United States, has the highest murder rate in the world. According to the International Crisis Group, the most violent regions in Central America, particularly along the Guatemala–Honduras border, are highly correlated with an abundance of drug trafficking activity.

Violent crime

In many countries, the illegal drug trade is thought to be directly linked to violent crimes such as murder. This is especially true in all developing countries, such as Honduras, but is also an issue for many developed countries worldwide. In the late 1990s in the United States the Federal Bureau of Investigation estimated that 5% of murders were drug-related. In Colombia, Drug violence can be caused by factors such as, the economy, poor governments, and no authority within the law enforcement.

After a crackdown by US and Mexican authorities in the first decade of the 21st century as part of tightened border security in the wake of the September 11 attacks, border violence inside Mexico surged. The Mexican government estimates that 90% of the killings are drug-related.

A report by the UK government's Drug Strategy Unit that was leaked to the press, stated that due to the expensive price of highly addictive drugs heroin and cocaine, drug use was responsible for the great majority of crime, including 85% of shoplifting, 70–80% of burglaries and 54% of robberies. It concluded that «[t]he cost of crime committed to support illegal cocaine and heroin habits amounts to £16 billion a year in the UK»

Drug trafficking routes

South America

Venezuela has been a path to the United States and Europe for illegal drugs originating in Colombia, through Central America, Mexico and Caribbean countries such as Haiti, the Dominican Republic, and Puerto Rico.

According to the United Nations, there was an increase of cocaine trafficking through Venezuela since 2002. In 2005, the government of Hugo Chávez severed ties with the United States Drug Enforcement Administration (DEA), accusing its representatives of spying.Following the departure of the DEA from Venezuela and the expansion of DEA's partnership with Colombia in 2005, Venezuela became more attractive to drug traffickers. Between 2008 and 2012, Venezuela›s cocaine seizure ranking among other countries declined, going from being ranked fourth in the world for cocaine seizures in 2008 to sixth in the world in 2012.

On 18 November 2016, following what was known as the Narcosobrinos incident, Venezuelan President Nicolás Maduro's two nephews were found guilty of trying to ship drugs into the United States so they could "obtain a large amount of cash to help their family stay in power".

West Africa

Cocaine produced in Colombia and Bolivia increasingly has been shipped via West Africa (especially in Cape Verde, Mali, Benin, Togo, Nigeria, Cameroon, Guinea-Bissau and Ghana). The money is often laundered in countries such as Nigeria, Ghana and Senegal.

According to the Africa Economic Institute, the value of illicit drug smuggling in Guinea-Bissau is almost twice the value of the country's GDP. Police officers are often bribed. A police officer›s normal monthly wage of $93 is less than 2% of the value of 1 kilogram (2.2 lb) of cocaine (€7000 or $8750 The money can also be laundered using real estate. A house is built using illegal funds, and when the house is sold, legal money is earned. When drugs are sent over land, through the Sahara, the drug traders have been forced to cooperate with terrorist organizations, such as Al Qaida in Islamic Maghreb.

Eastern and southern Africa

Heroin is increasingly trafficked from Afghanistan to Europe and America through eastern and southern African countries. This path is known as the "southern route" or "smack track." Repercussions of this trade include burgeoning heroin use and political corruption among intermediary African nations.

Asia

Drugs in Asia traditionally traveled the southern routes – the main caravan axes of Southeast Asia and Southern China – and include the former opium-producing countries of Thailand, Iran, and Pakistan. After the 1990s, particularly after the Cold War ended, borders were opened and trading and customs agreements were signed so that the routes expanded to include China, Central Asia, and Russia. There is, therefore, a diversified drug trafficking routes available today, particularly in the heroin trade and these thrive due to the continuous development of new markets. A large amount of drugs are smuggled into Europe from Asia. The main sources of these drugs are Afghanistan, along with countries that constituted the so-called Golden Crescent. From these producers, drugs are smuggled into the West and Central Asia to its destinations in Europe and the United States. Iran is now the route for smugglers, having been previously a primary trading route, due to its large-scale and costly war against drug trafficking. The Border Police Chief of Iran said that his country «is a strong barrier against the trafficking of illegal drugs to Caucasus, especially the Republic of Azerbaijan.» The drugs produced by the Golden Triangle of Myanmar, Laos, and Thailand, on the other hand, pass through the southern routes to feed the Australian, U.S., and Asian markets.

Online

Drugs are increasingly traded online on the dark web on darknet markets.

Profits

Statistics about profits from the drug trade are largely unknown due to its illicit nature. In its 1997 World Drugs Report the United Nations Office on Drugs and Crime estimated the value of the market at $4 trillion, ranking drugs alongside arms and oil among the world's largest traded goods. An online report published by the UK Home Office in 2007 estimated the illicit drug market in the UK at £4–6.6 billion a year

In December 2009 United Nations Office on Drugs and Crime Executive Director Antonio Maria Costa claimed illegal drug money saved the banking industry from collapse. He claimed he had seen evidence that the proceeds of organized crime were «the only liquid investment capital» available to some banks on the brink of collapse during 2008. He said that a majority of the $352 billion (£216bn) of drug profits was absorbed into the economic system as a result:

"In many instances, the money from drugs was the only liquid investment capital. In the second half of 2008, liquidity was the banking system's main problem and hence liquid capital became an important factor...Inter-bank loans were funded by money that originated from the drugs trade and other illegal activities...there were signs that some banks were rescued that way".

Costa declined to identify countries or banks that may have received any drug money, saying that would be inappropriate because his office is supposed to address the problem, not apportion blame.

Though street-level drug sales are widely viewed as lucrative, a study by Sudhir Venkatesh suggested that many low-level employees receive low wages. In a study he made in the 1990s working closely with members of the Black Gangster Disciple Nation in Chicago, he found that one gang (essentially a franchise) consisted of a leader (a college graduate named J.T.), three senior officers, and 25 to 75 street level salesmen ('foot soldiers') depending on season. Selling crack cocaine, they took in approximately $32,000 per month over a six-year period. This was spent as follows: $5,000 to the board of twenty directors of the Black Gangster Disciple Nation, who oversaw 100 such gangs for approximately $500,000 in monthly income. Another $5,000 monthly was paid for cocaine, and $4,000 for other non-wage expenses. J.T. took $8,500 monthly for his own salary. The remaining $9,500 monthly went to pay the employees a $7 per hour wage for officers and a $3.30 per hour wage for foot soldiers. Contrary to a popular image of drug sales as a lucrative profession, many of the employees were living with their mothers by necessity. Despite this, the gang had four times as many unpaid members who dreamed of becoming foot soldiers.

Free trade link

There are several arguments on whether or not free trade has a correlation to an increased activity in the illicit drug trade. Currently, the structure and operation of the illicit drug industry is described mainly in terms of an international division of labor. Free trade can open new markets to domestic producers who would otherwise resort to exporting illicit drugs. Additionally, extensive free trade among states increases cross-border drug enforcement and coordination between law enforcement agencies in different countries. However, free trade also increases the sheer volume of legal cross-border trade and provides cover for drug smuggling—by providing ample opportunity to conceal illicit cargo in legal trade. While international free trade continues to expand the volume of legal trade, the ability to detect and interdict drug trafficking is severely diminished. Towards the late 1990s, the top ten seaports in the world processed 33.6 million containers. Free trade has fostered integration of financial markets and has provided drug traffickers with more opportunities to launder money and invest in other activities. This strengthens the drug industry while weakening the efforts of law enforcement to monitor the flow of drug money into the legitimate economy. Cooperation among cartels expands their scope to distant markets and strengthens their abilities to evade detection by local law enforcement.Additionally, criminal organizations work together to coordinate money-laundering activities by having separate organizations handle specific stages of laundering process. One organization structures the process of how financial transactions will be laundered, while another criminal group provides the "dirty" money to be cleaned. By fostering expansion of trade and global transportation networks, free trade encourages cooperation and formation of alliances among criminal organizations across different countries. The drug trade in Latin America emerged in the early 1930s. It saw significant growth in the Andean countries, including Peru, Bolivia, Chile, Ecuador, Colombia and Venezuela. The underground market in the early half of the 20th century mainly had ties to Europe. After World War II, the Andean countries saw an expansion of trade, specifically with cocaine.

Drug trafficking by country

United States

Background

The effects of the illegal drug trade in the United States can be seen in a range of political, economic and social aspects. Increasing drug related violence can be tied to the racial tension that arose during the late 20th century along with the political upheaval prevalent throughout the 1960s and 70s. The second half of the 20th century was a period when increased wealth, and increased discretionary spending, increased the demand for illicit drugs in certain areas of the United States. Large-scale drug trafficking is one of the few capital crimes, and may result in a death sentence prescribed at the federal level.

Political impact

A large generation, the baby boomers, came of age in the 1960s. Their social tendency to confront the law on specific issues, including illegal drugs, overwhelmed the understaffed judicial system. The federal government attempted to enforce the law, but with meager effect.

Marijuana was a popular drug seen through the Latin American trade route in the 1960s. Cocaine became a major drug product in the later decades. Much of the cocaine is smuggled from Colombia and Mexico via Jamaica. This led to several administrations combating the popularity of these drugs. Due to the influence of this development on the U.S. economy, the Reagan administration began «certifying» countries for their attempts at controlling drug trafficking. This allowed the United States to intervene in activities related to illegal drug transport in Latin America. Continuing into the 1980s, the United States instated stricter policy pertaining to drug transit through sea. As a result, there was an influx in drug-trafficking across the Mexico–U.S. border. This increased the drug cartel activity in Mexico. By the early 1990s, so much as 50% of the cocaine available in the United States market originated from Mexico, and by the 2000s, over 90% of the cocaine in the United States was imported from Mexico. In Colombia, however, there was a fall of the major drug cartels in the mid-1990s. Visible shifts occurred in the drug market in the United States. Between the 1996 and 2000, U.S. cocaine consumption dropped by 11%.

In 2008, the U.S. government initiated another program, known as the Merida Initiative, to help combat drug trafficking in Mexico. This program increased U.S. security assistance to $1.4 billion over several years, which helped supply Mexican forces with "high-end equipment from helicopters to surveillance technology". Despite U.S. aid, Mexican «narcogangs» continue to outnumber and outgun the Mexican Army, allowing for continued activities of drug cartels across the U.S.–Mexico border.

Social impacts

Although narcotics are illegal in the US, they have become integrated into the nation's culture and are seen as a recreational activity by sections of the population. Illicit drugs are considered to be a commodity with strong demand, as they are typically sold at a high value. This high price is caused by a combination of factors that include the potential legal ramifications that exist for suppliers of illicit drugs and their high demand. Despite the constant effort by politicians to win the war on drugs, the US is still the world's largest importer of illegal drugs.

Throughout the 20th century, narcotics other than cocaine also crossed the Mexican border, meeting the US demand for alcohol during the 1920s Prohibition, opiates in the 1940s, marijuana in the 1960s, and heroin in the 1970s. Most of the U.S. imports of drugs come from Mexican drug cartels. In the United States, around 195 cities have been infiltrated by drug trafficking that originated in Mexico. An estimated $10bn of the Mexican drug cartel›s profits come from the United States, not only supplying the Mexican drug cartels with the profit necessary for survival, but also furthering America›s economic dependence on drugs.

Demographics

With a large wave of immigrants in the 1960s and onwards, the United States saw an increased heterogeneity in its public. In the 1980s and 90s, drug related homicide was at a record high. This increase in drug violence became increasingly tied to these ethnic minorities. Though the rate of violence varied tremendously among cities in America, it was a common anxiety in communities across urban America. An example of this could be seen in Miami, a city with a host of ethnic enclaves. Between 1985 and 1995, the homicide rate in Miami was one of the highest in the nation—four times the national homicide average. This crime rate was correlated with regions with low employment and was not entirely dependent on ethnicity.

The baby boomer generation also felt the effects of the drug trade in their increased drug use from the 1960s to 80s. Along with substance abuse, criminal involvement, suicide and murder were also on the rise. Due to the large amount of baby boomers, commercial marijuana use was on the rise. This increased the supply and demand for marijuana during this time period.

Mexico

Political influences

Corruption in Mexico has contributed to the domination of Mexican cartels in the illicit drug trade. Since the beginning of the 20th century, Mexico›s political environment allowed the growth of drug-related activity. The loose regulation over the transportation of illegal drugs and the failure to prosecute known drug traffickers and gangs increased the growth of the drug industry. Toleration of drug trafficking has undermined the authority of the Mexican government and has decreased the power of law enforcement officers in regulation over such activities. These policies of tolerance fostered the growing power of drug cartels in the Mexican economy and have made drug traders wealthier. Many states in Mexico lack policies that establish stability in governance. There also is a lack of local stability, as mayors cannot be re-elected. This requires electing a new mayor each term. Drug gangs have manipulated this, using vacuums in local leadership to their own advantage.

In 1929, the Institutional Revolutionary Party (PRI) was formed to resolve the chaos resulting from the Mexican Revolution. Over time, this party gained political influence and had a major impact on Mexico's social and economic policies. The party created ties with various groups as a power play in order to gain influence, and as a result created more corruption in the government. One such power play was an alliance with drug traffickers. This political corruption obscured justice, making it difficult to identify violence when it related to drugs. By the 1940s, the tie between the drug cartels and the PRI had solidified. This arrangement created immunity for the leaders of the drug cartels and allowed drug trafficking to grow under the protection of the government officials. During the 1990s, the PRI lost some elections to the new National Action Party(PAN). Chaos again emerged as elected government in Mexico changed drastically. As the PAN party took control, drug cartel leaders took advantage of the ensuing confusion and used their existing influence to further gain power. Instead of negotiating with the central government as was done with the PRI party, drug cartels utilized new ways to distribute their supply and continued operating through force and intimidation. As Mexico became more democratized, the corruption fell from a centralized power to the local authorities. Cartels began to bribe local authorities, thus eliminating the structure and rules placed by the government—giving cartels more freedom. As a response, Mexico saw an increase in violence caused by drug trafficking.

The corruption cartels created resulted in distrust of government by the Mexican public. This distrust became more prominent after the collapse of the PRI party. In response, the presidents of Mexico, in the late twentieth century and early twenty-first century, implemented several different programs relating to law enforcement and regulation. In 1993, President Salinas created the National Institute for the Combat of Drugs in Mexico. From 1995–1998, President Zedillo established policies regarding increased punishment of organized crime, allowing "[wire taps], protected witnesses, covert agents and seizures of goods", and increasing the quality of law enforcement at the federal level. From 2001–2005, President Vicente Fox created the Federal Agency of Investigation. These policies resulted in the arrests of major drug-trafficking bosses:

Mexico's economy

Over the past few decades drug cartels have become integrated into Mexico's economy. Approximately 500 cities are directly engaged in drug trafficking and nearly 450,000 people are employed by drug cartels. Additionally, the livelihood of 3.2 million people is dependent on the drug cartels. Between local and international sales, such as to Europe and the United States, drug cartels in Mexico see a $25–30bn yearly profit, a great deal of which circulates through international banks such as HSBC. Drug cartels are fundamental in local economics. A percentage of the profits seen from the trade are invested in the local community. Such profits contribute to the education and healthcare of the community.While these cartels bring violence and hazards into communities, they create jobs and provide income for its many members.

Culture of drug cartels

Major cartels saw growth due to a prominent set culture of Mexican society that created the means for drug capital. One of the sites of origin for drug trafficking within Mexico, was the state of Michoacán. In the past, Michoacán was mainly an agricultural society. This provided an initial growth of trade. Industrialization of rural areas of Mexico facilitated a greater distribution of drugs, expanding the drug market into different provinces. Once towns became industrialized, cartels such as the Sinaloa Cartel started to form and expand. The proliferation of drug cartel culture largely stemmed from the ranchero culture seen in Michoacán. Ranchero culture values the individual as opposed to the society as a whole. This culture fostered the drug culture of valuing the family that is formed within the cartel. This ideal allowed for greater organization within the cartels. Gangs play a major role in the activity of drug cartels. MS-13 and the 18th Street gang are notorious for their contributions and influence over drug trafficking throughout Latin America. MS-13 has controlled much of the activity in the drug trade spanning from Mexico to Panama Female involvement is present in the Mexican drug culture. Although females are not treated as equals to males, they typically hold more power than their culture allows and acquire some independence. The increase in power has attracted females from higher social classes. Financial gain has also prompted women to become involved in the illegal drug market. Many women in the lower levels of major drug cartels belong to a low economic class. Drug trafficking offers women an accessible way to earn income. Females from all social classes have become involved in the trade due to outside pressure from their social and economic environments.

Colombia

Political ties

It was common for smugglers in Colombia to import liquor, alcohol, cigarettes and textiles, while exporting cocaine. Personnel with knowledge of the terrain were able to supply the local market while also exporting a large amount of product. The established trade that began in the 1960s involved Peru, Bolivia, Colombia, Venezuela and Cuba. Peasant farmers produced coca paste in Peru and Bolivia, while Colombian smugglers would process the coca paste into cocaine in Colombia, and trafficked product through Cuba. This trade route established ties between Cuban and Colombian organized crime. From Cuba, cocaine would be transported to Miami, Florida; and Union City, New Jersey. Quantities of the drug were then smuggled throughout the US. The international drug trade created political ties between the involved countries, encouraging the governments of the countries involved to collaborate and instate common policies to eradicate drug cartels. Cuba stopped being a center for transport of cocaine following the establishment of a communist government in 1959. As a result, Miami and Union City became the sole locations for trafficking. The relations between Cuban and Colombian organized crime remained strong until the 1970s, when Colombian cartels began to vie for power. In the 1980s and 90s, Colombia emerged as a key contributor of the drug trade industry in the Western Hemisphere. While the smuggling of drugs such as marijuana, poppy, opium and heroin became more ubiquitous during this time period, the activity of cocaine cartels drove the development of the Latin American drug trade. The trade emerged as a multinational effort as supplies (i.e. coca plant substances) were imported from countries such as Bolivia and Peru, were refined in Colombian cocaine labs and smuggled through Colombia, and exported to countries such as the US.

Colombia's economy

Colombia has had a significant role in the illegal drug trade in Latin America. While active in the drug trade since the 1930s, Colombia's role in the drug trade did not truly become dominant until the 1970s. When Mexico eradicated marijuana plantations, demand stayed the same. Colombia met much of the demand by growing more marijuana. Grown in the strategic northeast region of Colombia, marijuana soon became the leading cash crop in Colombia. This success was short-lived due to anti-marijuana campaigns that were enforced by the US military throughout the Caribbean. Instead, drug traffickers in Colombia continued their focus on the exportation of cocaine. Having been an export of Colombia since the early 1950s, cocaine remained popular for a host of reasons. Colombia›s location facilitated its transportation from South America into Central America, and then to its destination of North America. This continued into the 1990s, when Colombia remained the chief exporter of cocaine. The business of drug trafficking can be seen in several stages in Colombia towards the latter half of the 20th century. Colombia served as the dominant force in the distribution and sale of cocaine by the 1980s. As drug producers gained more power, they became more centralized and organized into what became drug cartels. Cartels controlled the major aspects of each stage in the traffic of their product. Their organization allowed cocaine to be distributed in great amounts throughout the United States. By the late 1980s, intra-industry strife arose within the cartels. This stage was marked by increased violence as different cartels fought for control of export markets. Despite this strife, this power struggle led to then having multiple producers of coca leaf farms. This in turn caused an improvement in quality control and reduction of police interdiction in the distribution of cocaine. This also led to cartels attempting to repatriate their earnings which would eventually make up 5.5% of Colombia›s GDP. This drive to repatriate earnings led to the pressure of legitimizing their wealth, causing an increase in violence throughout Colombia.

Throughout the 1980s, estimates of illegal drug value in Colombia ranged from $2bn to $4bn. This made up about 7–10% of the $36bn estimated GNP of Colombia during this decade. In the 1990s, the estimates of the illegal drug value remained roughly within the same range (~$2.5bn). As the Colombian GNP rose throughout the 90›s ($68.5bn in 1994 and $96.3bn in 1997), illegal drug values began to comprise a decreasing fraction of the national economy. By the early 1990s, although Colombia led in the exportation of cocaine, it found increasing confrontations within its state. These confrontations were primarily between cartels and government institutions. This led to a decrease in the drug trade›s contribution to the GDP of Colombia; dropping from 5.5% to 2.6%. Though a contributor of wealth, the distribution of cocaine has had negative effects on the socio-political situation of Colombia and has weakened its economy as well.

Social impacts

By the 1980s, Colombian cartels became the dominant cocaine distributors in the US. This led to the spread of increased violence throughout both Latin America and Miami. In the 1980s, two major drug cartels emerged in Colombia: the Medellin and Cali groups. Throughout the 90›s however, several factors led to the decline of these major cartels and to the rise of smaller Colombian cartels. The U.S. demand for cocaine dropped while Colombian production rose, pressuring traffickers to find new drugs and markets. In this time period, there was an increase in activity of Caribbean cartels that led to the rise of an alternate route of smuggling through Mexico. This led to the increased collaboration between major Colombian and Mexican drug traffickers. Such drastic changes in the execution of drug trade in Colombia paired with the political instabilities and rise of drug wars in Medellin and Cali, gave way for the rise of the smaller Colombian drug trafficking organizations (and the rise of heroin trade). As the drug trade›s influence over the economy increased, drug lords and their networks grew in their power and influence in society. The occurrences in drug-related violence increased during this time period as drug lords fought to maintain their control in the economy.Typically a drug cartel had support networks that consisted of a number of individuals. These people individuals ranged from those directly involved in the trade (such as suppliers, chemists, transporters, smugglers, etc.) as well as those involved indirectly in the trade (such as politicians, bankers, police, etc.). As these smaller Colombian drug cartels grew in prevalence, several notable aspects of the Colombian society gave way for further development of the Colombian drug industry. For example, until the late 1980s, the long-term effects of the drug industry were not realized by much of society. Additionally, there was a lack of regulation in prisons where captured traffickers were sent. These prisons were under-regulated, under-funded, and under-staffed, which allowed for the formation of prison gangs, for the smuggling of arms/weapons/etc., for feasible escapes, and even for captured drug lords to continue running their businesses from prison.

Trade in specific drugs

Cannabis

While the recreational use of (and consequently the distribution of) cannabis is illegal in most countries throughout the world, it is available by prescription or recommendation in many places, including Canada and 10 of the 50 US states (although importation and distribution is still federally prohibited). Beginning in 2014, Uruguay became the first country to legalize cultivation, sale, and consumption of cannabis for recreational use for adult residents. In 2018, Canada became the only second country to legalize use, sale and cultivation of cannabis. The first few weeks were met with extremely high demand, most shops being out of stock after operating for only four days.

Cannabis use is tolerated in some areas, most notably the Netherlands which has legalized the possession and licensed sale (but not cultivation) of the drug. Many nations have decriminalized the possession of small amounts of marijuana. Due to the hardy nature of the cannabis plant, marijuana is grown all across the world and is today the world's most popular illegal drug with the highest level of availability. Cannabis is grown legally in many countries for industrial, non-drug use (known as hemp) as well. Cannabis-hemp may also be planted for other non-drug domestic purposes, such as seasoning that occurs in Aceh.

The demand for cannabis around the world, coupled with the drug's relative ease of cultivation, makes the illicit cannabis trade one of the primary ways in which organized criminal groups finance many of their activities. In

Mexico, for example, the illicit trafficking of cannabis is thought to constitute the majority of many of the cartels' earnings, and the main way in which the cartels finance many other illegal activities; including the purchase of other illegal drugs for trafficking, and for acquiring weapons that are ultimately used to commit murders (causing a burgeoning in the homicide rates of many areas of the world, but particularly Latin America).

Some studies show that the increased legalization of cannabis in the United States (beginning in 2012 with Washington Initiative 502 and Colorado Amendment 64) has led Mexican cartels to smuggle less cannabis in exchange for more heroin.

Alcohol

Alcohol, in the context of alcoholic beverages rather than denatured alcohol, is illegal in a number of Muslim countries, such as Saudi Arabia, and this has resulted in a thriving illegal trade in alcohol. The manufacture, sale, transportation, importation and exportation of alcoholic beverage were illegal in the United States during the time known as the Prohibition in the 1920s and early 1930s.

Heroin

Up until around 2004 the majority of the world's heroin was produced in an area known as the Golden Triangle. However, by 2007, 93% of the opiates on the world market originated in Afghanistan. This amounted to an export value of about US$64 billion, with a quarter being earned by opium farmers and the rest going to district officials, insurgents, warlords and drug traffickers. Another significant area where poppy fields are grown for the manufacture of heroin is Mexico.

According to the United States Drug Enforcement Administration, the price of heroin is typically valued 8 to 10 times that of cocaine on American streets, making it a high-profit substance for smugglers and dealers. In Europe (except the transit countries Portugal and the Netherlands), for example, a purported gram of street heroin, usually consisting of 700–800 mg of a light to dark brown powder containing 5–10% heroin base, costs €30–70, making the effective value per gram of pure heroin €300–700. Heroin is generally a preferred product for smuggling and distribution—over unrefined opium due to the cost-effectiveness and increased efficacy of heroin.

Because of the high cost per volume, heroin is easily smuggled. A US quarter-sized (2.5 cm) cylindrical vial can contain hundreds of doses. From the 1930s to the early 1970s, the so-called French Connection supplied the majority of US demand. Allegedly, during the Vietnam War, drug lords such as Ike Atkinson used to smuggle hundreds of kilograms of heroin to the US in coffins of dead American soldiers (see Cadaver Connection). Since that time it has become more difficult for drugs to be imported into the US than it had been in previous decades, but that does not stop the heroin smugglers from getting their product across US borders. Purity levels vary greatly by region with Northeastern cities having the most pure heroin in the United States. On

17 October 2018 police in Genoa Italy, discovered 270 kg of heroin hidden in a ship coming from the Iranian southern port of Bandar Abbas. The ship had already passed and stopped at Hamburg in Germanyand Valencia in Spain.

Penalties for smuggling heroin or morphine are often harsh in most countries. Some countries will readily hand down a death sentence (e.g. Singapore) or life in prison for the illegal smuggling of heroin or morphine, which are both internationally Schedule I drugs under the Single Convention on Narcotic Drugs Lacing is the act of adding one or more substances to another. Some street drugs are commonly laced with other chemicals for various reasons, but it is most commonly done so as to bulk up the original product or to sell other, cheaper drugs in the place of something more expensive. Individuals sometimes lace their own drugs with another substance to combine or alter the physiological or psychoactive effects.

Reasons for lacing

Drugs may be sold to end users who are unaware they have been laced or are unaware what was used to lace them. At various points in the supply chain, in order to maximize profitability, many drugs are adulterated with cutting agents. Substances with similar physical and/or chemical properties can be used so the end product most closely resembles what it is purported to be. Inert substances with similar physical properties can be used to increase weight without changing the look and feel. Less expensive or easier to obtain compounds with similar chemical properties may be used to lace heavily adulterated drugs while still maintaining some psychoactive potency.

Drugs may also be laced with the end user being made aware of the lacing. In this case, rather than as an adulteration, the lacing is intended to make the product more desirable. Sometimes less potent, often less expensive drugs, are laced with a small amount of a more potent, often more expensive drug. This may be used to facilitate the ingestion of drugs or to allow the simultaneous ingestion of multiple drugs. Cigarettes laced with PCP allow users to take in the liquid PCP through smoking and some multi drug users report intentionally buying marijuana laced with methamphetamine.

It is possible that drug users may accidentally purchase a product without knowing that it has been laced with a more potent drug, but psychiatrist Dr Bill MacEwan believes that drug dealers in British Columbia are intentionally lacing cannabis with methamphetamine to make it more addictive. He had some psychiatric patients that claimed they only smoked potbut their drug tests were positive for methamphetamine use.

Commonly laced drugs

Cocaine

The most common adulterants found in 1998 in samples in Rome, Italy were lidocaine and caffeine. Cocaine is sometimes mixed with methylamphetamine, methylphenidate, and ephedrine, but is usually mixed with non psychoactive chemicals such as mannitol, inositol, pectin, glucose, lactose, saccharin, white rice flour, and maltodextrin. Other local anesthetics such as procaine are very commonly used.

US Drug Enforcement Administration and state testing laboratories report that more than 70% of the illicit cocaine analyzed in July 2009 was positive for levamisole, an antiparasitic drug used by veterinarians to treat worm infestations. This represents an increase over previous reports indicating that levamisole contaminated only 30% of cocaine seized by the Drug Enforcement Administration from July to September 2008. Furthermore, a recent analysis found that almost 80% of the individuals who test positive for cocaine also test positive for levamisoleLevamisole used as an adulterant in cocaine has resulted in 20 confirmed or probable cases of agranulocytosis, including 2 deaths, according to an alert from the Substance Abuse and Mental Health Services Administration.

The emergence of fentanyl-laced cocaine has led to an increase in cocaine overdose fatalities in New York City.

Marijuana and Hashish

Though marijuana is less likely to be adulterated than hard drugs are, it still occurs, and has been reported in several countries.

In the Netherlands two chemical analogs of Sildenafil (Viagra) were found in adulterated marijuana.

In 2008, 30 German teenagers were hospitalized after the marijuana which they smoked was found to have been contaminated with lead (presumably metallic lead particles), which was added in order to increase its weight.

Rarely, cannabis (especially that of low quality) is laced with PCP, particularly in the United States. However, it is not always done surreptitiously. Dealers who do so often (but not always) advertise their wares as being "enhanced" with other substances, and charge more money than they would otherwise, even if they do not say exactly what the lacing agents are. Such concoctions are often called "fry", "wet", "illy", "sherm", "water-water", "dust(ed)", "super weed", "grecodine" or other names.

Ecstasy

Black market ecstasy pills are frequently found to contain other drugs in place of or in addition to methylenedioxymethylamphetamine (MDMA). Since the slang term «ecstasy» usually refers only to MDMA, any pill which contains other compounds may be considered adulterated. 3,4-Methylenedioxyamphetamine (MDA), methylenedioxyethamphetamine (MDEA), amphetamine, methylamphetamine, benzylpiperazine (BZP), trifluoromethylphenylpiperazine (TFMPP), caffeine, ephedrine, pseudoephedrine, and dextromethorphan (DXM) are all commonly found in pills being sold as ecstasy. Less common drugs in ecstasy include diphenhydramine, acetaminophen, 5-MeO-DiPT, 2C-B, procaine, and phencyclidine (PCP). Ecstasy pills sometimes contain dimethylamylamine to increase its stimulant effects. Ecstasy pills might also contain a low dose of 2C-I to potentiate its euphoric effects. Pharmaceutical pills are sometimes sold as ecstasy, as well as pills that contain no psychoactive chemicals at all. Ecstasy sometimes contains 10 mg to 20 mg of baclofen to reduce overheating caused by ecstasy. para-Methoxyamphetamine (PMA or «Dr. Death», a drug that causes so much overheating that it can kill within 40 minutes) is sometimes sold as ecstasy. There is one published case of an ecstasy tablet being adulterated with 8 mg of strychnine, a toxic alkaloid which was used in very low doses (less than 1 mg) as a stimulant and performance-enhancing drug in the past. Recently, several groups advocating for drug safety through education have made reagent testing products available to confirm what substances there are.

LSD

LSD is virtually never laced with other chemicals, but other lysergamides such as ALD-52 are sometimes sold as LSD-25. DOB, DOI, and other closely related drugs are sometimes sold as LSD. Several other highly potent hallucinogens such as Bromo-DragonFLY or 25I-NBOMe can be found in the form of blotters. LSD is also tasteless in normal dosages, so detection is only possible after ingestion or reagent testing. For these reasons, it is not uncommon to find blotters sold as LSD completely devoid of psychoactive substances.

Heroin

Heroin is commonly cut with quinine, caffeine, dimethocaine, procaine, lactose, inositol, dextrose, mannitol, and starch. Other opioids are sometimes sold as heroin or cut with heroin. Fentanyl sold as or laced into heroin has made the news in the past due to the numerous fatalities it causes when it appears on the market. Recently, Fentanyl and close analogues have been produced in pure powder form for very cheap. Dealers may cut with or sell heroin with Fentanyl due to the street cost of Fentanyl versus the cost of heroin. The potency of such mixtures (especially if made carelessly) can be far above that of pure heroin, and users frequently overdose due to this.

There are several test kits that are available online and also sold at some head shops. These kits claim to be able to identify common adulterants in ecstasy.

Professional lab tests

There are services available for testing the contents of an ecstasy pill that can tell the user what chemicals are contained in the pill and at what ratio. The results are then posted on their website along with every other pill that they have tested. The tests are considered to be highly accurate. Their services were at one time free, but when they ran out of funding they had to charge a fee for every pill tested.

Methamphetamine

Methamphetamine is another popular drug among distributors. Three common street names are «crystal meth», «meth», and «ice».

According to the Community Epidemiology Work Group, the number of clandestine methamphetamine laboratory incidents reported to the National Clandestine Laboratory Database decreased from 1999 to 2009. During this period, methamphetamine lab incidents increased in mid-western States (Illinois, Michigan, Missouri, and Ohio), and in Pennsylvania. In 2004, more lab incidents were reported in Missouri (2,788) and Illinois (1,058) than in California (764). In 2003, methamphetamine lab incidents reached new highs in Georgia (250), Minnesota (309), and Texas (677). There were only seven methamphetamine lab incidents reported in Hawaii in 2004, though nearly 59 percent of substance abuse treatment admissions (excluding alcohol) were for primary methamphetamine abuse during the first six months of 2004. As of 2007, Missouri leads the United States in drug-lab seizures, with 1,268 incidents reported. Often canine units are used for detecting rolling meth labs which can be concealed on large vehicles, or transported on something as small as a motorcycle. These labs are more difficult to detect than stationary ones, and can often be obscured among legal cargo in big trucks.

Methamphetamine is sometimes used intraveneously, placing users and their partners at risk for transmission of HIV and hepatitis C. «Meth» can also be inhaled, most commonly vaporized on aluminum foil or in a glass pipe. This method is reported to give «an unnatural high» and a «brief intense rush».

In South Africa methamphetamine is called "tik" or "tik-tik"."Known locally as "tik," the drug was virtually unknown as late as 2003. Now, it is the country's main drug of abuse, even when alcohol is included. " Children as young as eight are abusing the substance, smoking it in crude glass vials made from light bulbs. Since methamphetamine is easy to produce, the substance is manufactured locally in staggering quantities.

The government of North Korea currently operates methamphetamine production facilities. There, the drug is used as medicine because no alternatives are available; it also is smuggled across the Chinese border.

The Australian Crime Commission's illicit drug data report for 2011–2012 stated that the average strength of crystal methamphetamine doubled in most Australian jurisdictions within a 12-month period, and the majority of domestic laboratory closures involved small "addict-based" operations.

Temazepam

Temazepam, a strong hypnotic benzodiazepine, is illicitly manufactured in clandestine laboratories (called jellie labs) to supply the increasingly high demand for the drug internationally. Many clandestine temazepam labs are in Eastern Europe. The labs manufacture temazepam by chemically altering diazepam, oxazepam or lorazepam. «Jellie labs» have been identified and shut down in Russia, the Ukraine, Czech Republic, Latvia and Belarus.

Surveys in many countries show that temazepam, MDMA, nimetazepam, and methamphetamine rank among the top illegal drugs most frequently abused

Cocaine

Cocaine is a highly prominent drug among many drug dealers and manufacturers. The cocaine black market distribution industry is worth more than 85 billion dollars. It has been a heavily fought over and massively produced. Around 1.1 million kilograms of cocaine were made in 2009 and it is believed to have been consumed by around 17 million people worldwide. This drug's mass trade is believed to have been possible by notorious drug dealing kingpin Joaquín "El Chapo" Guzmán who ran the Sinaloa Cartel.Drug trafficking organizations

Drug trafficking organizations are defined by the United States Department of Justice as, «complex organizations with highly defined command-and-control structures that produce, transport, and/or distribute large quantity «Law enforcement reporting indicates that Mexican DTOs maintain drug distribution networks, or supply drugs to distributors, in at least 230 U.S. cities.» The use of weapons and fear are commonplace in trafficking which often lead to other crimes in the process. The structures of many of these organizations are of a para-military nature using armed combatants to protect their stock of illegal drugs from growth to delivery.

In 1914, the Harrison Narcotic Act was passed by congress making a medical prescription necessary for products with high levels of opiate or narcotics.» With laws against the use of un-prescribed drugs such as opium, cocaine, morphine, and heroin now in effect, the black market grew to continue supply to addicted or prospective users. Rising domestic enforcement of illegal growing and production operations, coupled with increasing legislation against illegal drugs, forced suppliers outside the country. Drug trafficking organizations from nations with lesser, or no drug laws emerged with the opportunity to make large profits from illegal trafficking into the United States. These organized crime syndicates would use any means necessary to exploit the weak border protection of the US. The drugs were shipped, flown, and trucked into the country and distributed from within. In many cases, «American mercenaries provided their services as pilots making trips between over 150 clandestine landing strips in South America and the US. In a 1986 Report from the President›s Commission on Organized Crime, it was believed that nearly 2/3 of the cocaine from Colombia was flown into the country.» Rampant drug epidemics and rising gang dealing would eventually lead to a massive operationalization of drug enforcement. The US formed federal agencies and initiatives such as the «Drug Enforcement Administration(DEA) in 1973, and High Intensity Drug Trafficking Area centers with the Anti-Drug Abuse Act of 1988, coordinating efforts to slow the flow across borders and within the country." These agencies, along with academics, would formally define the groups that traffic drugs and study their operations.

Organization and structure

Structure

Over the past few decades, drug trafficking organizations have increased in number and diversified in structure. They range from family based operations in which secrecy is essential, and where trafficking of large shipments are discreetly sent to associates across the border, to organizations involving hundreds of players with different roles. This varying structure can often make it difficult to identify the groups as each has a different MO and scale. In 1998, Mangai Natarajan, a professor at John Jay College of Criminal Justice, "studied court records of 39 trafficking organizations in New York City to classify drug syndicates into four main types. "Freelance" networks are composed of small nonhierarchical entrepreneurial groupings of individuals; "family businesses" are cohesive organizations with clear structure and authority and trust based on family ties; "communal businesses" are flexible organizations bound together by a common tie such as ethnicity, religion, nationality, or neighborhood residence; and "corporations" are large organizations in which there is a formal hierarchy and a well-defined division of labor." While these «corporations» are obviously the most organized, they often take years of investigation to trace up to the head operator. Many times these organizations are run from outside the country and therefore extradition and conflicting laws may prohibit the investigation. Another perspective argues that DTOs are politico-military groups that operate in failed states and have political agendas. Situations such as Mexico and Afghanistan today may support this claim, and perhaps, extend further connecting funds to terrorist groups.

Mexican DTOs

Mexican drug trafficking organizations have taken control of the US market in recent years, superseding Dominican and Colombian groups that held it for decades. These groups began as hierarchical with clear and defined leadership and a ladder of command down to the street dealer. In response to increasing law enforcement efforts and understanding of this system, many Mexican DTOs have shifted their command structure to an equally organized, but more independent system of decentralized cells. According to a High Intensity Drug Trafficking Areas Initiative (HIDTA) in the Midwest, the Mexican DTOs have "compartmentalized duties, employed advanced security and communications techniques, gathered intelligence, and used violence and intimidation to control organization members and secure smuggling territories." With a state of virtual lawlessness, futile domestic enforcement efforts, and rampant corruption fueled by the drug money, Mexico has grown into a massive drug producer. Production is unmatched when it comes to marijuana, heroin, and cocaine with methamphetamines an increasing trend.

Colombian and Dominican DTOs

Colombian and Dominican DTOs operate in hierarchical command structures and often launder money into non-drug legitimate industries such as real estate and high income businesses as an investigation by ICE learned in 2010 where a multibillion-dollar Colombian DTO was taken down. Controlling the US market for many years, these groups established undetectable transportation techniques and became deeply connected to domestic gangs.

The insurgence of Mexican DTOs has brought increased violence and competition for large cities and territory control. Heroin and cocaine are the primary drugs produced in the countries which have been under the control of cartels for decades.

Asian DTOs

Asian DTOs have filled in the gaps left by the major players by producing and trafficking MDMA known commonly on the street as ecstasy or X. «While once a competitive supplier of heroin, the groups have avoided strife by targeting the high potency marijuana market growing in both Canada and the US to avoid border raids.»

Impact of DTOs

Finance, violence and terrorism

While an exact financial figure is not known to US authorities, DTOs are believed to make tens of billions of dollars annually depending on size of the organization. With this staggering income from illegal trade, the longevity and persistence of these organizations is understandable. For groups based in economically struggling regions, the illegal trafficking of drugs is a tempting and extremely profitable illegitimate business with little domestic risk. A variety of methods are used to conceal and move the cash made from the network of drug deals. Money laundering techniques involve the wiring and constant movement of funds from different banks and accounts. This technique makes tracking the money more difficult, and can cost banks millions in losses each year. Aside from financial detriment, these groups can be very violent extending their police record to countless offences. In a constant struggle for territory and control of the market, DTOs will not hesitate to use deadly force against rival organizations, or threats to their business. The use of automatic weapons, threats, and bribery are common in maintaining control. «Narcoterrorism" is not a new threat but has become a domestic fear for the US after the attacks on September 11. With the formation of terrorism task forces and intelligence community initiatives, a greater understanding of the relationship between drug trade and terrorism has taken place.

Many terrorist organizations have the drug trade as their major income - for instance the Taliban controlled 96% of Afghanistan's poppy fields and made opium its largest source of taxation which became one of the mainstays of Taliban income and their war economy. According to Rashid, "drug money funded the weapons, ammunition and fuel for the war." In the New York Times, the Finance Minister of the United Front, Wahidullah Sabawoon, declared the Taliban had no annual budget but that they "appeared to spend US$300 million a year, nearly all of it on war." He added that the Taliban had come to increasingly rely on three sources of money: "poppy, the Pakistanis and bin Laden." According to Alfred McCoy, during the Cold War the CIA provided Afghan drug lord allies such as Gulbuddin Hekmatyar with transport, arms, and political protection in the fight against Soviet forces in

Afghanistan. According to Loretta Napoleoni terrorism later shifted from being mainly state sponsored to gaining financial independence from their sponsors and becoming self-financed.

In a CBS news article, the Chief of Operations for the US Drug Enforcement Administration Michael Braun called "groups like the FARC, the Taliban, Hamas and Hezbollah: "hybrids" stating that they are one part terrorist organization, and are becoming one part global drug trafficking cartel." With this new «hybrid» threat, the violence aimed at political impact meets the already violent world of drug trafficking in a perfect storm. These narco-terrorist groups have been linked to car bombings, hostage situations, and mass killings of police and politicians which opposed the operation and could perhaps pose the greatest threat to the US in the future.

Gang involvement

Operationally, DTOs rely on street gangs to distribute the product to their customers. This collaboration supports turf wars between rival gangs like the Bloods and Crips that ensures their participation in the drug trade. These gangs which make headlines daily, rely on the illegal drug trade to support their gangs across the US. The money generated by this process, among other factors, draws youth into the gang lifestyle continuing the cycle of violence on the street.

Combating drug trafficking organizations

Enforcement

With emerging involvement in these organizations, law enforcement agencies from all levels have stepped up operations against high intensity drug trafficking. Beginning with Vice units in Florida and other border states, law enforcement has grown exponentially in counter narcotics. Currently there is a large network of agencies, police, military, initiatives, and even private sector involvement to combat DTOs. Federal agencies such as the DEA, FBI, ICE, Border Patrol, and even the National Guard, work independently but cohesively to analyze and investigate organizations with the most impact. These agencies are dependent on local and state law enforcement officers who have the street interactions with members of the drug world. This data is collected and disseminated to initiatives such as HIDTAs which were formed as switchboards for drug Intel in target regions of the US. Using a wealth of knowledge, and ever improving technology in networks and analysis, law enforcement efforts finding greater success in dismantling organizations in the US.

Public health

Another approach has been initiated using campaigns for anti drug use in an attempt to reduce the demand for illegal drugs from within. This public health approach utilized TV programs and advertisements, as well as D.A.R.E. programs which are aimed at youth with the hope of prevention before enforcement.

Social Effects of Drugs on Society

The social effects of drugs on society are horrific. Drug abuse results in crime, depleted resources, injuries, worsened livelihoods and the deprivation of childcare and healthcare to innocent citizens.

How does drug abuse affect the community?

It costs everyone money

According to DrugRehab.org, drug and alcohol abuse rake up an annual fee of nearly $600 billion. Abusing drugs and alcohol comes with many side effects, requiring support and resources from health care, lost revenue, damages and health care. The ripple effects of drug use include sexual assault, prison sentences, foster care placement, child abuse and work-related injuries. The more society abuses drugs, the more we pay for it as a whole.

It monopolizes health care resources

Every year, drug abuse costs the healthcare industry over $180 billion. Health care is responsible for rehabilitation programs and services, mental disorders and injuries related to drug abuse or addiction.

Drug abuse demands tax dollars and hospital resources that could be directed toward other more positively beneficial efforts and life-saving endeavors.

It disrupts the family unit

Drug abuse takes an extensive toll on the family, which in turn has a negative impact on society. Studies show the tendency of one family member to abuse drugs or alcohol and this one family member's problem causes tension amongst all members.

If a parent is misusing drugs or alcohol, it creates strain in the spousal (if any) relationship, driving the parent's partner into frustration and fatigue, possibly resulting in a lack of effort at work, in parenting, in friendships or in the ability to care for himself or herself.

A parent abusing drugs always leads to the children receiving inadequate care. This results in poorer childhood health, reduced academic performance, neglected emotional support and more.

As the children of a drug abuser are denied basic necessities of parenting (often including shelter and food), their involvement in and contribution to society, later on, is hindered. In some cases, the emotional burden is too great, causing the affected children to turn to drugs or alcohol as a coping mechanism and recreating the cyclical negative process.

When one child in the family is addicted to or abusing drugs, it affects everyone. Parenting efforts and financial resources tend to go toward helping the one child, neglecting the needs of the other seemingly stable kids in the family. The stable children are denied necessary parenting attention and fail to be pushed toward their potential that would lead to greater positive influence in society in their adulthood.

It results in crime

Over half of federal prison occupancy is accounted for by individuals with incarcerations related to drug abuse or addiction. Each year, drug-related incarcerations in state prisons cost taxpayers $45 billion as well as $144 million in federal prison incarcerations.

More crimes are committed by individuals under the use of drugs and alcohol, costing society its resources, time, efforts and safety.

Everybody else has to work harder

Drug abusers bring down the productivity at work.

They are late, absent or mentally impaired on the job, requiring other employees to make up for their lack of productivity. Straining the work capacity of fellow employees triggers irritation and exhaustion in these employees, which has a ripple effect on their relationships with partners, family and friends and eventually, on their ability to function optimally at work.

These consequences of drug abuse on society are not necessary outcomes of every drug abuse situation, but they are unfortunately the common result and just some examples of how substance abuse worsen feelings of stress. Abusing drugs takes a toll on everyone, stemming from the abuser to close connections, family, work, health care and society as a whole.

If you or a loved one is facing drug addiction or abuse, reach out to United Recovery Project. We have the knowledge, resources, experience, and facilities necessary to help you or your loved ones get through this drug-related trying time. Contact us today.

6

Drug Prohibition Law

Drug prohibition law is prohibition-based law by which governments prohibit, except under licence, the production, supply, and possession of many, but not all, substances which are recognized as drugs, and which corresponds to international treaty commitments in the Single Convention on Narcotic Drugs 1961, the Convention on Psychotropic Substances 1971, and the United Nations Convention Against Illicit Traffic in Narcotic Drugs and Psychotropic Substances 1988.

When produced, supplied or possessed under licence, otherwise prohibited drugs are known as controlled drugs. The aforementioned legislation is the cultural institution and social fact that de facto divides world drug trade as illegal vs legal, according to geopolitical issues. The United Nations has its own drug control programme, as part of the United Nations Office on Drugs and Crime (UNODC), which was formerly called the United Nations Office for Drug Control and Crime Prevention (ODCCP), and the Commission on Narcotic Drugs is the central drug policy-making body within the United Nations system.

The International Narcotics Control Board (INCB) is an independent and quasi-judicial control organ for the implementation of the United Nations drug control conventions. It is important to note that there are several different sets of «schedules», or lists, of controlled drugs. One is the INCB schedules (four schedules numbered I-IV), while another is the United States› Controlled Substances Act schedules of controlled substances (five schedules, numbered I-V). Other countries also have different classifications and numbers of lists, such as those of the United Kingdom and Canada.

History and founding principles

Drug prohibition law is based on the view that some drugs, notably opium poppy, coca, and substances derived from these plants, are so addictive or dependence inducing and so dangerous, in terms of potential effects on the health, morality and behaviour of users, that they should be rarely, if ever, used.

Psychotropic substances covered by drug control law include psilocybin mushrooms and lysergic acid diethylamide (LSD).

The following treaties are no longer in force, being superseded in 1961 by the Single Convention on Narcotic Drugs:

- International Opium Convention, signed at The Hague on 23 January 1912
- Agreement concerning the Manufacture of, Internal Trade in and Use of Prepared Opium, signed at Geneva on 11 February 1925
- Convention for Limiting the Manufacture and Regulating the Distribution of Narcotic Drugs, signed at Geneva on 13 July 1931
- Agreement for the Control of Opium Smoking in the Far East, signed at Bangkok on 27 November 1931

Licensing

Otherwise prohibited drugs may be licensed for medical, research and industrial purposes.

Pharmaceutical companies, also known as drug companies, work under drug control licenses.

Hemp production from the Cannabis plant is an example of an industrial purpose.

Recreational and self-medicational drug use

Recreational use and self-medicational use are not licensed under drug prohibition laws, although other drugs, not covered by such laws, may be legally available for this purpose. Alcohol and tobacco are notable examples of legally available recreational drugs. Aspirin is an example of a drug legally available for self-medicational purposes.

Health, moral, and behavior issues, and legal issues, are associated with alcohol and tobacco use, but these are not addressed through drug prohibition laws.

Addiction to a prohibited drug may not be considered a legitimate reason for using it, even if the drug is obtained from a licensed source, or a substitute may be provided, for example, methadone instead of heroin. Generally, however, those addicted to prohibited drugs are expected to find other ways of coping with their addictions, or to risk suffering the law enforcement penalties associated with illegal possession.

Enforcement

There is an extensive illegal trans-national industry supplying prohibited drugs for recreational use. Thus, while drug prohibition laws remain in force, there is perpetual law enforcement action directed against the illegal industry, which also impacts supply for self-medication.

Although it is directed against illegal recreational drugs, and not against drugs licensed under prohibition laws or against drugs beyond the scope of prohibition laws, the law enforcement is sometimes called the war on drugs.

Criticism

Drug prohibition is responsible for enriching "organised criminal networks", according to some critics while the hypothesis that the prohibition of drugs generates violence is consistent with research done over long time-series and cross-country facts.

In the United Kingdom, where the principal piece of drug prohibition legislation is the Misuse of Drugs Act 1971, criticism includes:

- Drug classification: making a hash of it?, Fifth Report of Session 2005–06, House of Commons Science and Technology Committee, which said that the present system of drug classification is based on historical assumptions, not scientific assessment
- Development of a rational scale to assess the harm of drugs of potential misuse, David Nutt, Leslie A. King, William Saulsbury, Colin Blakemore, The Lancet, 24 March 2007, said the act is "not fit for purpose" and "the exclusion of alcohol and tobacco from the Misuse of Drugs Act is, from a scientific perspective, arbitrary"
- The Drug Equality Alliance (DEA) argue that the Government is administering the Act arbitrarily, contrary to its purpose, contrary to the original wishes of Parliament and therefore illegally. They are currently assisting and supporting several legal challenges to this alleged maladministration.

Prohibition

Prohibition is the act or practice of forbidding something by law; more particularly the term refers to the banning of the manufacture, storage (whether in barrels or in bottles), transportation, sale, possession, and consumption of alcoholic beverages. The word is also used to refer to a period of time during which such bans are enforced.

History

Some kind of limitation on the trade in alcohol can be seen in the Code of Hammurabi (ca.1772 BCE) specifically banning the selling of beer for money. It could only be bartered for barley: «If a beer seller do not receive barley as the price for beer, but if she receive money or make the beer a measure smaller than the barley measure received, they shall throw her into the water.»

In the Western world, one of the great moral issues of the nineteenth century was slavery, but once that battle was won, social moralists turned to their next targets, one of which was prohibition. In the early twentieth century, much of the impetus for the prohibition movement in the Nordic countries and North America came from moralistic convictions of pietistic Protestants. Prohibition movements in the West coincided with the advent of women's suffrage, with newly empowered women as part of the political process strongly supporting policies that curbed alcohol consumption.

The first half of the 20th century saw periods of prohibition of alcoholic beverages in several countries:

- 1907 to 1948 in Prince Edward Island, and for shorter periods in other provinces in Canada
- 1907 to 1992 in the Faroe Islands; limited private imports from Denmark were allowed from 1928
- 1914 to 1925 in the Russian Empire and the Soviet Union
- 1915 to 1933 in Iceland (beer was still prohibited until 1989)
- 1916 to 1927 in Norway (fortified wine and beer were also prohibited from 1917 to 1923)
- 1919 in the Hungarian Soviet Republic, March 21 to August 1; called szesztilalom
- 1919 to 1932 in Finland (called kieltolaki, "ban law")
- 1920 to 1933 in the United States

After several years, prohibition failed in North America and elsewhere. Rum-running or bootlegging became widespread, and organized crime took control of the distribution of alcohol. Distilleries and breweries in Canada, Mexico and the Caribbean flourished as their products were either consumed by visiting Americans or illegally exported to the United States. Chicago became notorious as a haven for prohibition dodgers during the time known as the Roaring Twenties. Prohibition generally came to an end in the late 1920s or early 1930s in most of North America and Europe, although a few locations continued prohibition for many more years.

In some countries where the dominant religion forbids the use of alcohol, the production, sale, and consumption of alcoholic beverages is prohibited or restricted today. For example, in Saudi Arabia and Libya alcohol is banned; in Pakistan and Iran it is illegal with exceptions.

Asia[

Afghanistan

Sale of alcohol is banned in Afghanistan.

Bangladesh

In Bangladesh, alcohol is somewhat prohibited due to its proscription in the Islamic faith. However, the purchase and consumption is allowed in the country. The Garo tribe consume a type of rice beer, and Christians in this country drink and purchase wine for their holy communion.

Brunei

In Brunei, alcohol consumption and sale is banned in public. Non-Muslims are allowed to purchase a limited amount of alcohol from their point of embarcation overseas for their own private consumption, and non-Muslims who are at least the age of 18 are allowed to bring in not more than two bottles of liquor (about two litres) and twelve cans of beer per person into the country.

India

In India alcohol is a state subject and individual states can legislate prohibition, but currently most states do not have prohibition and sale/ consumption is freely available in 25 out of 29 states. Prohibition is in force in the states of Gujarat, Bihar and Nagaland, parts of Manipur, and the union territory of Lakshadweep. All other States and union territories of Indiapermit the sale of alcohol.

Election days and certain national holidays such as Independence Day are meant to be dry days when liquor sale is not permitted but consumption is allowed. Some Indian states observe dry days on major religious festivals/ occasions depending on the popularity of the festival in that region

Iran]

Since the 1979 Islamic Revolution, the sale and consumption of alcohol is banned in Iran. All people are banned from drinking alcohol but some people trade and sell it illegally.

Indonesia

Alcohol sales are banned in small shops and convenience stores.

Kuwait

The consumption, importation and brewing of, and trafficking in liquor is strictly against the law.

Malaysia

Alcohol is banned only for Muslims in Malaysia due to its Islamic faith and sharia law. Nevertheless, alcoholic products can easily be found in supermarkets, specialty shops, and convenience stores all over the country. Non-halal restaurants also typically sell alcohol.

Maldives

The Maldives ban the import of alcohol, x-raying all baggage on arrival. Alcoholic beverages are available only to foreign tourists on resort islands and may not be taken off the resort.

Pakistan[

Pakistan allowed the free sale and consumption of alcohol for three decades from 1947, but restrictions were introduced by Zulfikar Ali Bhutto just weeks before he was removed as prime minister in 1977. Since then, only members of non-Muslim minorities such as Hindus, Christians and Zoroastrians are allowed to apply for alcohol permits. The monthly quota is dependent upon one›s income, but usually is about five bottles of liquor or 100 bottles of beer. In a country of 180 million, only about 60 outlets are allowed to sell alcohol. The Murree Brewery in Rawalpindi was once the only legal brewery, but today there are more. The ban officially is enforced by the country›s Islamic Ideology Council, but it is not strictly policed. Members of religious minorities, however, often sell their liquor permits to Muslims as part of a continuing black market trade in alcohol.

Philippines[

There are only restrictions during elections in the Philippines. Alcohol is prohibited from purchase two days prior to an election. The Philippine [Commission on Elections] may opt to extend the liquor ban. In the 2010 elections, the liquor ban was a minimum two days; in the 2013 elections, there was a proposal that it be extended to five days. This was overturned by the Supreme Court.

Other than election-related prohibition, alcohol is freely sold to anyone above the legal drinking age.

Saudi Arabia

The sale, consumption, importation and brewing of, and trafficking in liquor is strictly against the law.

Sri Lanka[

In 1955 Sri Lanka passed a law prohibiting adult women from buying alcohol. In January 2018, Finance Minister Mangala Samaraweera announced that the law would be amended, allowing women to legally consume alcohol and work in venues that sell alcohol. The legalization was overruled by President Maithripala Sirisena several days later.

Thailand[

Alcohol is prohibited from being sold during election time, from 6 pm the day prior to voting, until the end of the day of voting itself. Alcohol is also prohibited on major Buddhist holy days, and sometimes on Royal Commemoration days, such as birthdays.

Thailand also enforces time-limited bans on alcohol on a daily basis. Alcohol can only be legally purchased in stores or restaurants between 11 am–2 pm and 5 pm–midnight. This law is enforced by all major retailers (most notably 7-Eleven) and restaurants but is frequently ignored by the smaller 'mom and pop' stores. Hotels and resorts are exempt from the rules.

The consumption of alcohol is also banned at any time within 200 meters of a filling station (where sale of alcohol is also illegal), schools, temples or hospitals as well as on board any type of road vehicle regardless of whether it is being consumed by the driver or passenger.

At certain times of the year – Thai New Year (Songkran) as an example – the government may also enforce arbitrary bans on the sale and consumption of alcohol in specific public areas where large scale festivities are due to take place and large crowds are expected.

Europe

Czech Republic

On 14 September 2012, the government of the Czech Republic banned all sales of liquor with more than 20% alcohol. From this date on it was illegal to sell such alcoholic beverages in shops, supermarkets, bars, restaurants, gas stations, e-shops etc. This measure was taken in response to the wave of methanol poisoning cases resulting in the deaths of 18 people in the Czech Republic. Since the beginning of the «methanol affair" the total number of deaths has increased to 25. The ban was to be valid until further notice, though restrictions were eased towards the end of September. The last bans on Czech alcohol with regard to the poisoning cases were lifted on 10 October 2012, when neighbouring Slovakia and Poland allowed its import once again.

Nordic countries

The Nordic countries, with the exception of Denmark, have had a strong temperance movement since the late 1800s, closely linked to the Christian revival movement of the late 19th century, but also to several worker organisations. As an example, in 1910 the temperance organisations in Sweden had some 330,000 members, which was about 6% of a population of 5.5 million. This heavily influenced the decisions of Nordic politicians in the early 20th century.

In 1907, the Faroe Islands passed a law prohibiting all sale of alcohol, which was in force until 1992. Very restricted private importation from Denmark was allowed from 1928 on.

In 1914, Sweden put in place a rationing system, the Bratt System, in force until 1955. A referendum in 1922 rejected an attempt to enforce total prohibition.

In 1915, Iceland instituted total prohibition. The ban for wine was lifted in 1922 and spirits in 1935, but beer remained prohibited until 1989 (circumvented by mixing light beer and spirits).

In 1916, Norway prohibited distilled beverages, and in 1917 the prohibition was extended to also include fortified wine and beer. The wine and beer ban was lifted in 1923, and in 1927 the ban of distilled beverages was also lifted.

In 1919, Finland enacted prohibition, as one of the first acts after independence from the Russian Empire. Four previous attempts to institute prohibition in the early 20th century had failed due to opposition from the tsar. After a development similar to the one in the United States during its prohibition, with large-scale smuggling and increasing violence and crime rates, public opinion turned against the prohibition, and after a national referendum where 70% voted for a repeal of the law, prohibition was ended in early 1932.

Today, all Nordic countries (with the exception of Denmark) continue to have strict controls on the sale of alcohol which is highly taxed (dutied) to the public. There are government monopolies in place for selling spirits, wine, and stronger beers in Norway (Vinmonopolet), Finland (Alko), Sweden (Systembolaget), Iceland (Vínbúðin), and the Faroe Islands (Rúsdrekkasøla Landsins). Bars and restaurants may, however, import alcoholic beverages directly or through other companies.

Alcoholic beverages in Sweden and Algoth Niska

Greenland, which is part of the Kingdom of Denmark, does not share its easier controls on the sale of alcohol. Greenland has (like Denmark) sales in food shops, but prices are high. Private import when traveling from Denmark is only allowed in small quantities.

Russian Empire and the Soviet Union

In the Russian Empire, a limited version of a Dry Law was introduced in 1914. It continued through the turmoil of the Russian Revolution of 1917 and the Russian Civil War into the period of Soviet Russia and the Soviet Union until 1925.

United Kingdom

Although the sale or consumption of commercial alcohol has never been prohibited by law in the United Kingdom, historically, various groups in the UK have campaigned for the prohibition of alcohol; including the Society of Friends (Quakers), The Methodist Church and other non-conformists, as well as temperance movements such as Band of Hope and temperance Chartist movements of the nineteenth century.

Formed in 1853 and inspired by the Maine law in the United States, the United Kingdom Alliance aimed at promoting a similar law prohibiting the sale of alcohol in the UK. This hard-line group of prohibitionists was opposed by other temperance organisations who preferred moral persuasion to a legal ban. This division in the ranks limited the effectiveness of the temperance movement as a whole. The impotence of legislation in this field was demonstrated when the Sale of Beer Act 1854 which restricted Sunday opening hours had to be repealed, following widespread rioting. In 1859, a prototype prohibition bill was overwhelmingly defeated in the House of Commons.

On 22 March 1917, during the First World War at a crowded meeting in the Queen's Hall in London (chaired by Alfred Booth) many influential people including Agnes Weston spoke, or letters from them were read out, against alcohol consumption, calling for prohibition; General Sir Reginald Hart wrote to the meeting that «Every experienced officer knew that practically all unhappiness and crime in the Army is due to drink». At the meeting, Lord Channing said that it was a pity that the whole Cabinet did not follow the example of King George V and Lord Kitchener when in 1914 those two spoke calling for complete prohibition for the duration of the war.

North America

Canada

Indigenous peoples in Canada were subject to prohibitory alcohol laws under the Indian Act of 1876. Sections of the Indian Act regarding liquor were not repealed for over a hundred years, until 1985.

An official, but non-binding, federal referendum on prohibition was held in 1898. Prime Minister Wilfrid Laurier's government chose not to introduce a federal bill on prohibition, mindful of the strong antipathy in Quebec. As a result, Canadian prohibition was instead enacted through laws passed by the provinces during the first twenty years of the 20th century, especially during the 1910s. However, Canada did enact a national prohibition from 1918 to 1920, as a temporary wartime measure. Much of the rum-running during prohibition took place in Windsor, Ontario. The provinces later repealed their prohibition laws, mostly during the 1920s, although some local municipalities remain dry.

Mexico

Some communities in the Chiapas state of southern Mexico are under the control of the radical leftist Zapatista Army of National Liberation, and often ban alcohol as part of what was described as "a collective decision". This prohibition has been used by many villages as a way to decrease domestic violence and has generally been favored by women. However, this prohibition is not recognized by federal Mexican law as the Zapatista movement is strongly opposed by the federal government.

The sale and purchase of alcohol is prohibited on and the night before certain national holidays, such as Natalicio de Benito Juárez (birthdate of Benito Juárez) and Día de la Revolución, which are meant to be dry nationally. The same "dry law" applies to the days before presidential elections every six years.

United States

Prohibition in the United States focused on the manufacture, transportation, and sale of alcoholic beverages; however, exceptions were made for medicinal and religious uses. Alcohol consumption was never illegal under federal law. Nationwide Prohibition did not begin in the United States until January 1920, when the Eighteenth Amendment to the U.S. Constitution went into effect. The 18th amendment was ratified in 1919, and was repealed in December 1933 with the ratification of the Twenty-first Amendment.

Temperance movement

Concern over excessive alcohol consumption began during the American colonial era, when fines were imposed for drunken behavior and for selling liquor without a license. In the eighteenth century, when drinking was a part of everyday American life, Protestantreligious groups, especially the Methodists, and health reformers, including Benjamin Rush and others, urged Americans to curb their drinking habits for moral and health reasons. In particular, Benjamin Rush believed Americans were drinking hard spirits in excess, so he created «A Moral and Physical Thermometer,» displaying the progression of behaviors caused by the consumption of various alcohols. By the 1840s the temperance movement was actively encouraging individuals to immediately stop drinking. Music (a completely new genre) was composed and performed in support of the efforts, both in social contexts and in response to state legislation attempts to regulate alcohol. Many took a pledge of total abstinence (teetotalism) from drinking distilled liquor as well as beer and wine. However, the issue of slavery, and then the Civil War, overshadowed the temperance movement, and temperance groups petered out until they found new life in the 1870s.

Prohibition was a major reform movement from the 1870s until the 1920s, when nationwide prohibition went into effect. Prohibition was supported by evangelical Protestant churches, especially the Methodists, Baptists, Presbyterians, Disciples of Christ, Congregationalists, Quakers, and Scandinavian Lutherans. Opposition came from Catholics, Episcopalians, and German Lutherans. Kansas and Maine were early adopters of statewide prohibition. Following passage of the Maine law, Delaware, Ohio, Illinois, Rhode Island, Minnesota, Massachusetts, Connecticut, Pennsylvania, and New York, among others, soon passed statewide prohibition legislation; however, a number of these laws were overturned.

Women served a special role in the temperance movement. Along with prostitution, alcohol was a vice that kept men out of their homes and caused them to oppress their wives. Carrie Nation, a middle-aged woman living in Kansas in the early 1900s, grew tired of the moral protesting and began a campaign destroying bars first in Kansas and later across the entire United States. She said once that "almost everyone who was in jail was directly or indirectly there from the influence of intoxicating drinks," which encapsulated people›s negative attitudes towards alcohol at the time. Nation also said, after she destroyed a painting of a nude woman, «It is very significant that the pictures of naked women are in saloons. Women are stripped of everything by them. Her husband is torn from her, she is robbed of her sons, her home, her food, and her virtue, and then they strip her clothes off and hang her up bare of all things!»

As temperance groups continued to promote prohibition, other groups opposed increased alcohol restrictions. For example, Chicago's citizens fought against enforcing Sunday closings laws in the 1850s, which included mob violence. It was also during this time when patent medicines, many of which contained alcohol, gained popularity. During the American Civil War efforts at increasing federal revenue included imposition of taxes on liquor and beer. The liquor industry responded to the taxes by forming an industry lobby, the United States Brewers Association, that succeeded in reducing the tax rate on beer from $1 to 60 cents. The Women's Crusade of 1873 and the Woman's Christian Temperance Union (WCTU), founded in 1874, «marked the formal entrance of women into the temperance movement.» Organizations such as the Women›s Christian Temperance Movement were a venue through which certain women organized and demanded political action, well before they were granted the vote. The WCTU and the Prohibition Party, organized in 1869, remained major players in the temperance movement until the early twentieth century, when the Anti-Saloon League, formed in 1895, emerged as the movement's leader.

Between 1880 and 1890, although several states enacted local option laws that allowed counties or towns to go dry by referendum, only six states had statewide prohibition by state statute or constitutional amendment. The League, with the support of evangelical Protestant churches and other Progressive-era reformers continued to press for prohibition legislation.

Opposition to prohibition was strong in America›s urban industrial centers, where a large, immigrant, working-class population generally opposed it, as did Jewish and Catholic religious groups. In the years leading up to World War I, nativism, American patriotism, distrust of immigrants, and anti-German sentiment became associated with the prohibition movement. Through the use of pressure politics on legislators, the League and other temperance reformers achieved the goal of nationwide prohibition by emphasizing the need to destroy the moral corruption of the saloons and the political power of the brewing industry, and to reduce domestic violence in the home. By 1913 nine states had stateside prohibition and thirty-one others had local option laws in effect, which included nearly fifty percent of the U.S. population. At that time the League and other reformers turned their efforts toward attaining a constitutional amendment and grassroots support for nationwide prohibition.

18th Amendment to the Constitution

In December 1917, Congress submitted a constitutional amendment on nationwide prohibition to the states for ratification. The new constitutional amendment prohibited «the manufacture, sale, or transportation of intoxicating liquors within, the importation thereof into, or the exportation thereof from the United States and all territory subject to the jurisdiction thereof for beverage purposes». It was ratified and became law on January 16, 1919, assuring its passage into law. On October 28, 1919, Congress passed the National Prohibition Act, also known as the Volstead Act, which provided enabling legislation to implement the Eighteenth Amendment. When the National Prohibition Act was passed on October 28, 1919, thirty-three of the forty-eight states were already dry. After a year›s required delay, national prohibition began on January 16, 1920.

During the first years of Prohibition, the new law was enforced in regions such as the rural South and western states, where it had popular support; however, in large urban cities and small industrial or mining towns, residents defied or ignored the law. The Ku Klux Klan was a major supporter of Prohibition; once it was passed they helped with its enforcement. For example, in 1923, Klansmen traded pistol shots with bootleggers, burned down roadhouses, and whipped liquor sellers, and anybody else who broke the moral code. The Prohibition was effective in reducing per-capita consumption, and consumption remained lower for a quarter-century after Prohibition had been repealed.

Prohibition reduced alcohol consumption but did not stop it. Drinking itself was never illegal, although manufacturing and sale of alcoholic beverages was outlawed, so people who had bought alcohol before January 16, 1920, could and did continue to serve it privately. In addition, the illicit market soon grew to about two-thirds its pre-Prohibition levels. Illegal stills flourished in remote rural areas as well as city slums, and large quantities were smuggled from Canada. Bootlegging – and the related speakeasies – became a major business activity for organized crime groups, under leaders such as Al Capone in Chicago and Lucky Luciano in New York City.Indeed, Capone became a national symbol of Prohibition's violent side and was a top target for President Hoover.

Repeal

Prohibition lost support during the Great Depression, which started in 1929. So-called "wets" – people in favor of repeal – argued that legal sales would reduce violent gang crime, increase employment and raise tax revenues. The repeal movement was initiated and financed by the Association Against the Prohibition Amendment, who worked to elect Congressmen who agreed to support repeal. The group's wealthy supporters included John D. Rockefeller, Jr., S. S. Kresge, and the Du Pont family, among others, who had abandoned the dry cause. Pauline Sabin, a wealthy Republican who founded the Women's Organization for National Prohibition Reform (WONPR), argued that Prohibition should be repealed because it made the United States a nation of hypocrites and undermined its respect for the rule of law. This hypocrisy and the fact that women had initially led the prohibition movement convinced Sabin to establish the WONPR. Their efforts eventually led to the repeal of prohibition. When Sabin's fellow Republicans would not support her efforts, she went to the Democrats, who switched their support of the dry cause to endorse repeal under the leadership of liberal politicians such as Fiorello La Guardia and Franklin D. Roosevelt. Sabin and her supporters emphasized that repeal would generate enormous sums of much-needed tax revenue, and weaken the base of organized crime.

Repeal of Prohibition was accomplished with the ratification of the Twenty-first Amendment on December 5, 1933. Under its terms, states were allowed to set their own laws for the control of alcohol.

Aftermath

Following repeal, public interest in an organized prohibition movement dwindled. However, it survived for a while in a few southern and border states. To this day, there are still counties and parishes within the US known as "dry", where the sale of alcohol – liquor, and sometimes wine and beer – is prohibited. Some such counties/parishes/municipalities have adopted "Moist county" policies, however, in order to expand tax revenue. Some municipalities regulate when alcohol can be sold; an example is restricting or banning sales on Sunday, under the so-called «blue laws".

South America

Venezuela

In Venezuela, twenty-four hours before every election, the government prohibits the sale and distribution of alcoholic beverages throughout the national territory, including the restriction to all dealers, liquor stores, supermarkets, restaurants, wineries, pubs, bars, public entertainment, clubs and any establishment that markets alcoholic beverages. This is done to prevent violent alcohol-induced confrontations because of the high political polarization.

The same is done during Holy Week as a measure to reduce the alarming rate of road traffic accidents during these holidays.

Oceania

Australia

The Australian Capital Territory (then the Federal Capital Territory) was the first jurisdiction in Australia to have prohibition laws. In 1911, King O'Malley, then Minister of Home Affairs, shepherded laws through Parliament preventing new issue or transfer of licences to sell alcohol, to address unruly behaviour among workers building the new capital city. Prohibition was partial, since possession of alcohol purchased outside of the Territory remained legal and the few pubs that had existing licences could continue to operate. The Federal Parliament repealed the laws after residents of the Federal Capital Territory voted for the end of them in a 1928 plebiscite.

Since then, some local councils have enacted local dry zones in which possession or consumption of alcohol is forbidden. Nearly all dry zones are only a district within a larger community. Notable among those remaining in existence is the Adelaide city centre.

More recently, alcohol has been prohibited in many remote indigenous communities. Penalties for transporting alcohol into these «dry» communities are severe and can result in confiscation of any vehicles involved; in dry areas within the Northern Territory, all vehicles used to transport alcohol are seized.

New Zealand

In New Zealand, prohibition was a moralistic reform movement begun in the mid-1880s by the Protestant evangelical and Nonconformist churches and the Woman's Christian Temperance Union and after 1890 by the Prohibition League. It assumed that individual virtue was all that was needed to carry the colony forward from a pioneering society to a more mature one, but it never achieved its goal of national prohibition. However, both the Church of England and the largely Irish Catholic Church rejected prohibition as an intrusion of government into the church›s domain, while the growing labor movement saw capitalism rather than alcohol as the enemy.

Reformers hoped that the women's vote, in which New Zealand was a pioneer, would swing the balance, but the women were not as well organized as in other countries. Prohibition had a majority in a national referendum in 1911, but needed a 60% vote to pass. The movement kept trying in the 1920s, losing three more referenda by close votes; it managed to keep in place a 6pm closing hour for pubs and Sunday closing. The Depression and war years effectively ended the movement. but their 6pm closing hour remained until October 1967 when it was extended to 10pm.

For many years, referenda were held for individual towns or electorates, often coincident with general elections. The ballots determined whether these individual areas would be "dry" – that is, alcohol could not be purchased or consumed in public in these areas. One notable example was the southern city of Invercargill, which was dry from 1907 to 1943. People wanting alcohol usually travelled to places outside the city (such as the nearby township of Lorneville or the town of Winton) to drink in the local pubs or purchase alcohol to take back home. The last bastion of this 'dry' area remains in force in the form of a licensing trust which still to this day governs the sale of liquor in Invercargill. The city does not allow the sale of alcohol (beer and wine included) in supermarkets unlike the remainder of New Zealand, and all form of alcohol regardless of the sort can only be sold in bars and liquor stores.

Prohibition was of limited success in New Zealand as—like in other countries—it led to organised bootlegging. The most famous bootlegged alcohol in New Zealand was that produced in the Hokonui Hills close to the town of Gore (not coincidentally, the nearest large town to Invercargill). Even today, the term «Hokonui» conjures up images of illicit whisky to many New Zealanders.

A drug overdose (or simply overdose or OD) is the ingestion or application of a drug or other substance in quantities greater than are recommended. Typically it is used for cases when a risk to health will potentially result. An overdose may result in a toxic state or death.

Classification

The word "overdose" implies that there is a common safe dosage and usage for the drug; therefore, the term is commonly only applied to drugs, not poisons, even though some poisons are harmless at a low enough dosage. Drug overdose is caused to commit suicide, the result of intentional or unintentional misuse of medication. Intentional misuse leading to overdose can include using prescribed or unprescribed drugs in excessive quantities in an attempt to produce euphoria.

Usage of illicit drugs of unexpected purity, in large quantities, or after a period of drug abstinence can also induce overdose. Cocaine users who inject intravenously can easily overdose accidentally, as the margin between a pleasurable drug sensation and an overdose is small. Unintentional misuse can include errors in dosage caused by failure to read or understand product labels. Accidental overdoses may also be the result of over-prescription, failure to recognize a drug›s active ingredient, or unwitting ingestion by children. A common unintentional overdose in young children involves multi-vitamins containing iron. Iron is a component of the hemoglobin molecule in blood, used to transport oxygen to living cells. When taken in small amounts, iron allows the body to replenish hemoglobin, but in large amounts it causes severe pH imbalances in the body. If this overdose is not treated with chelation therapy, it can lead to death or a permanent coma. The term 'overdose' is often misused as a descriptor for adverse drug reactions or negative drug interactions due to mixing multiple drugs simultaneously.

Signs and symptoms

Signs and symptoms of an overdose vary depending on the drug or exposure to toxins. The symptoms can often be divided into differing toxidromes. This can help one determine what class of drug or toxin is causing the difficulties.

Symptoms of opioid overdoses include slow breathing, heart rate and pulse. Opioid overdoses can also cause pinpoint pupils, and blue lips and nails due to low levels of oxygen in the blood. A person experiencing an opioid overdose might also have muscle spasms, seizures and decreased consciousness. A person experiencing an opiate overdose usually will not wake up even if their name is called or if they are shaken vigorously.

First modern drug regulations

The first modern law in Europe for the regulating of drugs was the Pharmacy Act 1868 in the United Kingdom. There had been previous moves to establish the medical and pharmaceutical professions as separate, self-regulating bodies, but the General Medical Council, established in 1863, unsuccessfully attempted to assert control over drug distribution. The Act set controls on the distribution of poisons and drugs. Poisons could only be sold if the purchaser was known to the seller or to an intermediary known to both, and drugs, including opium and all preparations of opium or of poppies, had to be sold in containers with the seller's name and address. Despite the reservation of opium to professional control, general sales did continue to a limited extent, with mixtures with less than 1 per cent opium being unregulated.

After the legislation passed, the death rate caused by opium immediately fell from 6.4 per million population in 1868 to 4.5 in 1869. Deaths among children under five dropped from 20.5 per million population between 1863 and 1867, to 12.7 per million in 1871, and further declined to between 6 and 7 per million in the 1880s.

In the United States, the first drug law was passed in San Francisco in 1875, banning the smoking of opium in opium dens. The reason cited was "many women and young girls, as well as young men of respectable family, were being induced to visit the Chinese opium-smoking dens, where they were ruined morally and otherwise." This was followed by other laws throughout the country, and federal laws which barred Chinese people from trafficking in opium. Though the laws affected the use and distribution of opium by Chinese immigrants, no action was taken against the producers of such products as laudanum, a tincture of opium and alcohol, commonly taken as a panacea by white Americans. The distinction between its use by white Americans and Chinese immigrants was thus based on the form in which it was ingested: Chinese immigrants tended to smoke it, while it was often included in various kinds of generally liquid medicines often (but not exclusively) used by people of European descent. The laws targeted opium smoking, but not other methods of ingestion.

Britain also passed the All-India Opium Act of 1878, which similarly formalized social distinctions, by limiting recreational opium sales to registered Indian opium-eaters and Chinese opium-smokers and prohibiting its sale to workers from Burma.

Following passage of a regional law in 1895, Australia's Aboriginals Protection and Restriction of the Sale of Opium Act 1897 addressed opium addiction among Aborigines, though it soon became a general vehicle for depriving them of basic rights by administrative regulation. Opium sale was prohibited to the general population in 1905, and smoking and possession was prohibited in 1908.

Despite these laws, the late 19th century saw an increase in opiate consumption. This was due to the prescribing and dispensing of legal opiates by physicians and pharmacists to relieve painful menstruation. It is estimated that between 150,000 and 200,000 opiate addicts lived in the United States at the time, and a majority of these addicts were women.

Changing attitudes and the drug prohibition campaign

Since Britain's victory over the Qing Empire in the First Opium War, British traders had sold large amounts of opium to the Chinese to balance their trade. Attitudes towards the morality of this business were slow to change, but in 1874 the Society for the Suppression of the Opium Trade was formed in England by Quakers led by the Rev. Frederick Storrs-Turner. By the 1890s, increasingly strident campaigns were waged by Protestant missionaries in China for its abolition. The first such society was established at the 1890 Shanghai Missionary Conference, where British and American representatives, including John Glasgow Kerr, Arthur E. Moule, Arthur Gostick Shorrock and Griffith John, agreed to establish the Permanent Committee for the Promotion of Anti-Opium Societies.

Due to increasing pressure in the British parliament, the Liberal government under William Ewart Gladstone approved the appointment of a Royal Commission on Opium to India in 1893. The commission was tasked with ascertaining the impact of India›s opium exports to the Far East, and to advise whether the trade should be ended and opium consumption itself banned in India or not. After an extended inquiry the Royal Commission rejected the claims made by the anti-opiumists in regard to the harm wrought to India by this traffic and the issue was buried for another 15 years.

The missionary organizations were outraged over the Royal Commission on Opium's conclusions and set up the Anti-Opium League in China; the league gathered data from every Western-trained medical doctor in China and published Opinions of Over 100 Physicians on the Use of Opium in China. This was the first anti-drug campaign to be based on scientific principles, and it had a tremendous impact on the state of educated opinion in the West. In England, the home director of the China Inland Mission, Benjamin Broomhall, was an active opponent of the opium trade, writing two books to promote the banning of opium smoking: The Truth about Opium Smoking and The

Chinese Opium Smoker. In 1888, Broomhall formed and became secretary of the Christian Union for the Severance of the British Empire with the Opium Traffic and editor of its periodical, National Righteousness. He lobbied the British Parliament to stop the opium trade. He and James Laidlaw Maxwell appealed to the London Missionary Conference of 1888 and the Edinburgh Missionary Conference of 1910 to condemn the continuation of the trade. As Broomhall lay dying, an article from The Times was read to him with the welcome news that an international agreement had been signed ensuring the end of the opium trade within two years.

In 1906, a motion to 'declare the opium trade "morally indefensible" and remove Government support for it', initially unsuccessfully proposed by Arthur Pease in 1891, was put before the House of Commons. This time the motion passed. The Chinese government banned opium soon afterwards.

These changing attitudes led to the founding of the International Opium Commission in 1909. An International Opium Convention was signed by 13 nations at The Hague on January 23, 1912 during the First International Opium Conference. This was the first international drug control treaty and it was registered in the League of Nations Treaty Series on January 23, 1922. The Convention provided that «The contracting Powers shall use their best endeavours to control, or to cause to be controlled, all persons manufacturing, importing, selling, distributing, and exporting morphine, cocaine, and their respective salts, as well as the buildings in which these persons carry such an industry or trade.»

The treaty became international law in 1919 when it was incorporated into the Treaty of Versailles. The role of the Commission was passed to the League of Nations, and all signatory nations agreed to prohibit the import, sale, distribution, export, and use of all narcotic drugs, except for medical and scientific purposes.

Prohibition

In the UK the Defence of the Realm Act 1914, passed at the onset of the First World War, gave the government wide-ranging powers to requisition property and to criminalise specific activities. A moral panic was whipped up by the press in 1916 over the alleged sale of drugs to the troops of the British Indian Army. With the temporary powers of DORA, the Army Council quickly banned the sale of all psychoactive drugs to troops, unless required for medical reasons. However, shifts in the public attitude towards drugs—they were beginning to be associated with prostitution, vice and immorality—led the government to pass further unprecedented laws, banning and criminalising the possession and dispensation of all narcotics, including opium and cocaine. After the war, this legislation was maintained and strengthened with the passing of the Dangerous Drugs Act 1920. Home Office control was extended to include raw opium, morphine, cocaine, ecogonine and heroin.

Hardening of Canadian attitudes toward Chinese opium users and fear of a spread of the drug into the white population led to the effective criminalization of opium for nonmedical use in Canada between 1908 and the mid-1920s.

The Mao Zedong government nearly eradicated both consumption and production of opium during the 1950s using social control and isolation. Ten million addicts were forced into compulsory treatment, dealers were executed, and opium-producing regions were planted with new crops. Remaining opium production shifted south of the Chinese border into the Golden Triangle region. The remnant opium trade primarily served Southeast Asia, but spread to American soldiers during the Vietnam War, with 20 percent of soldiers regarding themselves as addicted during the peak of the epidemic in 1971. In 2003, China was estimated to have four million regular drug users and one million registered drug addicts.

In the USA, the Harrison Act was passed in 1914, and required sellers of opiates and cocaine to get a license. While originally intended to regulate the trade, it soon became a prohibitive law, eventually becoming legal precedent that any prescription for a narcotic given by a physician or pharmacist – even in the course of medical treatment for addiction – constituted conspiracy to violate the Harrison Act. In 1919, the Supreme Court ruled in Doremus that the Harrison Act was constitutional and in Webb that physicians could not prescribe narcotics solely for maintenance. In Jin Fuey Moy v. United States, the court upheld that it was a violation of the Harrison Act even if a physician provided prescription of a narcotic for an addict, and thus subject to criminal prosecution. This is also true of the later Marijuana Tax Act in 1937. Soon, however, licensing bodies did not issue licenses, effectively banning the drugs.

The American judicial system did not initially accept drug prohibition. Prosecutors argued that possessing drugs was a tax violation, as no legal licenses to sell drugs were in existence; hence, a person possessing drugs must have purchased them from an unlicensed source. After some wrangling, this was accepted as federal jurisdiction under the interstate commerce clause of the U.S. Constitution.

Alcohol prohibition

The prohibition of alcohol commenced in Finland in 1919 and in the United States in 1920. Because alcohol was the most popular recreational drug in these countries, reactions to its prohibition were far more negative than to the prohibition of other drugs, which were commonly associated with ethnic minorities, prostitution, and vice. Public pressure led to the repeal of alcohol prohibition in Finland in 1932, and in the United States in 1933. Residents of many provinces of Canada also experienced alcohol prohibition for similar periods in the first half of the 20th century.

In Sweden, a referendum in 1922 decided against an alcohol prohibition law (with 51% of the votes against and 49% for prohibition), but starting in 1914 (nationwide from 1917) and until 1955 Sweden employed an alcohol rationing system with personal liquor ration books («motbok").

War on Drugs

In response to rising drug use among young people and the counterculture movement, government efforts to enforce prohibition were strengthened in many countries from the 1960s onward. Support at an international level for the prohibition of psychoactive drug use became a consistent feature of United States policy during both Republican and Democratic administrations, to such an extent that US support for foreign governments has often been contingent on their adherence to US drug policy. Major milestones in this campaign include the introduction of the Single Convention on Narcotic Drugs in 1961, the Convention on Psychotropic Substances in 1971 and the United Nations Convention Against Illicit Traffic in Narcotic Drugs and Psychotropic Substances in 1988. A few developing countries where consumption of the prohibited substances has enjoyed longstanding cultural support, long resisted such outside pressure to pass legislation adhering to these conventions. Nepal only did so in 1976.

In 1972, United States President Richard Nixon announced the commencement of the so-called «War on Drugs». Later, President Reagan added the position of drug czar to the President's Executive Office. In 1973, New York introduced mandatory minimum sentences of 15 years to life imprisonment for possession of more than 113 grams (4 oz) of a so-called hard drug, called the Rockefeller drug laws after New York Governor and later Vice President Nelson Rockefeller. Similar laws were introduced across the United States.

California's broader 'three strikes and you're out' policy adopted in 1994 was the first mandatory sentencing policy to gain widespread publicity and was subsequently adopted in most United States jurisdictions. This policy mandates life imprisonment for a third criminal conviction of any felony offense. A similar ‹three strikes› policy was introduced to the United Kingdom by the Conservative government in 1997. This legislation enacted a mandatory minimum sentence of seven years for those convicted for a third time of a drug trafficking offense involving a class A drug.

Calls for legalization, relegalization or decriminalization

The terms relegalization, legalization, and decriminalization are used with very different meanings by different authors, something that can be confusing when the claims are not specified. Here are some variants:

- Sales of one or more drugs (e.g., marijuana) for personal use become legal, at least if sold in a certain way.
- Sales of an extracts with a specific substance become legal sold in a certain way, for example on prescription.
- Use or possession of small amounts for personal use do not lead to incarceration if it is the only crime, but it is still illegal; the court or the prosecutor can impose a fine. (In that sense, Sweden both legalized and supported drug prohibition simultaneously.)
- Use or possession of small amounts for personal use do not lead to

incarceration. The case is not treated in an ordinary court, but by a commission that may recommend treatment or sanctions including fines. (In that sense, Portugal both legalized and supported drug prohibitions).

In the 2010s, movements have grown around the world proposing the relegalization and decriminalization of drugs. For instance, there is a movement for cannabis legalization in Canada, as well as the Marijuana Party of Canada. Drug liberalization policies are often supported by proponents of liberalism and libertarianism on the grounds of individual freedom. There are also growing countermovements. Prohibition of drugs is supported by proponents of conservative values but also by many other types of NGO›s that are not linked to conservative political parties. A growing number of NGO organizations in many countries have joined the international network World Federation Against Drugs. WFAD members support the United Nations narcotics conventions.

In 2002, five (former) police officers created Law Enforcement Against Prohibition, a NGO that has gained a lot of media attention, showing that support for a regulation of drug sales also comes from the "other side" of the drug war and that maintaining a global corruption pyramid for the tax-free Mafia monopoly isn't a good idea, compared to controlling access, age and quality. The former Director of the Office of National Drug Control Policy, the Drug Czar John P. Walters, has described the drug problem in the United States as a "public health challenge", and he has publicly eschewed the notion of a "war on drugs". He has supported additional resources for substance abuse treatment and has touted random student drug testing as an effective prevention strategy. However, the actions of the Office of National Drug Control Policy continue to belie the rhetoric of a shift away from primarily enforcement-based responses to illegal drug use.

On February 22, 2008 the President of Honduras, Manuel Zelaya, called on the world to legalize drugs, in order, he said, to prevent the majority of violent murders occurring in Honduras. Honduras is used by cocaine smugglers as a transiting point between Colombia and the US. Honduras, with a population of 7 million, suffers an average of 8–10 murders a day, with an estimated 70% being a result of this international drug trade. The same problem is occurring in Guatemala, El Salvador, Costa Rica and Mexico, according to Zelaya. In January 2012 Colombian President Juan Manuel Santos made a plea to the United States and Europe to start a global debate about legalizing drugs. This call was echoed by the Guatemalan President Otto Pérez Molina, who announced his desire to legalize drugs, saying "What I have done is put the issue back on the table."

In a report dealing with HIV in June 2014, the World Health Organization (WHO) of the UN called for the decriminalization of drugs particularly including injected ones. This conclusion put WHO at odds with broader long-standing UN policy favoring criminalization. Eight states of the United

States (Alaska, California, Colorado, Maine, Massachusetts, Nevada, Oregon, and Washington), as well as the District of Columbia, have legalized the sale of marijuana for personal recreational use as of 2017, despite the fact that recreational use remains illegal under U.S. federal law. The conflict between state and federal law is, as of 2018, unresolved.

Drug prohibition laws

The following individual drugs, listed under their respective family groups (e.g., barbiturates, benzodiazepines, opiates), are the most frequently sought after by drug users and as such are prohibited or otherwise heavily regulated for use in many countries:

- Among the barbiturates, pentobarbital (Nembutal), secobarbital (Seconal), and amobarbital (Amytal)
- Among the benzodiazepines, temazepam (Restoril; Normison; Euhypnos), flunitrazepam (Rohypnol; Hypnor; Flunipam), and nimetazepam (Erimin)
- Cannabis products, e.g., marijuana, hashish, and hashish oil
- Among the dissociatives, phencyclidine (PCP), and ketamine are the most sought after.
- hallucinogens such as LSD, mescaline, peyote, and psilocybin
- Empathogen-entactogen drugs like MDMA («ecstasy»)
- Among the narcotics, it is opiates such as morphine and codeine, and opioids such as diacetylmorphine (Heroin), hydrocodone (Vicodin; Hycodan), oxycodone (Percocet; Oxycontin), hydromorphone (Dilaudid), and oxymorphone (Opana).
- Sedatives such as GHB and methaqualone (Quaalude)
- Stimulants such as cocaine, amphetamine (Adderall), dextroamphetamine (Dexedrine), methamphetamine (Desoxyn), methcathinone, and methylphenidate (Ritalin).

The regulation of the above drugs varies in many countries. Alcohol possession and consumption by adults is today widely banned only in Islamic countries and certain states of India. The United States, Finland, and Canada banned alcohol in the early part of the 20th century; this was called Prohibition. Although alcohol prohibition was repealed in these countries at a national level, there are still parts of the United States that do not allow alcohol sales, even though alcohol possession may be legal. Bhutan is the only country in the world where possession and use of tobacco is illegal. New Zealand has banned the importation of chewing tobacco as part of the Smoke-free Environments Act 1990. In some parts of the world, provisions are made for the use of traditional sacraments like ayahuasca, iboga, and peyote. In Gabon, Africa, iboga (tabernanthe iboga) has been declared a national treasure and is used in rites of the Bwiti religion. The active ingredient, ibogaine, is proposed as a treatment of opioid withdrawal and various substance use disorders.

In countries where alcohol and tobacco are legal, certain measures are frequently undertaken to discourage use of these drugs. For example, packages of alcohol and tobacco sometimes communicate warnings directed towards the consumer, communicating the potential risks of partaking in the use of the substance. These drugs also frequently have special sin taxes associated with the purchase thereof, in order to recoup the losses associated with public funding for the health problems the use causes in long-term users. Restrictions on advertising also exist in many countries, and often a state holds a monopoly on manufacture, distribution, marketing, and/or the sale of these drugs.

Legal dilemmas

In the United States, there is considerable legal debate about the impact these laws have had on Americans' civil rights. Critics claim that the War on Drugs has lowered the evidentiary burden required for a legal search of a suspect's dwelling or vehicle, or to intercept a suspect's communications However, many of the searches that result in drug arrests are often «commissions» to search a person or the person›s propertyPeople who consent to a search, knowing full well that they possess contraband, generally consent because they are ignorant of the fact that they have the right to decline permission to search Under the laws of most U.S. states, police are not required to disclose to suspects that they have the right to decline a search. Even when a suspect does not give permission to search, police are often known to state in arrest affidavits and even provide sworn testimony that the suspect consented to the search, secure in the knowledge that a judge will normally weigh all questions of credibility in favour of law enforcement and against the accusedSimilarly, in cases where the accused does not consent to a search, courts have generally held police to a very low standard of reasonable suspicion and/or probable cause in drug cases, essentially endorsing «fishing expeditions» by stop-and-search highway interdiction police

The sentencing statutes in the United States Code that cover controlled substances are notoriously intricate For example, a first-time offender convicted in a single proceeding for selling marijuana three times, and found to have carried a gun on him all three times (even if it were not used) is subject to a minimum sentence of 55 years in federal prison.

Drug sentencing guidelines under state law in America are generally much less harsh than the federal sentencing guidelines, although great irregularities exist. The vast majority of drug felonies and almost all drug misdemeanors in the United States are prosecuted at the state level. The federal government tends to prosecute only drug trafficking cases involving large amounts of drugs, or cases which have been referred to federal prosecutors by local district attorneys seeking the harsher sentences provided under the federal sentencing guidelines. In rare instances, some defendants are prosecuted both federally and by the state for the same drug trafficking conduct. The United States Supreme Court has ruled that a defendant does not face double jeopardy if he is convicted and sentenced by both the state and federal government for the same underlying criminal conduct. Sometimes, crimes not directly related to drug use and sale. For example, the United States recently brought charges against club owners for maintaining a place of business where a) ecstasy is known to be frequently consumed; b) paraphernalia associated with the use of ecstasy is sold and/or widely tolerated (such as glow sticks and pacifiers); and c) "chill-out rooms" are created, where ecstasy users can cool down (ecstasy users in club settings tend to dance for extended periods of time, raising the user's blood temperature These are being challenged in court by organizations such as the American Civil Liberties Union (ACLU) and Drug Policy Alliance. Drug prohibition has created several legal dilemmas. For example, many countries allow the use of undercover law enforcement officers solely or primarily for the enforcement of laws against use of certain drugs. Many of these officers are allegedly allowed to commit crimes if it is necessary to maintain the secrecy of the investigation, or in order to collect adequate evidence for a conviction Some people have criticized this practice as failing to ensure equality under the law because it grants police officers the right to commit crimes that no other citizen could commit without potential consequences.

Another legal dilemma is the creation in several countries of a legal loopholes allowing for arbitrary arrest and prosecution This is the result of several drugs such as Dimethyltryptamine, GHB, and morphine being illegal to possess but also inherently present in all humans as a result of endogenous synthesis. Since some jurisdictions classify possession of drugs to include having the drug present in the blood in any concentration, all residents of such countries are technically in possession of multiple illegal drugs at all timesThe War on Drugs has stimulated the creation of international law enforcement agencies (such as Interpol), mostly in Western countries. This has occurred because a large volume of illicit drugs come from Third-World countries.

Social control

The role of drugs in the exercise of political control is also coming under increasing discussion. Control can be through prohibition or supply. The total or even partial prohibition of drugs gives the government considerable leverage for other types of control. An example would be the selective application of drug laws ... against selected components of the population such as members of certain minority groups or political organizations

Academic Noam Chomsky argues that drug laws are currently, and have historically, been used by the state to oppress sections of society it opposes:

Very commonly substances are criminalized because they're associated with what's called the dangerous classes, poor people, or working people. So for example in England in the 19th century, there was a period when gin was criminalized and whiskey wasn›t, because gin is what poor people drink.

Legal highs and prohibition

In 2013 the European Monitoring Centre for Drugs and Drug Addiction reported that there are 280 new legal drugs, known as legal highs, available in Europe. One of the best known, mephedrone, was banned in the United Kingdom in 2010. On November 24, 2010, the U.S. Drug Enforcement

Administration announced it would use emergency powers to ban many synthetic cannabinoids within a month. An estimated 73 new psychoactive synthetic drugs appeared on the UK market in 2012. The response of the Home Office has been to create a temporary class drug order which bans the manufacture, import and supply but not the possession of named substances.

Penalties

United States

Drug possession is the crime of having one or more illegal drugs in one's possession, either for personal use, distribution, sale or otherwise. Illegal drugs fall into different categories and sentences vary depending on the amount, type of drug, circumstances, and jurisdiction. In the U.S., the penalty for illegal drug possession and sale can vary from a small fine to a prison sentence. In some states, marijuana possession is considered to be a petty offense, with the penalty being comparable to that of a speeding violation. In some municipalities, possessing a small quantity of marijuana in one's own home is not punishable at all. Generally, however, drug possession is an arrestable offense, although first-time offenders rarely serve jail time. Federal law makes even possession of "soft drugs", such as cannabis, illegal, though some local governments have laws contradicting federal laws.

In the U.S., the War on Drugs is thought to be contributing to a prison overcrowding problem. In 1996, 59.6% of prisoners were drug-related criminals. The U.S. population grew by about +25% from 1980 to 2000. In that same 20 year time period, the U.S. prison population tripled, making the U.S. the world leader in both percentage and absolute number of citizens incarcerated. The United States has 5% of the world›s population, but 25% of the prisoners.

About 90% of United States prisoners are incarcerated in state jails. In 2016, about 200,000, under 16%, of the 1.3 million people in these state jails, were serving time for drug offenses. 700,000 were incarcerated for violent offenses.

Australia

A Nielsen poll in 2012 found that only 27% of voters favoured decriminalisation. Australia has steep penalties for growing and using drugs even for personal use. with Western Australia having the toughest laws. There is an associated anti-drug culture amongst a significant number of Australians. Law enforcement targets drugs, particularly in the party scene. In 2012, crime statistics in Victoria revealed that police were increasingly arresting users rather than dealers, and the Liberal government banned the sale of bongs that year.

The Netherlands

In the Netherlands, cannabis and other "soft" drugs are partly decriminalised in small quantities. The Dutch government treats the problem as more of a public health issue than a criminal issue. Contrary to popular belief, cannabis is still illegal, mostly to satisfy the country's agreements with the United Nations Coffee shops that sell cannabis to people 18 or above are tolerated in some cities, and pay taxes like any other business for their cannabis and hashish sales, although distribution is a grey area that the authorities would rather not go into as it is not decriminalised. Many «coffee shops» are found in Amsterdam and cater mainly to the large tourist trade; the local consumption rate is far lower than in the US. Netherlands has the highest antidrug related public expenditure per capita of all countries in EU (139 EUR per capita, 2004Similarly to the rest of the European Union member states and American democracies, controlled drugs are illegal in the Netherlands. Nevertheless, illegal drugs are consumed worldwide, causing concern in the international community. According to the United Nations Drug Control Programme, results in the 2001 World Drug Report estimate «that the extent of drug abuse in the world involves about 180 million people, which represents 3% of the global population. The majority of drug users (80%) used cannabis, followed by amphetamine-type stimulants such as methamphetamine, amphetamine and substances of the ecstasy group (16%), cocaine (8%), heroin (5%) and other opiates (2%)».

The administrative bodies responsible for enforcing the drug policies include the Ministry of Health, Welfare and Sport, the Ministry of Justice, the Ministry of the Interior and Kingdom Relations, and the Ministry of Finance. Local authorities also shape local policy, within the national framework. The prohibition policy is heavily influenced by the international community (through the United Nations), especially the neighboring states of France and Germany, which pressure the kingdom to be more strict, for they are directly affected through the illegal trafficking of narcotics coming from the NetherlandsLegally, possession, manufacturing, trafficking, importation and exportation are forbidden. Nonetheless, it is not an offense to use drugs (Ministry of Foreign Affairs, 2003). There are different penalties involved when breaking the law, which may include a monetary fine, imprisonment, or both. To apply the law, the government differentiates between "soft" and "hard" drugs. Soft drugs are considered to produce less harm to both the individual and society, these being used mainly for folk medicine and recreational purposes. This category encompasses cannabis (nederwiet), hashish and some fungi. Hard drugs are considered to cause considerable personal harm through addiction and physical detriment, as well as nuisance to society, by increasing crime and deteriorating families. Cocaine, heroin, etc. belong to this categoryAlong with these two categories, there is a pyramid of priority when it comes to prosecution by law enforcement agencies.

- The handling and trade of hard drugs is on the zenith, being a joint target not only by the Netherlands, but also by the international community. This can be punished by maximum sentences of twelve years of imprisonment and/or a fine of up to €45,000 The second priority is given to the production and trade of soft drugs. Deviation from the AHOJ-G criteria for coffee shops may result in up to four years of imprisonment and/or a fine of €45,000.

- The third priority focuses on hard drug users. Instead of labelling the users of hard drugs as "criminals", the state aims to rehabilitate users and prevent others from becoming addicted. However, disturbance to society caused by the consumption of hard drugs can result in one year of prison and/or a €11,250 fine. Lastly, individuals possessing more than five grams for personal consumption, or disturbing the public, can go to prison for one month and/or be fined €2,250 There are varying rules within these categories, for example the amount possessed, the role played in the transaction and the intent of the goods Regarding coffee shops, the line between law and practice thins. A coffee shop is a heavily controlled business establishment where individuals can purchase a personal dose of soft drugs in the form of joints, pastry, drinks and packages. In theory, these shops must abide by governmental and local regulations, as well as meet the AHOJ-G criteria, an acronym for: No Advertising, Hard drugs, Nuisance of any kind, Jongeren (minors under 18), and a limit of five grams per transaction. Additionally, the maximum stock at any time is five hundred grams. Local governments may impose additional rules, such as closing times, zoning (coffee shops may not be close to schools), and parking restrictions. The rationale behind coffee shops is to keep citizens away from the hard drugs scene, bringing them to a safe, social, and regulated environment

When analysing the Dutch model, both disadvantages and advantages can be drawn when comparing the results with other countries. On a moral argument, tolerating soft drugs can be seen as the defeat of the government against hedonism. Additionally, decades of growing and perfecting cannabis and hashish has resulted in increased levels of the main active hallucinogenic constituent tetrahydrocannabinol (THC), as levels have doubled, making the derived products more powerful, and therefore requiring less to achieve the desired effect The coffee shop will lose its license if it caught selling to minors. Though there was a slight increase of use at the beginning, the rates balanced out some years later. The presence of coffee shops does not translate in public urge for experimentation. In fact, most people that did not consume drugs before the enhancement of the policy continue not to use them.

When compared to other countries, Dutch drug consumption falls in the European average at six per cent regular use (twenty-one per cent at some point in life) and considerably lower than the Anglo-Saxon countries headed by the United States with an eight per cent recurring use (thirty-four at some point in life). Experts have come to the conclusion that the policies applied do not play a striking role in these statistics, though there is debate over this issue (CEDRO, 2004). While there has been talk for over a decade about preventing foreigners from entering Dutch cannabis coffeeshops by requiring customers to possess a 'weedpass', this legislation has not been enacted, so Dutch coffeeshops continue to sell cannabis openly to both locals and foreigners. However a small number of southern municipalities (including Roosendaal and Maastricht) in the Netherlands now require customers to carry identification proving that they are resident in the Netherlands.

Asia

Indonesia

Indonesia carries a maximum penalty of death for drug dealing, and a maximum of 15 years prison for drug use. In 2004, Australian citizen Schappelle Corby was convicted of smuggling 4.4 kilograms of cannabis into Bali, a crime that carried a maximum penalty of death. Her trial reached the verdict of guilty with a punishment of 20 years imprisonment. Corby claimed to be an unwitting drug mule. Australian citizens known as the "Bali Nine" were caught smuggling heroin. Two of the nine, Andrew Chan and Myuran Sukumaran, were executed April 29, 2015 along with six other foreign nationals. In August 2005, Australian model Michelle Leslie was arrested with two ecstasy pills. She pleaded guilty to possession and in November 2005 was sentenced to 3 months imprisonment, which she was deemed to have already served, and was released from prison immediately upon her admission of guilt on the charge of possession.

Republic of China (Taiwan

Taiwan carries a maximum penalty of death for drug trafficking, while smoking tobacco and wine are classified as legal entertainment drug. The Department of Health is in charge of drug prohibition.

Methods of law enforcement

Because the possession of drugs is called a "victimless crime" by some analysts, as it can be committed in privacy, the enforcement of prohibitionist laws requires methods of law enforcement to inspect private property. In societies with strong property laws or individual rights, this may present a risk for conflicts or violations of rights. Disrupting the market relies on eradication, interdiction and domestic law enforcement efforts. Through cooperation with governments such as those of Colombia, Mexico and Afghanistan, coca (the plant source for cocaine) and poppy (the plant source for opium and heroin) are eradicated by the United States and other allies such as the United Kingdom, so that the crops cannot be processed into narcotics. Eradication can be accomplished by aerial spraying or manual eradication. However, the eradication is only temporary as the harvest fields can usually be replanted after a certain amount of time.

The government of Colombian President Álvaro Uribe has resisted criticism of aerial spraying of coca and poppy and has seen major reductions in both crops according to the United Nations Office of Crime and Drugs (See also Plan Colombia). In 2003, over 1,300 square kilometers of mature coca were sprayed and eradicated in Colombia, where at the start of the year, approximately 1,450 square kilometers had been planted. This strategic accomplishment prevented the production over 500 tonnes of cocaine, sufficient to supply all the cocaine users in both US and Europe for one year. Further, it eliminated upward of $100 million of illicit income in Colombia. No effect on prices or availability in the marketplace has been noted, and the actual number of acres of coca planted seems to have actually increased, largely shifting to more remote areas or into neighboring countries. Aerial spraying also has the unintended consequence of destroying legitimate crop fields in the process.

Interdiction is carried out primarily by aerial and naval armed forces patrolling known trafficking zones. From South America to the United States most drugs traverse either the Caribbean Sea or the Eastern Pacific, usually in "go-fast" boats that carry drug cargos and engines and little else. Drugs have also been smuggled in makeshift submarines. In 2015, a submarine with 12,000 pounds of cocaine was seized by the US Coast Guard off of the coast of Central America. This was the largest US drug seizure to date.

Investigation on drug trafficking often begins with the recording of unusually frequent deaths by overdose, monitoring financial flows of suspected traffickers, or by finding concrete elements while inspecting for other purposes. For example, a person pulled over for traffic violations may have illicit drugs in his or her vehicle, thus leading to an arrest and/or investigation of the source of the materials. The United States federal government has placed a premium on disrupting the large drug trafficking organizations that move narcotics into and around the United States, while state and local law enforcement focus on disrupting street-level drug dealing gangs.

Drug control strategy

Present drug control efforts utilize several techniques in the attempt to achieve their goal of eliminating illegal drug use:

- Disrupting the market for drugs
- Prevention efforts that rely on community activism, public information campaigns to educate the public on the potential dangers of drug use
- Law-enforcement efforts against elements of the supply chain, through surveillance and undercover work
- Providing effective and targeted substance abuse treatment to dependent users

Alternatives to prohibition

On February 11, 2009 a document called Drugs and democracy in Latin America: Towards a paradigm shift was signed by several Latin American political figures, intellectuals, writers and journalists as commissioners of the Latin American Initiative on Drugs and Democracy. The document questions the war on drugs and points out its failures. It also indicates that prohibition has come with an extensive social cost, especially to the countries that take part in the production of illicit drugs. Although controversial, the document does not endorse either the production or consumption of drugs but recommends for both a new and an alternative approach. The document argues that drug production and consumption has become a social taboo that inhibits the public debate because of its relationship to crime and as consequence it confines consumers to a small circle where they become more vulnerable to the actions of organized crime. The authors also demand for a close review to the prohibitive strategies of the United States and the study of the advantages and limits of the damage reduction strategy followed by the European Union. The proposal uses three paradigms as an alternative:

- The treatment of consumption as a problem of public health.
- The reduction of consumption through the dissemination of information and prevention.
- A new focus towards organized crime.

The document favors the European policies towards drug consumption since according to the authors it is more humane and efficient. The signers of this document are: Fernando Henrique Cardoso, Ernesto Zedillo, César Gaviria, Paulo Coelho, Enrique Santos, Mario Vargas Llosa, Moisés Naím, Tomas Eloy Martinez

In a number of countries, though not the United States at present (2017), there are supervised injection sites, in which a nurse is present to ensure cleanliness and quickly treat overdoses. It is a form of harm reduction.

Two years later in mid-2011, the core of the Initiative and its commission were extended and endorsed in a report issued by the Global Commission on Drug Policy. Joining the three former presidents of Colombia, Brazil and Mexico and Nobel Prize for Literature winner Llosa on the Global Commission were former U.S. Secretary of State George P. Shultz and Federal Reserve chair Paul Volcker; Carlos Fuentes, Mexican writer and public intellectual; John C. Whitehead, formerly of Goldman Sachs; and Kofi Annan, former Secretary-General of the United Nations.

Diagnosis

The substance that has been taken may often be determined by asking the person. However, if they will not, or cannot, due to an altered level of consciousness, provide this information, a search of the home or questioning of friends and family may be helpful.

Examination for toxidromes, drug testing, or laboratory test may be helpful. Other laboratory test such as glucose, urea and electrolytes, paracetamol levels and salicylate levels are typically done. Negative drug-drug interactions have sometimes been misdiagnosed as an acute drug overdose, occasionally leading to the assumption of suicide.

Prevention

The distribution of naloxone to injection drug users and other opioid drug users decreases the risk of death from overdose. The Centers for Disease Control and Prevention (CDC) estimates that U.S. programs for drug users and their caregivers prescribing take-home doses of naloxone and training on its utilization are estimated to have prevented 10,000 opioid overdose deaths. Healthcare institution-based naloxone prescription programs have also helped reduce rates of opioid overdose in the U.S. state of North Carolina, and have been replicated in the U.S. military. Nevertheless, scale-up of healthcare-based opioid overdose interventions is limited by providers' insufficient knowledge and negative attitudes towards prescribing take-home naloxone to prevent opioid overdose. Programs training police and fire personnel in opioid overdose response using naloxone have also shown promise in the U.S.

Management

Stabilization of the victim's airway, breathing, and circulation (ABCs) is the initial treatment of an overdose. Ventilation is considered when there is a low respiratory rate or when blood gases show the person to be hypoxic. Monitoring of the patient should continue before and throughout the treatment process, with particular attention to temperature, pulse, respiratory rate, blood pressure, urine output, electrocardiography (ECG) and O saturation. Poison control centers and medical toxicologists are available in many areas to provide guidance in overdoses to both physicians and the general public.

Antidotes

Specific antidotes are available for certain overdoses. For example, naloxone is the antidote for opiates such as heroin or morphine. Similarly, benzodiazepine overdoses may be effectively reversed with flumazenil. As a nonspecific antidote, activated charcoal is frequently recommended if available within one hour of the ingestion and the ingestion is significant. Gastric lavage, syrup of ipecac, and whole bowel irrigation are rarely used.

Epidemiology and statistics

In the United States, 70,200 people died from drug overdoses in 2017, which was an increase of about 10 percent over 2016. Since 2000, the U.S. drug overdose death rate has gone from 6.2 per 100,000 people in 2000 to 14.7 per 100,000 in 2014.

The National Center for Health Statistics report that 19,250 people died of accidental poisoning in the U.S. in the year 2004 (8 deaths per 100,000 population).

In 2008 testimony before a Senate subcommittee, Leonard J. Paulozzi, a medical epidemiologist at the Centers for Disease Control and Prevention stated that in 2005 more than 22,000 American lives were lost due to overdoses, and the number is growing rapidly. Paulozzi also testified that all available evidence suggests that unintentional overdose deaths are related to the increasing use of prescription drugs, especially opioid painkillers. However, the vast majority of overdoses are also attributable to alcohol. It is very rare for a victim of an overdose to have consumed just one drug. Most overdoses occur when drugs are ingested in combination with alcohol.

Drug overdose was the leading cause of injury death in 2013. Among people 25 to 64 years old, drug overdose caused more deaths than motor vehicle traffic crashes. There were 43,982 drug overdose deaths in the United States in 2013. Of these, 22,767 (51.8%) were related to prescription drugs.

The 22,767 deaths relating to prescription drug overdose in 2013, 16,235 (71.3%) involved opioid painkillers, and 6,973 (30.6%) involved benzodiazepines. Drug misuse and abuse caused about 2.5 million emergency department (ED) visits in 2011. Of these, more than 1.4 million ED visits were related to prescription drugs. Among those ED visits, 501,207 visits were related to anti-anxiety and insomnia medications, and 420,040 visits were related to opioid analgesics

Drug cartel

A drug cartel is any criminal organization with the intention of supplying drug trafficking operations. They range from loosely managed agreements among various drug traffickers to formalized commercial enterprises. The term was applied when the largest trafficking organizations reached an agreement to coordinate the production and distribution of cocaine. Since that agreement was broken up, drug cartels are no longer actually cartels, but the term stuck and it is now popularly used to refer to any criminal narcotics related organization.

The basic structure of a drug cartel is as follows:

- Falcons (Spanish: Halcones): Considered as the "eyes and ears" of the streets, the "falcons" are the lowest rank in any drug cartel. They are responsible for supervising and reporting the activities of the police, the military, and rival groups.
- Hitmen (Spanish: Sicarios): The armed group within the drug cartel, responsible for carrying out assassinations, kidnappings, thefts, and extortions, operating protection rackets, and defending their plaza (turf) from rival groups and the military.
- Lieutenants (Spanish: Teniente): The second highest position in the drug cartel organization, responsible for supervising the hitmen and falcons within their own territory. They are allowed to carry out low-profile murders without permission from their bosses.
- Drug lords (Spanish: Capos): The highest position in any drug cartel, responsible for supervising the entire drug industry, appointing territorial leaders, making alliances, and planning high-profile murders.

There are other operating groups within the drug cartels. For example, the drug producers and suppliers, although not considered in the basic structure, are critical operators of any drug cartel, along with the financiers and money launderers. In addition, the arms suppliers operate in a completely different circle, and are technically not considered part of the cartel›s logistics.

Drug legalization

Drug legalization calls for a return to the pre-20th century situation in which almost all drugs were legal. This would require ending government-enforced prohibition on the distribution or sale and personal use of specified (or all) currently banned drugs. Proposed ideas range from full legalization which would completely remove all forms of government control, to various forms of regulated legalization, where drugs would be legally available, but under a system of government control which might mean for instance:

- Mandated labels with dosage and medical warnings,
- Restrictions on advertising,
- Age limitations,
- Restrictions on amount purchased at one time,
- Requirements on the form in which certain drugs would be supplied,
- Ban on sale to intoxicated persons,
- Special user licenses to purchase particular drugs.
- A possible clinical setting for the consumption of some intravenous drugs and/or supervised consumption.

The regulated legalization system would probably have a range of restrictions for different drugs, depending on their perceived risk, so while some drugs would be sold over the counter in pharmacies or other licensed establishments, drugs with greater risks of harm might only be available for sale on licensed premises where use could be monitored and emergency medical care made available. Examples of drugs with different levels of regulated distribution in most countries include: caffeine (coffee, tea), nicotine (tobacco), and ethyl alcohol (beer, wine, spirits).

Full legalization is often proposed by groups such as libertarians who object to drug laws on moral grounds, while regulated legalization is suggested by groups such as Law Enforcement Against Prohibition who object to the drug laws on the grounds that they fail to achieve their stated aims and instead greatly worsen the problems associated with use of prohibited drugs, but who acknowledge that there are harms associated with currently prohibited drugs which need to be minimized. Not all proponents of drug re-legalization necessarily share a common ethical framework, and people may adopt this viewpoint for a variety of reasons. In particular, favoring drug legalization does not imply approval of drug use.

Drug decriminalization

Drug decriminalization calls for reduced control and penalties compared to existing laws. Proponents of drug decriminalization generally support the use of fines or other punishments to replace prison terms, and often propose systems whereby illegal drug users who are caught would be fined, but would not receive a permanent criminal record as a result. A central feature of drug decriminalization is the concept of harm reduction.

Drug decriminalization is in some ways an intermediate between prohibition and legalization, and has been criticized as being "the worst of both worlds", in that drug sales would still be illegal, thus perpetuating the problems associated with leaving production and distribution of drugs to the criminal underworld, while also failing to discourage illegal drug use by removing the criminal penalties that might otherwise cause some people to choose not to use drugs. However, there are many that argue that the decriminalization of possession of drugs would redirect focus of the law enforcement system of any country to put more effort into arresting dealers and big time criminals, instead of arresting minor criminals for mere possession, and thus be more effective.

In 2001 Portugal began treating use and possession of small quantities of drugs as a public health issue. This means rather than incarcerating those in possession they are referred to a treatment program. The drugs are still illegal, the police just handles the situation differently. This also decreases the amount of money the government spends fighting a war on drugs and money spent keeping drug users incarcerated. "As noted by the EMCDDA, across Europe in the last decades, there has been a movement toward "an approach that distinguishes between the drug trafficker, who is viewed as a criminal, and the drug user, who is seen more as a sick person who is in need of treatment" (EMCDDA 2008, 22).6 A number of Latin American countries have similarly moved to reduce the penalties associated with drug use and personal possession" (Laqueur, 2015, p. 748). Portugal is the first country that has decriminalized the possession of small amounts of drugs, to positive results. Anyone caught with any type of drug in Portugal, if it is for personal consumption, will not be imprisoned.

Economics

There are numerous economic and social impacts of the criminalization of drugs. Prohibition increases crime (theft, violence, corruption) and drug price and increases potency. In many developing countries the production of drugs offers a way to escape poverty. Milton Friedman estimated that over 10,000 deaths a year in the US are caused by the criminalization of drugs, and if drugs were to be made legal innocent victims such as those shot down in drive by shootings, would cease or decrease. The economic inefficiency and ineffectiveness of such government intervention in preventing drug trade has been fiercely criticised by drug-liberty advocates. The War on Drugs of the United States, that provoked legislation within several other Western governments, has also garnered criticism for these reasons.

Prices and consumption

Much of the debate surrounding the economics of drug legalization centers on the shape of the demand curve for illegal drugs and the sensitivity of consumers to changes in the prices of illegal drugs. Proponents of drug legalization often assume that the quantity of addictive drugs consumed is unresponsive to changes in price; however, studies into addictive, but legal, substances like alcohol and cigarettes, have shown that consumption can be quite responsive to changes in prices. In the same study, economists Michael Grossman and Frank J. Chaloupka estimated that a 10% reduction in the price of cocaine would lead to a 14% increase in the frequency of cocaine use. This increase indicates that consumers are responsive to price changes in the cocaine market. There is also evidence that in the long run, consumers are much more responsive to price changes than in the short run, but other studies have led to a wide range of conclusions.

Considering that legalization would likely lead to an increase in the supply of drugs, the standard economic model predicts that the quantity of drugs consumed would rise and the prices would fall. However, Andrew E. Clark, an economist who has studied the effects of drug legalization, suggests that a specific tax, or sin tax, would counteract the increase in consumption.

Associated costs

Proponents of drug prohibition argue that many negative externalities, or third party costs, are associated with the consumption of illegal drugs., Externalities like violence, environmental effects on neighborhoods, increased health risks and, increased healthcare costs are often associated with the illegal drug market. Opponents of prohibition argue that many of those externalities are created by current drug policies. They believe that much of the violence associated with drug trade is due to the illegal nature of drug trade, where there is no mediating authority to solve disputes peacefully and legally. The illegal nature of the market also affects the health of consumers by making it difficult to acquire syringes, which often leads to needle sharing. Prominent economist Milton Friedman argues that prohibition of drugs creates many negative externalities like increased incarceration rates, the undertreatment of chronic pain, corruption, disproportional imprisonment of African Americans, compounding harm to users, the destruction of inner cities and harm to foreign countries. Proponents of legalization also argue that prohibition decrease the quality of the drugs made, which often leads to more physical harm, like accidental overdoses and poisoning, to the drug users. Steven D. Levitt and Ilyana Kuziemko point to the over crowding of prisons as another negative side effect of the war on drugs. They believe that by sending such a large number of drug offenders to prison, the war on drugs has reduced the prison space available for other offenders. This increased incarceration rate not only costs tax payers more to maintain, it could possibly increase crime by crowding violent offenders out of prison cells and replacing them with drug offenders.

Direct costs

A Harvard economist, Jeffrey Miron, estimated that ending the war on drugs would inject 76.8 billion dollars into the US economy in 2010 alone. He estimates that the government would save $41.3 billion for law enforcement and the government would gain up to $46.7 billion in tax revenue.

Since the war on drugs began under the administration of President Richard Nixon, the federal drug-fighting budget has increased from $100 million in 1970 to $15.1 billion in 2010, with a total cost estimated near 1 trillion dollars over 40 years. In the same time period an estimated 37 million nonviolent drug offenders have been incarcerated. $121 billion was spent to arrest these offenders and $450 billion to incarcerate them.

Size of the illegal drug market

According to 2013 data from the United Nations Office on Drugs and Crime (UNODC) and European crime-fighting agency Europol, the annual global drugs trade is worth around $435 billion a year, with the annual cocaine trade worth $84 billion of that amount.

Drug misuse can be harmful to your health in both the short term and the long term, and could possibly lead to addiction.

New psychoactive substances (NPS) called 'legal highs')

What are NPS?

NPS, such as mephedrone (meow meow) and spice, used to be available to buy legally in "head shops" (shops that sell drug paraphernalia) or online.

Since the Psychoactive Substances Act came into effect on May 26 2016 it has been illegal to supply any NPS in the UK for human consumption. This includes selling them or giving them away for free.

Alcohol, medicines, nicotine, caffeine and poppers (alkyl nitrites) are exempt from the act.

How do NPS make you feel?

The main effects of almost all psychoactive drugs, including NPS, fall into three categories:

"downers" or sedatives

psychedelics or hallucinogens

Synthetic cannabinoids, which can have both sedative and psychedelic effects, are sometimes separated out into their own category. They have been a big part of the NPS market and have been particularly problematic and harmful.

Even NPS that look similar or have similar names can vary in strength and can have different effects on different people.

How do NPS affect your health?

For lots of NPS, there has been little or no research into the short- or long-term health risks from human consumption and some risks aren't yet known.

Forensic testing of NPS has shown that they often contain different substances to what the packaging says, or mixtures of different substances.

This means you can never be sure what you are taking or what the effects might be.

Risks include:

- NPS can reduce your inhibitions, so you may do potentially harmful things you wouldn't normally do.
- They can cause paranoia, coma, seizures and, in rare cases, death.
- You can never be sure of what is in an NPS, so you can't be sure what you've bought or been given, or what effect it's likely to have on you or your friends.

Cannabis (hash, weed, grass, skunk, marijuana)

What is cannabis?

Cannabis is a calming drug that also alters perceptions. It›s seen as «natural» because it›s made from the cannabis plant, but that doesn›t mean it›s safe. It can be smoked, often with tobacco, in a «joint» or «spliff», or in a pipe or «bong». It can also be drunk as a «tea» or eaten when mixed with food, such as biscuits or cakes.

How does cannabis make you feel?

Cannabis can make you feel relaxed and happy, but sometimes makes people feel lethargic, very anxious and paranoid, and even psychotic.

How does cannabis affect your health?

Cannabis has been linked to mental health problems such as schizophrenia and, when smoked, to lung diseases including asthma.

It affects how your brain works, so regular use can make concentration and learning very difficult. Frequent use can have a negative effect on your fertility.

It is also dangerous to drive after taking cannabis. Mixing it with tobacco is likely to increase the risk of heart disease and lung cancer.

Can cannabis be addictive?

Yes, it is possible to become psychologically dependent on cannabis. And some people do experience withdrawal symptoms when they stop taking it.

Cocaine (powder cocaine, coke, crack)

What is cocaine?

Powder cocaine (coke), freebase and crack are all types of cocaine, and all are powerful stimulants. Freebase and crack can be smoked, and powder cocaine can be snorted in lines. Both cocaine powder and crack can also be prepared for injecting.

How does cocaine make you feel?

Cocaine gives the user energy, a feeling of happiness and being wide awake, and an overconfidence that can lead to taking risks. The effects are short-lived, so more drug is taken, which is often followed by a nasty "comedown" that makes you feel depressed and unwell, sometimes for several days.

How does cocaine affect your health?

If you take cocaine, it's possible to die of an overdose from overstimulating the heart and nervous system, which can lead to a heart attack. It can be more risky if mixed with alcohol.

Taking cocaine is particularly risky if you have high blood pressure or already have a heart condition. If you›re pregnant, cocaine can harm your baby and even cause miscarriage. If you›ve had previous mental health problems, it can increase the chance of these returning.

If you snort cocaine, it can damage the cartilage of your nose over time. If you inject it, you are at higher risk of dying as the result of an overdose, and your veins and body tissues can be seriously damaged. You put yourself at risk of catching HIV or hepatitis if you share needles.

Can cocaine be addictive?

Yes, cocaine is highly addictive and can cause a very strong psychological dependence. For advice on getting help for cocaine addiction, go to Cocaine: get help. The Cocaine Anonymous websitealso offers further advice.

Ecstasy (MDMA, pills, crystal, E)

What is ecstasy?

Ecstasy is a "psychedelic" stimulant drug usually sold as tablets, but it's sometimes dabbed on to gums or snorted in its powder form. It's also known as MDMA or "crystal".

How does ecstasy make you feel?

Ecstasy can make you feel alert, affectionate and chatty, and can make music and colours seem more intense. Taking ecstasy can also cause anxiety, confusion, paranoia and even psychosis.

How does ecstasy affect your health?

Long-term use has been linked with memory problems, depression and anxiety. Ecstasy use affects the body›s temperature control and can lead to dangerous overheating and dehydration.

But a balance is important as drinking too much fluid can also be very dangerous for the brain, particularly because ecstasy tends to stop your body producing enough urine, so your body retains the fluid. For more information on ecstasy, visit the FRANK website.

Is ecstasy addictive?

Ecstasy can be addictive, as users can develop a psychological dependence on this drug. It is also possible to build up a tolerance to the drug and need to take more and more to get the same effect.

Speed (amphetamine, billy, whizz)

What is speed?

Speed is the street name for drugs based on amphetamine, and is a stimulant drug. It's usually an off-white or pink powder that's either dabbed on to gums, snorted or swallowed in paper.

How does speed make you feel?

Speed can make you feel alert, confident and full of energy, and can reduce appetite. But it can make you agitated and aggressive, and can cause confusion, paranoia and even psychosis. You can also become very depressed and lethargic for hours or days after a period of heavy use.

How does speed affect your health?

Taking speed can be dangerous for the heart, as it can cause high blood pressure and heart attacks. It can be more risky if mixed with alcohol, or if it's used by people who have blood pressure or heart problems.

Injecting speed is particularly dangerous, as death can occur from overdose. Speed is usually very impure and injecting it can cause damage to veins and tissues, which can also lead to serious infections in the body and bloodstream. Any sharing of injecting equipment adds the risk of catching hepatitis C and HIV.

History

The cultivation, use and trade of psychoactive and other drugs has occurred since the dawn of civilization. In the 20th century, the United States government led a major renewed surge in drug prohibition called the «War on Drugs." It was only in the 20th Century that Britain and the United States outlawed cannabis. The British had gone to war with China in the 19th Century in what became known as the First and Second Opium Wars to protect their valuable trade in narcotics.

Motivations claimed by supporters of drug prohibition laws across various societies and eras have included religious observance, allegations of violence by racial minorities, and public health concerns. Those who are not proponents of anti-drug legislation characterize these motivations as religious intolerance, racism, and public healthism.

Various proponents of drug liberalization wish to repeal these laws for reasons ranging from individual rights-based defenses of liberty, to consequentialist arguments against the economic and social outcomes of drug prohibition. Starting in the 20th century, large organized movements to overturn existing drug laws formed around the world. The most vocal of these groups exist in liberal democracies, and typically attract liberal and libertarian supporters, although drug liberalization itself is a non-partisan issue and may be supported by adherents of any ideology.

The campaign against alcohol prohibition culminated in the Twenty-first Amendment to the United States Constitution repealing prohibition on 5 December 1933, as well as liberalization in Canada, and some but not all of the other countries that enforced prohibition. However, many laws controlling the use of alcohol continue to exist even in these countries.

Current proponents of drug liberalization seek the repeal or softening of drug prohibition laws, most commonly cannabis but also including other controlled substances such as alcohol, tobacco, opiates, stimulants, psychedelics, dissociatives, prescription drugs, and others.

Around the world

Thailand

Although Thailand has a strict drug policy, in May 2018, the Cabinet approved draft legislation that allows for more research into the effects of drug marijuana on people. Thus, the Government Pharmaceutical Organization (GPO) will soon begin clinical trials of marijuana as a preliminary step in the production of drugs from this plant. These medical studies are considered exciting, new landmarks in the history of Thailand, because since 1979, marijuana is a drug and its use, storage and manufacture is illegal.

On November 9, 2018, the National Assembly of Thailand officially proposed to allow licensed medical use of marijuana, thereby legalizing what was previously considered a dangerous drug.

The National Assembly on Friday submitted its amendments to the Ministry of Health, which would place marijuana and vegetable kratom in the category allowing their licensed possession and distribution in regulated conditions. The ministry will review the amendments before sending them to the cabinet, which will return it to the National Assembly for a final vote. This process can be completed before the end of the year. Thus, Thailand may become the first Asian country to legalize medical cannabis. It is worth noting that the proposed changes will not allow recreational use of drugs. These actions were taken because of the growing interest in the use of marijuana and its components for the treatment of certain diseases.

Supporters of legalization argue that the legal market for marijuana in Thailand could increase to $5 billion by 2024.

Europe

Czech Republic

In the Czech Republic, until 31 December 1998 only drug possession "for other person" (i.e. intent to sell) was criminal (apart from production, importation, exportation, offering or mediation, which was and remains criminal) while possession for personal use remained legal.

On 1 January 1999, an amendment of the Criminal Code, which was necessitated in order to align the Czech drug rules with the Single Convention on Narcotic Drugs, became effective, criminalizing possession of "amount larger than small" also for personal use (Art. 187a of the Criminal Code) while possession of small amounts for personal use became a misdemeanor.

The judicial practice came to the conclusion that the "amount larger than small" must be five to ten times larger (depending on drug) than a usual single dose of an average consumer.

On 14 December 2009, the Government of the Czech Republic adopted Regulation No. 467/2009 Coll., that took effect on 1 January 2010, and specified what «amount larger than small" under the Criminal Code meant, effectively taking over the amounts that were already established by the previous judicial practice. According to the regulation, a person could possess up to 15 grams of marijuana or 1.5 grams of heroin without facing criminal charges. These amounts were higher (often many times) than in any other European country, possibly making the Czech Republic the most liberal country in the European Union when it comes to drug liberalization, apart from Portugal. Czech

Republic has also the highest prevalence of last years cannabis use among young adults (15-34) (18.5% in 2012) among the 30 counties reporting to the EMCDDA.

Under the Regulation No. 467/2009 Coll, possession of the following amounts or less of illicit drugs was to be considered smaller than large for the purposes of the Criminal Code and was to be treated as a misdemeanor subject to a fine equal to a parking ticket:

- Marijuana 15 grams (or five plants)
- Hashish 5 grams
- Magic mushrooms 40 pieces
- Peyote 5 plants
- LSD 5 tablets
- Ecstasy 4 tablets
- Amphetamine 2 grams
- Methamphetamine 2 grams
- Heroin 1.5 grams
- Coca 5 plants
- Cocaine 1 gram

In 2013, a District Court in Liberec was deciding a case of a person that was accused of criminal possession for having 3.25 grams of methamphetamine (1.9 grams of straight methamphetamine base), well over the Regulation›s limit of 2 grams. The court considered that basing a decision on mere Regulation would be unconstitutional and in breach of Article 39 of the Czech Charter of Fundamental Rights and Freedoms which states that «only a law may designate which acts constitute a crime and what penalties, or other detriments to rights or property, may be imposed for committing them" and proposed to the Constitutional Court to abolish the Regulation. In line with the District Courts› argument, the Constitutional Court abolished the Regulation effective from 23 August 2013, noting that the «amount larger than small" within the meaning of the Criminal Code may be designated only by the means of an Act of Parliament, and not a Governmental Regulation. Moreover, the Constitutional Court further noted that the Regulation merely took over already existing judicial practice of interpretation of what constitutes "amount larger than small" and thus its abolishment will not really change the criminality of drug possession in the country. Thus, the above-mentioned amounts from the now-not-effective Regulation remain as the base for consideration of police and prosecutors, while courts are not bound by the precise grammage.

Sale of any amount (not purchase) remains a criminal act. Possession of "amount larger than a small" of marijuana can result in a jail sentence of up to one year. For other illicit drugs, the sentence is up to two years. Trafficking as well as production (apart from growing up to five plants of marijuana) offenses carry stiffer sentences.

Medical use of cannabis on prescription has been legal and regulated since 1 April 2013.

France

Following a contentious debate France opened its first supervised injection centre on 11 October 2016. Marisol Touraine, the Minister of Health, declared that the centre was "a strong political response, for a pragmatic and responsible policy that brings high-risk people back towards the health system rather than stigmatizing them." The centre is located near the Gare du Nord in Paris.

Germany

In 1994 the Federal Constitutional Court ruled that drug addiction was not a crime, nor was the possession of small amounts of drugs for personal use. In 2000 the German narcotic law («BtmG») was changed to allow for supervised drug injection rooms. In 2002, a pilot study was started in seven German cities to evaluate the effects of heroin-assisted treatmenton addicts, compared to methadone-assisted treatment. The positive results of the study led to the inclusion of heroin-assisted treatment into the services of the mandatory health insurance in 2009. On 4 May 2016 the Cabinet of Germany decided to approve the measure for legal cannabis for seriously ill patients who have consulted with a doctor and «have no therapeutic alternative». German Health Minister, Hermann Gröhe, presented the legal draft on the legalization of medical cannabis to the cabinet which is expected to take effect early 2017.

Ireland

On 2 November 2015, Aodhán Ó Ríordáin, the minister in charge of the National Drugs Strategy, announced that Ireland planned to introduce supervised injection rooms.The minister also referenced that possession of controlled substances will be decriminalized although supply and production will remain criminalized. On July 12, 2017, the Health Committee of the Irish government rejected a bill that would have legalized medical cannabis.

Netherlands

- The drug policy of the Netherlands is based on 2 principles:
- Drug use is a public health issue, not a criminal matter

A distinction between hard and soft drugs exists

Cannabis remains a controlled substance in the Netherlands and both possession and production for personal use are still misdemeanors, punishable by fine. Cannabis coffee shopsare also illegal according to the statutes.

However, a policy of non-enforcement has led to a situation where reliance upon non-enforcement has become common, and because of this the courts have ruled against the government when individual cases were prosecuted.

Norway

On 14 June 2010, the Stoltenberg commission recommended implementing heroin assisted treatment and expanding harm reduction measures. On 18 June 2010, Knut Storberget, Minister of Justice and the Police announced that the ministry was working on new drug policy involving decriminalization by the Portugal model, which was to be introduced to parliament before the next general election. However, Storberget later changed his statements, saying the decriminalization debate is «for academics», instead calling for coerced treatment. In early March 2013, minister of health and care services Jonas Gahr Støre proposed to decriminalize the inhalation of heroin by 2014 as a measure to decrease drug overdoses. In 2011 there were 294 fatal overdoses, in comparison to only 170 traffic related deaths.

Portugal

In 2001, Portugal became the first European country to abolish all criminal penalties for personal drug possession, under Law 30/2000. In addition, drug users were to be provided with therapy rather than prison sentences. Research commissioned by the Cato Institute and led by Glenn Greenwald found that in the five years after the start of decriminalization, illegal drug use by teenagers had declined, the rate of HIV infections among drug users had dropped, deaths related to heroin and similar drugs had been cut by more than half, and the number of people seeking treatment for drug addiction had doubled. However, Peter Reuter, a professor of criminology and public policy at the University of Maryland, College Park, suggests that the heroin usage rates and related deaths may have been due to the cyclical nature of drug epidemics, but conceded that "decriminalization in Portugal has met its central goal. Drug use did not rise."

Ukraine

The use of marijuana in Ukraine is not prohibited, but the manufacture, storage, transportation and sale of cannabis and its derivatives are under administrative and criminal liability.

Speaking on the legalization of soft drugs in Ukraine has been going on for a long time. In June 2016, the Parliament received a bill on the legalization of marijuana for medical purposes. It dealt with changes to the current act "On narcotic drugs, psychotropic substances and precursors" and was registered number 4533. The document must examine the relevant committee, and then submit it to the government. It was expected that this would happen in the fall of 2016, but the bill was not considered.

In October 2018, a petition appeared on the website of electronic appeals to the President of Ukraine asking for the legalization of marijuana.

In October 2018, the State Service of Ukraine on Drugs and Drug Control issued the first license for the import and re-export of raw materials and products derived from cannabis. The corresponding licenses were obtained by the USA company C21. The company is also in the process of applying for additional licenses, including the cultivation of cannabis.

Latin America

In the late 2000s and early 2010s, advocacy for drug legalization has increased in Latin America. Spearheading the movement Uruguayan government announced in 2012 plans to legalize state-controlled sales of marijuana in order to fight drug-related crimes. Some countries in this region have already advanced towards depenalization of personal consumption.

Argentina

In August 2009, the Argentine supreme court declared in a landmark ruling that it was unconstitutional to prosecute citizens for having drugs for their personal use - «adults should be free to make lifestyle decisions without the intervention of the state». The decision affected the second paragraph of Article 14 of the country›s drug control legislation (Law Number 23,737) that punishes the possession of drugs for personal consumption with prison sentences ranging from one month to two years (although education or treatment measures can be substitute penalties). The unconstitutionality of the article concerns cases of drug possession for personal consumption that does not affect others

Brazil

In 2002 and 2006, Brazil went through legislative changes, resulting in a partial decriminalization of possession for personal use. Prison sentences no longer applied and were replaced by educational measures and community services. However, the 2006 law does not provide objective means to distinguish between users or traffickers. A disparity exists between the decriminalization of drug use and the increased penalization of selling drugs, punishable with a maximum prison sentences of 5 years for the sale of very minor quantities of drugs. Most of those incarcerated for drug trafficking are offenders caught selling small quantities of drugs, among them drug users who sell drugs to finance their drug habits. Since 2006, there's been a long debate whether the anti-drug law goes against the Constitution and principle of personal freedom. In 2009, the Supreme Federal Court re-opened to vote if the law is Constitutional, or if it goes against the Constitution specifically against personal Freedom of choice. Since each Minister inside the tribunal can take a personal time to evaluate the law, the voting can take years. In fact, the voting was re-opened in 2015, 3 ministers voted in favor, and then the law was again paused by another minister.

Colombia

Guatemalan President Otto Pérez Molina and Colombian President Juan Manuel Santos proposed the legalization of drugs in an effort to counter the failure of the War on Drugs, which was said to have yielded poor results at a huge cost. On 25 May 2016, the congress approved the legalization of marijuana for medical usage.

Costa Rica

Costa Rica has decriminalized drugs for personal consumption. Manufacturing or selling drugs is still a jailable offense.

Ecuador

According to the 2008 Constitution of Ecuador, in its Article 364, the Ecuadorian state does not see drug consumption as a crime but only as a health concern. Since June 2013 the state drugs regulatory office CONSEP has published a table which establishes maximum quantities carried by persons so as to be considered in legal possession and that person as not a seller of drugs. The «CONSEP established, at their latest general meeting, that the following quantities be considered the maximum consumer amounts: 10 grams of marijuana or hash, 4 grams of opiates, 100 milligrams of heroin, 5 grams of cocaine, 0.020 milligrams of LSD, and 80 milligrams of methamphetamine or MDMA».

Honduras

On 22 February 2008, Honduras President Manuel Zelaya, called on the United States to legalize drugs, in order, he said, to prevent the majority of violent murders occurring in Honduras. Honduras is used by cocaine smugglers as a transiting point between Colombia and the US. Honduras, with a population of 7 million suffers an average of 8–10 murders a day, with an estimated 70% being as a result of this international drug trade. The same problem is occurring in Guatemala, El Salvador, Costa Rica and Mexico, according to Zelaya.

Mexico

In April 2009, the Mexican Congress approved changes in the General Health Law that decriminalized the possession of illegal drugs for immediate consumption and personal use allowing a person to possess up to 5 g of marijuana or 500 mg of cocaine. The only restriction is that people in possession of drugs should not be within a 300-meter radius of schools, police departments, or correctional facilities. Opium, heroin, LSD, and other synthetic drugs were also decriminalized, it will not be considered as a crime as long as the dose does not exceed the limit established in the General Health Law. Many question this, as cocaine is as much synthesised as heroin, both are produced as extracts from plants. The law establishes very low amount thresholds and strictly defines personal dosage. For those arrested with more than the threshold allowed by the law this can result in heavy prison sentences, as they will be assumed to be small traffickers even if there are no other indications that the amount was meant for selling.

Uruguay

Uruguay is one of few countries that never criminalized the possession of drugs for personal use. Since 1974, the law establishes no quantity limits, leaving it to the judge's discretion to determine whether the intent was personal use. Once it is determined by the judge that the amount in possession was meant for personal use, there are no sanctions.

In June 2012, the Uruguayan government announced plans to legalize state-controlled sales of marijuana in order to fight drug-related crimes. The government also stated that they will ask global leaders to do the same.

On 31 July 2013, the Uruguayan House of Representatives approved a bill to legalize the production, distribution, sale, and consumption of marijuana by a vote of 50 to 46. The bill then passed the Senate, where the left-leaning majority coalition, the Broad Front, holds a comfortable majority, the bill was approved by the Senate by 16 to 13 on 10-December-2013. The bill was presented to the President José Mujica, also of the Broad Front coalition, who has supported legalization since June 2012. Relating this vote to the 2012 legalization of marijuana by the U.S. states Colorado and Washington, John Walsh, drug policy expert of the Washington Office on Latin America, stated that "Uruguay's timing is right. Because of last year's Colorado and Washington State votes to legalize, the U.S. government is in no position to browbeat Uruguay or others who may follow."

In July 2014, government officials announced that part of the implementation of the law (the sale of cannabis through pharmacies) is postponed to 2015, as "there are practical difficulties". Authorities will grow all the cannabis that can be sold legal. Concentration of THC shall be 15% or lower. In August 2014 an opposition presidential candidate, who was not elected in the November 2014 presidential elections, claimed that the new law was never going to be applied, as it was not workable. By the end of 2016 the government announced that the sale through pharmacies will be fully implemented during 2017.

North America

Canada

The cultivation of cannabis is currently legal in Canada, with exceptions only for Manitoba and Quebec. The recreational use of cannabis by the general public is legal with restrictions on smoking in public locations which vary by jurisdiction. The sale of marijuana seeds is also legal.

In 2001, The Globe and Mail reported that a poll found 47% of Canadians agreed with the statement, «The use of marijuana should be legalized» in 2000, compared to 26% in 1975. A more recent poll found that more than half of Canadians supported legalization. However, in 2007 Prime Minister Stephen Harper's government tabled Bill C-26 to amend the Controlled Drugs and Substances Act, 1996 to bring forth a more restrictive law with higher minimum penalties for drug crimes. Bill-26 died in committee after the dissolution of the 39th Canadian Parliament in September 2008, but the Bill had subsequently been resurrected by the government twice. In 2015, the Liberal Party of Canada campaigned on a promise to legalize marijuana and has since passed legislation making marijuana legal across Canada on 17 October 2018.

Since legalization, the country has set up an online framework to allow consumers to purchase a wide variety of merchandise ranging from herbs, extract, oil capsules, and paraphernalia. Most provinces are also providing a venue for purchase through physical brick and mortar stores. Despite legalization and government regulation in place, the initial objective of abolishing the underground and black market sales were not resolved.

United States

Throughout the United States, various people and groups have been pushing for the legalization of marijuana for medical reasons. Organizations such as NORML and the Marijuana Policy Project work to decriminalize possession, use, cultivation, and sale of marijuana by adults, even beyond medical uses. In 1996, 56% of California voters voted for California Proposition 215, legalizing the growing and use of marijuana for medical purposes. This created significant legal and policy tensions between federal and state governments. Since then, 20 more states and the District of Columbia have legalized and regulated medical marijuana. State laws in conflict with federal law about cannabis remain valid, and prevent state level prosecution, despite cannabis being illegal under federal law On 6 November 2012, Colorado and Washington state legalized possession of small amounts of marijuana for private recreational use, and created a process for writing rules for legal growing and commercial distribution of marijuana within each state.

Oceania

Australia

Australia has one of the highest percentages of marijuana smokers in the world. In 1993, HEMP (Help End Marijuana Prohibition) was established and continued the fight for law reform. In 2010, HEMP qualified as a political party and will be fielding candidates in elections where possible.

In 2011, the Cannabis Campaign seemed to experience a renaissance in Australia, no doubt due to developments worldwide, with many new groups appearing in different states, using social media as a conduit and forum. Since 1985, the Federal Government has run a declared "War on Drugs" and while initially Australia led the world in 'harm-minimization' approach, they have since lagged. In 2012, the think tank Australia 21, released a report on the decriminalization of drugs in Australia.

'Harm-minimization' approaches towards MDMA and ecstasy have also met opposition. A trial of drug checking at the popular Spilt Milk festival was cancelled in October 2017. While organizers have blamed this on a lack of documentation sources allege that political pressure caused the cancellation. Proponents argue that pill testing is an important service considering Australia having the highest per capita use of ecstasy globally as well as some of the most adulterated pills.

In October 2016, Australia legislated for some medicinal use cannabis.

Political parties

Many political parties support, to various degrees, and for various reasons, liberalising drug control laws, from liberal parties to far-left movements, as well as some pragmatic right-wing intellectuals. Drug liberalization is fundamental in the platforms of most libertarian parties.

In the UK in March 2016, the Liberal Democrats became the first major political party in the country to support the legalisation of cannabisThere are also numerous single issue marijuana parties devoted to campaign for the legalisation of cannabis exclusively.

Societal effects

The countries of drug production and transit are some of the most affected by the drug trade, though countries receiving the illegally imported substances are also adversely affected. For example, Ecuador has absorbed up to 300,000 refugees from Colombia who are running from guerrillas, paramilitaries and drug lords. While some applied for asylum, others are still illegal immigrants. The drugs that pass from Colombia through Ecuador to other parts of South America create economic and social problems.

Honduras, through which an estimated 79% of cocaine passes on its way to the United States, has the highest murder rate in the world. According to the International Crisis Group, the most violent regions in Central America, particularly along the Guatemala–Honduras border, are highly correlated with an abundance of drug trafficking activity.

Violent crime

In many countries, the illegal drug trade is thought to be directly linked to violent crimes such as murder. This is especially true in all developing countries, such as Honduras, but is also an issue for many developed countries worldwide. In the late 1990s in the United States the Federal Bureau of Investigation estimated that 5% of murders were drug-related. In Colombia, Drug violence can be caused by factors such as, the economy, poor governments, and no authority within the law enforcement.

After a crackdown by US and Mexican authorities in the first decade of the 21st century as part of tightened border security in the wake of the September 11 attacks, border violence inside Mexico surged. The Mexican government estimates that 90% of the killings are drug-related.

A report by the UK government's Drug Strategy Unit that was leaked to the press, stated that due to the expensive price of highly addictive drugs heroin and cocaine, drug use was responsible for the great majority of crime, including 85% of shoplifting, 70–80% of burglaries and 54% of robberies. It concluded that «[t]he cost of crime committed to support illegal cocaine and heroin habits amounts to £16 billion a year in the UK»

Drug trafficking routes

South America

Venezuela has been a path to the United States and Europe for illegal drugs originating in Colombia, through Central America, Mexico and Caribbean countries such as Haiti, the Dominican Republic, and Puerto Rico.

According to the United Nations, there was an increase of cocaine trafficking through Venezuela since 2002. In 2005, the government of Hugo Chávez severed ties with the United States Drug Enforcement Administration (DEA), accusing its representatives of spying.Following the departure of the

DEA from Venezuela and the expansion of DEA's partnership with Colombia in 2005, Venezuela became more attractive to drug traffickers. Between 2008 and 2012, Venezuela›s cocaine seizure ranking among other countries declined, going from being ranked fourth in the world for cocaine seizures in 2008 to sixth in the world in 2012.

On 18 November 2016, following what was known as the Narcosobrinos incident, Venezuelan President Nicolás Maduro's two nephews were found guilty of trying to ship drugs into the United States so they could "obtain a large amount of cash to help their family stay in power".

West Africa

Cocaine produced in Colombia and Bolivia increasingly has been shipped via West Africa (especially in Cape Verde, Mali, Benin, Togo, Nigeria, Cameroon, Guinea-Bissau and Ghana). The money is often laundered in countries such as Nigeria, Ghana and Senegal.

According to the Africa Economic Institute, the value of illicit drug smuggling in Guinea-Bissau is almost twice the value of the country's GDP. Police officers are often bribed. A police officer›s normal monthly wage of $93 is less than 2% of the value of 1 kilogram (2.2 lb) of cocaine (€7000 or $8750 The money can also be laundered using real estate. A house is built using illegal funds, and when the house is sold, legal money is earned. When drugs are sent over land, through the Sahara, the drug traders have been forced to cooperate with terrorist organizations, such as Al Qaida in Islamic Maghreb.

Eastern and southern Africa

Heroin is increasingly trafficked from Afghanistan to Europe and America through eastern and southern African countries. This path is known as the "southern route" or "smack track." Repercussions of this trade include burgeoning heroin use and political corruption among intermediary African nations.

Asia

Drugs in Asia traditionally traveled the southern routes – the main caravan axes of Southeast Asia and Southern China – and include the former opium-producing countries of Thailand, Iran, and Pakistan. After the 1990s, particularly after the Cold War ended, borders were opened and trading and customs agreements were signed so that the routes expanded to include China, Central Asia, and Russia. There is, therefore, a diversified drug trafficking routes available today, particularly in the heroin trade and these thrive due to the continuous development of new markets. A large amount of drugs are smuggled into Europe from Asia. The main sources of these drugs are Afghanistan, along with countries that constituted the so-called Golden Crescent. From these producers, drugs are smuggled into the West and Central Asia to its destinations in Europe and the United States. Iran is now the route for smugglers, having been previously a primary trading route, due to its large-scale and costly war against drug trafficking. The Border Police

Chief of Iran said that his country «is a strong barrier against the trafficking of illegal drugs to Caucasus, especially the Republic of Azerbaijan.» The drugs produced by the Golden Triangle of Myanmar, Laos, and Thailand, on the other hand, pass through the southern routes to feed the Australian, U.S., and Asian markets.

Online

Drugs are increasingly traded online on the dark web on darknet markets.

Statistics about profits from the drug trade are largely unknown due to its illicit nature. In its 1997 World Drugs Report the United Nations Office on Drugs and Crime estimated the value of the market at $4 trillion, ranking drugs alongside arms and oil among the world's largest traded goods. An online report published by the UK Home Office in 2007 estimated the illicit drug market in the UK at £4–6.6 billion a year

In December 2009 United Nations Office on Drugs and Crime Executive Director Antonio Maria Costa claimed illegal drug money saved the banking industry from collapse. He claimed he had seen evidence that the proceeds of organized crime were «the only liquid investment capital» available to some banks on the brink of collapse during 2008. He said that a majority of the $352 billion (£216bn) of drug profits was absorbed into the economic system as a result:

"In many instances, the money from drugs was the only liquid investment capital. In the second half of 2008, liquidity was the banking system's main problem and hence liquid capital became an important factor...Inter-bank loans were funded by money that originated from the drugs trade and other illegal activities...there were signs that some banks were rescued that way".

Costa declined to identify countries or banks that may have received any drug money, saying that would be inappropriate because his office is supposed to address the problem, not apportion blame.

Though street-level drug sales are widely viewed as lucrative, a study by Sudhir Venkatesh suggested that many low-level employees receive low wages. In a study he made in the 1990s working closely with members of the Black Gangster Disciple Nation in Chicago, he found that one gang (essentially a franchise) consisted of a leader (a college graduate named J.T.), three senior officers, and 25 to 75 street level salesmen ('foot soldiers') depending on season. Selling crack cocaine, they took in approximately $32,000 per month over a six-year period. This was spent as follows: $5,000 to the board of twenty directors of the Black Gangster Disciple Nation, who oversaw 100 such gangs for approximately $500,000 in monthly income. Another $5,000 monthly was paid for cocaine, and $4,000 for other non-wage expenses. J.T. took $8,500 monthly for his own salary. The remaining $9,500 monthly went to pay the employees a $7 per hour wage for officers and a $3.30 per hour wage for foot soldiers. Contrary to a popular image of drug sales as a lucrative profession, many of the employees were living with their mothers by necessity. Despite this, the gang had four times as many unpaid members who dreamed of becoming foot soldiers.

Free trade link

There are several arguments on whether or not free trade has a correlation to an increased activity in the illicit drug trade. Currently, the structure and operation of the illicit drug industry is described mainly in terms of an international division of labor. Free trade can open new markets to domestic producers who would otherwise resort to exporting illicit drugs. Additionally, extensive free trade among states increases cross-border drug enforcement and coordination between law enforcement agencies in different countries.However, free trade also increases the sheer volume of legal cross-border trade and provides cover for drug smuggling—by providing ample opportunity to conceal illicit cargo in legal trade. While international free trade continues to expand the volume of legal trade, the ability to detect and interdict drug trafficking is severely diminished. Towards the late 1990s, the top ten seaports in the world processed 33.6 million containers. Free trade has fostered integration of financial markets and has provided drug traffickers with more opportunities to launder money and invest in other activities. This strengthens the drug industry while weakening the efforts of law enforcement to monitor the flow of drug money into the legitimate economy. Cooperation among cartels expands their scope to distant markets and strengthens their abilities to evade detection by local law enforcement. Additionally, criminal organizations work together to coordinate money-laundering activities by having separate organizations handle specific stages of laundering process. One organization structures the process of how financial transactions will be laundered, while another criminal group provides the "dirty" money to be cleaned. By fostering expansion of trade and global transportation networks, free trade encourages cooperation and formation of alliances among criminal organizations across different countries. The drug trade in Latin America emerged in the early 1930s. It saw significant growth in the Andean countries, including Peru, Bolivia, Chile, Ecuador, Colombia and Venezuela. The underground market in the early half of the 20th century mainly had ties to Europe. After World War II, the Andean countries saw an expansion of trade, specifically with cocaine.

Drug trafficking by country

Background

The effects of the illegal drug trade in the United States can be seen in a range of political, economic and social aspects. Increasing drug related violence can be tied to the racial tension that arose during the late 20th century along with the political upheaval prevalent throughout the 1960s and 70s The second half of the 20th century was a period when increased wealth, and increased discretionary spending, increased the demand for illicit drugs in certain areas of the United States. Large-scale drug trafficking is one of the few capital crimes, and may result in a death sentence prescribed at the federal level.

Political impact

A large generation, the baby boomers, came of age in the 1960s. Their social tendency to confront the law on specific issues, including illegal drugs, overwhelmed the understaffed judicial system. The federal government attempted to enforce the law, but with meager effect.

Marijuana was a popular drug seen through the Latin American trade route in the 1960s. Cocaine became a major drug product in the later decades. Much of the cocaine is smuggled from Colombia and Mexico via Jamaica. This led to several administrations combating the popularity of these drugs. Due to the influence of this development on the U.S. economy, the Reagan administration began "certifying" countries for their attempts at controlling drug trafficking. This allowed the United States to intervene in activities related to illegal drug transport in Latin America. Continuing into the 1980s, the United States instated stricter policy pertaining to drug transit through sea. As a result, there was an influx in drug-trafficking across the Mexico–U.S. border. This increased the drug cartel activity in Mexico. By the early 1990s, so much as 50% of the cocaine available in the United States market originated from Mexico, and by the 2000s, over 90% of the cocaine in the United States was imported from Mexico. In Colombia, however, there was a fall of the major drug cartels in the mid-1990s. Visible shifts occurred in the drug market in the United States. Between the 1996 and 2000, U.S. cocaine consumption dropped by 11%.

In 2008, the U.S. government initiated another program, known as the Merida Initiative, to help combat drug trafficking in Mexico. This program increased U.S. security assistance to $1.4 billion over several years, which helped supply Mexican forces with "high-end equipment from helicopters to surveillance technology". Despite U.S. aid, Mexican «narcogangs» continue to outnumber and outgun the Mexican Army, allowing for continued activities of drug cartels across the U.S.–Mexico border.

Social impacts

Although narcotics are illegal in the US, they have become integrated into the nation's culture and are seen as a recreational activity by sections of the population. Illicit drugs are considered to be a commodity with strong demand, as they are typically sold at a high value. This high price is caused by a combination of factors that include the potential legal ramifications that exist for suppliers of illicit drugs and their high demand. Despite the constant effort by politicians to win the war on drugs, the US is still the world's largest importer of illegal drugs.

Throughout the 20th century, narcotics other than cocaine also crossed the Mexican border, meeting the US demand for alcohol during the 1920s Prohibition, opiates in the 1940s, marijuana in the 1960s, and heroin in the 1970s. Most of the U.S. imports of drugs come from Mexican drug cartels. In the United States, around 195 cities have been infiltrated by drug trafficking that originated in Mexico. An estimated $10bn of the Mexican drug cartel›s profits come from the United States, not only supplying the Mexican drug cartels with the profit necessary for survival, but also furthering America›s economic dependence on drugs.

Demographics]

With a large wave of immigrants in the 1960s and onwards, the United States saw an increased heterogeneity in its public. In the 1980s and 90s, drug related homicide was at a record high. This increase in drug violence became increasingly tied to these ethnic minorities. Though the rate of violence varied tremendously among cities in America, it was a common anxiety in communities across urban America. An example of this could be seen in Miami, a city with a host of ethnic enclaves. Between 1985 and 1995, the homicide rate in Miami was one of the highest in the nation—four times the national homicide average. This crime rate was correlated with regions with low employment and was not entirely dependent on ethnicity.

The baby boomer generation also felt the effects of the drug trade in their increased drug use from the 1960s to 80s. Along with substance abuse, criminal involvement, suicide and murder were also on the rise. Due to the large amount of baby boomers, commercial marijuana use was on the rise. This increased the supply and demand for marijuana during this time period.

Mexico

Political influences

Corruption in Mexico has contributed to the domination of Mexican cartels in the illicit drug trade. Since the beginning of the 20th century, Mexico›s political environment allowed the growth of drug-related activity. The loose regulation over the transportation of illegal drugs and the failure to prosecute known drug traffickers and gangs increased the growth of the drug industry. Toleration of drug trafficking has undermined the authority of the Mexican government and has decreased the power of law enforcement officers in regulation over such activities. These policies of tolerance fostered the growing power of drug cartels in the Mexican economy and have made drug traders wealthier. Many states in Mexico lack policies that establish stability in governance. There also is a lack of local stability, as mayors cannot be re-elected. This requires electing a new mayor each term. Drug gangs have manipulated this, using vacuums in local leadership to their own advantage.

In 1929, the Institutional Revolutionary Party (PRI) was formed to resolve the chaos resulting from the Mexican Revolution. Over time, this party gained political influence and had a major impact on Mexico's social and economic policies. The party created ties with various groups as a power play in order to gain influence, and as a result created more corruption in the government. One such power play was an alliance with drug traffickers. This political corruption obscured justice, making it difficult to identify violence when it related to drugs. By the 1940s, the tie between the drug cartels and the PRI had solidified. This arrangement created immunity for the leaders of the drug cartels and allowed drug trafficking to grow under the protection of the government officials. During the 1990s, the PRI lost some elections to the new National Action Party(PAN). Chaos again emerged as elected government in Mexico changed drastically. As the PAN party took control, drug cartel leaders took advantage of the ensuing confusion and used their existing influence to further gain power. Instead of negotiating with the central government as was done with the PRI party, drug cartels utilized new ways to distribute their supply and continued operating through force and intimidation. As Mexico became more democratized, the corruption fell from a centralized power to the local authorities. Cartels began to bribe local authorities, thus eliminating the structure and rules placed by the government—giving cartels more freedom. As a response, Mexico saw an increase in violence caused by drug trafficking.

The corruption cartels created resulted in distrust of government by the Mexican public. This distrust became more prominent after the collapse of the PRI party. In response, the presidents of Mexico, in the late twentieth century and early twenty-first century, implemented several different programs relating to law enforcement and regulation. In 1993, President Salinas created the National Institute for the Combat of Drugs in Mexico. From 1995–1998, President Zedillo established policies regarding increased punishment of organized crime, allowing "[wire taps], protected witnesses, covert agents and seizures of goods", and increasing the quality of law enforcement at the federal level. From 2001–2005, President Vicente Fox created the Federal Agency of Investigation. These policies resulted in the arrests of major drug-trafficking bosses:

Mexico's economy

Over the past few decades drug cartels have become integrated into Mexico's economy. Approximately 500 cities are directly engaged in drug trafficking and nearly 450,000 people are employed by drug cartels. Additionally, the livelihood of 3.2 million people is dependent on the drug cartels. Between local and international sales, such as to Europe and the United States, drug cartels in Mexico see a $25–30bn yearly profit, a great deal of which circulates through international banks such as HSBC. Drug cartels are fundamental in local economics. A percentage of the profits seen from the trade are invested in the local community. Such profits contribute to the education and healthcare of the community.While these cartels bring violence and hazards into communities, they create jobs and provide income for its many members.

Culture of drug cartels

Major cartels saw growth due to a prominent set culture of Mexican society that created the means for drug capital. One of the sites of origin for drug trafficking within Mexico, was the state of Michoacán. In the past, Michoacán was mainly an agricultural society. This provided an initial growth of trade. Industrialization of rural areas of Mexico facilitated a greater distribution of drugs, expanding the drug market into different provinces. Once towns became industrialized, cartels such as the Sinaloa Cartel started to form and expand. The proliferation of drug cartel culture largely stemmed from the ranchero culture seen in Michoacán. Ranchero culture values the individual as opposed to the society as a whole. This culture fostered the drug culture of valuing the family that is formed within the cartel. This ideal allowed for greater organization within the cartels. Gangs play a major role in the activity of drug cartels. MS-13 and the 18th Street gang are notorious for their contributions and influence over drug trafficking throughout Latin America. MS-13 has controlled much of the activity in the drug trade spanning from Mexico to Panama Female involvement is present in the Mexican drug culture. Although females are not treated as equals to males, they typically hold more power than their culture allows and acquire some independence. The increase in power has attracted females from higher social classes. Financial gain has also prompted women to become involved in the illegal drug market. Many women in the lower levels of major drug cartels belong to a low economic class. Drug trafficking offers women an accessible way to earn income. Females from all social classes have become involved in the trade due to outside pressure from their social and economic environments.

Colombia

Political ties

It was common for smugglers in Colombia to import liquor, alcohol, cigarettes and textiles, while exporting cocaine. Personnel with knowledge of the terrain were able to supply the local market while also exporting a large amount of product. The established trade that began in the 1960s involved Peru, Bolivia, Colombia, Venezuela and Cuba. Peasant farmers produced coca paste in Peru and Bolivia, while Colombian smugglers would process the coca paste into cocaine in Colombia, and trafficked product through Cuba. This trade route established ties between Cuban and Colombian organized crime. From Cuba, cocaine would be transported to Miami, Florida; and Union City, New Jersey. Quantities of the drug were then smuggled throughout the US. The international drug trade created political ties between the involved countries, encouraging the governments of the countries involved to collaborate and instate common policies to eradicate drug cartels. Cuba stopped being a center for transport of cocaine following the establishment of a communist government in 1959. As a result, Miami and Union City became the sole locations for trafficking. The relations between Cuban and Colombian organized crime remained strong until the 1970s, when Colombian cartels began to vie for power. In the 1980s and 90s, Colombia emerged as a key contributor of the drug trade industry in the Western Hemisphere. While the smuggling of drugs such as marijuana, poppy, opium and heroin became more ubiquitous during this time period, the activity of cocaine cartels drove the development of the Latin American drug trade. The trade emerged as a multinational effort as supplies (i.e. coca plant substances) were imported from countries such as Bolivia and Peru, were refined in Colombian cocaine labs and smuggled through Colombia, and exported to countries such as the US.

Colombia's economy

Colombia has had a significant role in the illegal drug trade in Latin America. While active in the drug trade since the 1930s, Colombia's role in the drug trade did not truly become dominant until the 1970s. When Mexico eradicated marijuana plantations, demand stayed the same. Colombia met much of the demand by growing more marijuana. Grown in the strategic northeast region of Colombia, marijuana soon became the leading cash crop in Colombia. This success was short-lived due to anti-marijuana campaigns that were enforced by the US military throughout the Caribbean. Instead, drug traffickers in Colombia continued their focus on the exportation of cocaine. Having been an export of Colombia since the early 1950s, cocaine remained popular for a host of reasons. Colombia›s location facilitated its transportation from South America into Central America, and then to its destination of North America. This continued into the 1990s, when Colombia remained the chief exporter of cocaine. The business of drug trafficking can be seen in several stages in Colombia towards the latter half of the 20th century.

Colombia served as the dominant force in the distribution and sale of cocaine by the 1980s. As drug producers gained more power, they became more centralized and organized into what became drug cartels. Cartels controlled the major aspects of each stage in the traffic of their product. Their organization allowed cocaine to be distributed in great amounts throughout the United States. By the late 1980s, intra-industry strife arose within the cartels. This stage was marked by increased violence as different cartels fought for control of export markets.

Despite this strife, this power struggle led to then having multiple producers of coca leaf farms. This in turn caused an improvement in quality control and reduction of police interdiction in the distribution of cocaine. This also led to cartels attempting to repatriate their earnings which would eventually make up 5.5% of Colombia›s GDP. This drive to repatriate earnings led to the pressure of legitimizing their wealth, causing an increase in violence throughout Colombia.

Throughout the 1980s, estimates of illegal drug value in Colombia ranged from \$2bn to \$4bn. This made up about 7–10% of the \$36bn estimated GNP of Colombia during this decade. In the 1990s, the estimates of the illegal drug value remained roughly within the same range (~\$2.5bn). As the Colombian GNP rose throughout the 90›s (\$68.5bn in 1994 and \$96.3bn in 1997), illegal drug values began to comprise a decreasing fraction of the national economy. By the early 1990s, although Colombia led in the exportation of cocaine, it found increasing confrontations within its state. These confrontations were primarily between cartels and government institutions. This led to a decrease in the drug trade›s contribution to the GDP of Colombia; dropping from 5.5% to 2.6%. Though a contributor of wealth, the distribution of cocaine has had negative effects on the socio-political situation of Colombia and has weakened its economy as well.

Social impacts

By the 1980s, Colombian cartels became the dominant cocaine distributors in the US. This led to the spread of increased violence throughout both Latin America and Miami. In the 1980s, two major drug cartels emerged in Colombia: the Medellin and Cali groups. Throughout the 90›s however, several factors led to the decline of these major cartels and to the rise of smaller Colombian cartels. The U.S. demand for cocaine dropped while Colombian production rose, pressuring traffickers to find new drugs and markets. In this time period, there was an increase in activity of Caribbean cartels that led to the rise of an alternate route of smuggling through Mexico. This led to the increased collaboration between major Colombian and Mexican drug traffickers. Such drastic changes in the execution of drug trade in Colombia paired with the political instabilities and rise of drug wars in Medellin and Cali, gave way for the rise of the smaller Colombian drug trafficking organizations (and the rise of heroin trade). As the drug trade›s influence over the economy increased, drug lords and their networks grew in their power and influence in society. The occurrences in drug-related violence increased during this time period as drug lords fought to maintain their control in the economy.Typically a drug cartel had support networks that consisted of a number of individuals. These people individuals ranged from those directly involved in the trade (such as suppliers, chemists, transporters, smugglers, etc.) as well as those involved indirectly in the trade (such as politicians, bankers, police, etc.). As these smaller Colombian drug cartels grew in prevalence, several notable aspects of the Colombian society gave way for further development of the Colombian drug industry. For example, until the late 1980s, the long-term effects of the drug industry were not realized by much of society. Additionally, there was a lack of regulation in prisons where captured traffickers were sent. These prisons were under-regulated, under-funded, and under-staffed, which allowed for the formation of prison gangs, for the smuggling of arms/weapons/etc., for feasible escapes, and even for captured drug lords to continue running their businesses from prison.

Trade in specific drugs

Cannabis

While the recreational use of (and consequently the distribution of) cannabis is illegal in most countries throughout the world, it is available by prescription or recommendation in many places, including Canada and 10 of the 50 US states (although importation and distribution is still federally prohibited). Beginning in 2014, Uruguay became the first country to legalize cultivation, sale, and consumption of cannabis for recreational use for adult residents. In 2018, Canada became the only second country to legalize use, sale and cultivation of cannabis. The first few weeks were met with extremely high demand, most shops being out of stock after operating for only four days.

Cannabis use is tolerated in some areas, most notably the Netherlands which has legalized the possession and licensed sale (but not cultivation) of the drug. Many nations have decriminalized the possession of small amounts of marijuana. Due to the hardy nature of the cannabis plant, marijuana is grown all across the world and is today the world's most popular illegal drug with the highest level of availability. Cannabis is grown legally in many countries for industrial, non-drug use (known as hemp) as well. Cannabis-hemp may also be planted for other non-drug domestic purposes, such as seasoning that occurs in Aceh.

The demand for cannabis around the world, coupled with the drug's relative ease of cultivation, makes the illicit cannabis trade one of the primary ways in which organized criminal groups finance many of their activities. In Mexico, for example, the illicit trafficking of cannabis is thought to constitute the majority of many of the cartels' earnings, and the main way in which the cartels finance many other illegal activities; including the purchase of other illegal drugs for trafficking, and for acquiring weapons that are ultimately used to commit murders (causing a burgeoning in the homicide rates of many areas of the world, but particularly Latin America).

Some studies show that the increased legalization of cannabis in the United States (beginning in 2012 with Washington Initiative 502 and Colorado Amendment 64) has led Mexican cartels to smuggle less cannabis in exchange for more heroin.

Alcohol

Alcohol, in the context of alcoholic beverages rather than denatured alcohol, is illegal in a number of Muslim countries, such as Saudi Arabia, and this has resulted in a thriving illegal trade in alcohol The manufacture, sale, transportation, importation and exportation of alcoholic beverage were illegal in the United States during the time known as the Prohibition in the 1920s and early 1930s.

Heroin

Up until around 2004 the majority of the world's heroin was produced in an area known as the Golden Triangle However, by 2007, 93% of the opiates on the world market originated in Afghanistan. This amounted to an export value of about US$64 billion, with a quarter being earned by opium farmers and the rest going to district officials, insurgents, warlords and drug traffickers. Another significant area where poppy fields are grown for the manufacture of heroin is Mexico.

According to the United States Drug Enforcement Administration, the price of heroin is typically valued 8 to 10 times that of cocaine on American streets, making it a high-profit substance for smugglers and dealers. In Europe (except the transit countries Portugal and the Netherlands), for example, a purported gram of street heroin, usually consisting of 700–800 mg of a light to dark brown powder containing 5–10% heroin base, costs €30–70, making the effective value per gram of pure heroin €300–700. Heroin is generally a preferred product for smuggling and distribution—over unrefined opium due to the cost-effectiveness and increased efficacy of heroin.

Because of the high cost per volume, heroin is easily smuggled. A US quarter-sized (2.5 cm) cylindrical vial can contain hundreds of doses. From the 1930s to the early 1970s, the so-called French Connection supplied the majority of US demand. Allegedly, during the Vietnam War, drug lords such as Ike Atkinson used to smuggle hundreds of kilograms of heroin to the US in coffins of dead American soldiers (see Cadaver Connection). Since that time it has become more difficult for drugs to be imported into the US than it had been in previous decades, but that does not stop the heroin smugglers from getting their product across US borders. Purity levels vary greatly by region with Northeastern cities having the most pure heroin in the United States. On 17 October 2018 police in Genoa Italy, discovered 270 kg of heroin hidden in a ship coming from the Iranian southern port of Bandar Abbas. The ship had already passed and stopped at Hamburg in Germanyand Valencia in Spain.

Penalties for smuggling heroin or morphine are often harsh in most countries. Some countries will readily hand down a death sentence (e.g. Singapore) or life in prison for the illegal smuggling of heroin or morphine, which are both internationally Schedule I drugs under the Single Convention on Narcotic Drugs

Methamphetamine

According to the Community Epidemiology Work Group, the number of clandestine methamphetamine laboratory incidents reported to the National Clandestine Laboratory Database decreased from 1999 to 2009. During this period, methamphetamine lab incidents increased in mid-western States (Illinois, Michigan, Missouri, and Ohio), and in Pennsylvania. In 2004, more lab incidents were reported in Missouri (2,788) and Illinois (1,058) than in California (764). In 2003, methamphetamine lab incidents reached new highs in Georgia (250), Minnesota (309), and Texas (677). There were only seven methamphetamine lab incidents reported in Hawaii in 2004, though nearly 59 percent of substance abuse treatment admissions (excluding alcohol) were for primary methamphetamine abuse during the first six months of 2004. As of 2007, Missouri leads the United States in drug-lab seizures, with 1,268 incidents reported. Often canine units are used for detecting rolling meth labs which can be concealed on large vehicles, or transported on something as small as a motorcycle. These labs are more difficult to detect than stationary ones, and can often be obscured among legal cargo in big trucks.

Methamphetamine is sometimes used intraveneously, placing users and their partners at risk for transmission of HIV and hepatitis C. «Meth» can also be inhaled, most commonly vaporized on aluminum foil or in a glass pipe. This method is reported to give «an unnatural high» and a «brief intense rush».

In South Africa methamphetamine is called "tik" or "tik-tik"."Known locally as "tik," the drug was virtually unknown as late as 2003. Now, it is the country's main drug of abuse, even when alcohol is included. " Children as young as eight are abusing the substance, smoking it in crude glass vials made from light bulbs. Since methamphetamine is easy to produce, the substance is manufactured locally in staggering quantities

The government of North Korea currently operates methamphetamine production facilities. There, the drug is used as medicine because no alternatives are available; it also is smuggled across the Chinese border.

The Australian Crime Commission's illicit drug data report for 2011–2012 stated that the average strength of crystal methamphetamine doubled in most Australian jurisdictions within a 12-month period, and the majority of domestic laboratory closures involved small "addict-based" operations.

Temazepam

Temazepam, a strong hypnotic benzodiazepine, is illicitly manufactured in clandestine laboratories (called jellie labs) to supply the increasingly high demand for the drug internationally. Many clandestine temazepam labs are in Eastern Europe. The labs manufacture temazepam by chemically altering diazepam, oxazepam or lorazepam. «Jellie labs» have been identified and shut down in Russia, the Ukraine, Czech Republic, Latvia and Belarus.

Surveys in many countries show that temazepam, MDMA, nimetazepam, and methamphetamine rank among the top illegal drugs most frequently abused.

Cocaine

Cocaine is a highly prominent drug among many drug dealers and manufacturers. The cocaine black market distribution industry is worth more than 85 billion dollars. It has been a heavily fought over and massively produced. Around 1.1 million kilograms of cocaine were made in 2009 and it is believed to have been consumed by around 17 million people worldwide. This drug's mass trade is believed to have been possible by notorious drug dealing kingpin Joaquín "El Chapo" Guzmán who ran the Sinaloa Cartel.

International coordination:

Interpol

United Nations Convention Against Illicit Traffic in Narcotic Drugs and Psychotropic Substances

Medical cannabis, or medical marijuana, is cannabis and cannabinoids that are prescribed by physicians for their patients. The use of cannabis as medicine has not been rigorously tested due to production and governmental restrictions, resulting in limited clinical research to define the safety and efficacy of using cannabis to treat diseases. Preliminary evidence suggests that cannabis can reduce nausea and vomiting during chemotherapy, improve appetite in people with HIV/AIDS, reduces chronic pain and muscle spasms and treats severe forms of epilepsy.

Short-term use increases the risk of minor and major adverse effects. Common side effects include dizziness, feeling tired, vomiting, and hallucinations. Long-term effects of cannabis are not clear. Concerns include memory and cognition problems, risk of addiction, schizophrenia in young people, and the risk of children taking it by accident.

The Cannabis plant has a history of medicinal use dating back thousands of years in many cultures. Some American medical organizations have requested removal of cannabis from the list of Schedule I controlled substances maintained by the United States federal government, followed by regulatory and scientific review. Others oppose its legalization, such as the American Academy of Pediatrics.

Medical cannabis can be administered through various methods, including capsules, lozenges, tinctures, dermal patches, oral or dermal sprays, cannabis edibles, and vaporizing or smoking dried buds. Synthetic cannabinoids are available for prescription use in some countries, such as dronabinol and nabilone. Countries that allow the medical use of whole-plant cannabis include Australia, Canada, Chile, Colombia, Germany, Greece, Israel, Italy, the Netherlands, Peru, Poland, Portugal, and Uruguay. In the United States, 33 states and the District of Columbia have legalized cannabis for medical purposes, beginning with the passage of California's Proposition 215in 1996. Although cannabis remains prohibited for any use at the federal level, the Rohrabacher–Farr amendment was enacted in December 2014, limiting the ability of federal law to be enforced in states where medical cannabis has been legalized.

Classification

Many different cannabis strains are collectively called medical cannabis. Since many varieties of the cannabis plant and plant derivatives all share the same name, the term medical cannabis is ambiguous and can be misunderstood. A Cannabis plant includes more than 400 different chemicals, of which about 70 are cannabinoids. In comparison, typical government-approved medications contain only one or two chemicals. The number of active chemicals in cannabis is one reason why treatment with cannabis is difficult to classify and study.

A 2014 review stated that the variations in ratio of CBD-to-THC in botanical and pharmaceutical preparations determines the therapeutic vs psychoactive effects (CBD attenuates THC's psychoactive effects) of cannabis products.

Medical uses

Medical cannabis has several potential beneficial effects. Evidence is moderate that it helps in chronic pain and muscle spasms. Low quality evidence suggests its use for reducing nausea during chemotherapy, improving appetite in HIV/AIDS, improving sleep, and improving tics in Tourette syndrome. When usual treatments are ineffective, cannabinoids have also been recommended for anorexia, arthritis, migraine, and glaucoma. It is unclear whether American states might be able mitigate the adverse effects of the opioid epidemic by prescribing medical cannabis as an alternative pain managament drug.

It is recommended that cannabis use be stopped in pregnancy.

Nausea and vomiting

Medical cannabis is somewhat effective in chemotherapy-induced nausea and vomiting (CINV) and may be a reasonable option in those who do not improve following preferential treatment. Comparative studies have found cannabinoids to be more effective than some conventional antiemetics such as prochlorperazine, promethazine, and metoclopramide in controlling CINV, but these are used less frequently because of side effects including dizziness, dysphoria, and hallucinations. Long-term cannabis use may cause nausea and vomiting, a condition known as cannabinoid hyperemesis syndrome.

A 2016 Cochrane review said that cannabinoids were «probably effective» in treating chemotherapy-induced nausea in children, but with a high side-effect profile (mainly drowsiness, dizziness, altered moods, and increased appetite). Less common side effects were «ocular problems, orthostatic hypotension, muscle twitching, pruritis, vagueness, hallucinations, lightheadedness and dry mouth».

HIV/AIDS

Evidence is lacking for both efficacy and safety of cannabis and cannabinoids in treating patients with HIV/AIDS or for anorexia associated with AIDS. As of 2013, current studies suffer from effects of bias, small sample size, and lack of long-term data.

Pain

A 2017 review found only limited evidence for the effectiveness of cannabis in relieving chronic pain in several conditions. Another review found tentative evidence for use of cannabis in treating peripheral neuropathy, but little evidence of benefit for other types of long term pain.

When cannabis is inhaled to relieve pain, blood levels of cannabinoids rise faster than when oral products are used, peaking within three minutes and attaining an analgesic effect in seven minutes. A 2014 review found limited and weak evidence that smoked cannabis was effective for chronic non-cancer pain. A 2015 meta-analysis found that inhaled medical cannabis was effective in reducing neuropathic pain in the short term for one in five to six patients. Another 2015 review found limited evidence that medical cannabis was effective for neuropathic pain when combined with traditional analgesics.

A 2011 review considered cannabis to be generally safe, and it appears safer than opioids in palliative care.

Neurological conditions

Cannabis' efficacy is not clear in treating neurological problems, including multiple sclerosis (MS) and movement problems. The combination of Δ9-tetrahydrocannabinol (THC) and cannabidiol (CBD) extracts give subjective relief of spasticity, though objective post-treatment assessments do not reveal significant changes. Evidence also suggests that oral cannabis extract is effective for reducing patient-centered measures of spasticity. A trial of cannabis is deemed to be a reasonable option if other treatments have not been effective. Its use for MS is approved in ten countries. A 2012 review found no problems with tolerance, abuse, or addiction. In the United States, cannabidiol, one of the canaboids found in the marijuana plant, has been approved for treating two severe forms of epilepsy, Lennox-Gastaut syndrome and Dravet syndrome.

Posttraumatic stress disorder

There is tentative evidence that medical cannabis is effective at reducing posttraumatic stress disorder symptoms, but, as of 2017, there is insufficient evidence to confirm its effectiveness for this condition.

Adverse effects

Medical use

There is insufficient data to draw strong conclusions about the safety of medical cannabis. Typically, adverse effects of medical cannabis use are not serious; they include tiredness, dizziness, increased appetite, and cardiovascular and psychoactive effects. Other effects can include impaired short-term memory; impaired motor coordination; altered judgment; and paranoia or psychosis at high doses. Tolerance to these effects develops over a period of days or weeks. The amount of cannabis normally used for medicinal purposes is not believed to cause any permanent cognitive impairment in adults, though long-term treatment in adolescents should be weighed carefully as they are more susceptible to these impairments. Withdrawal symptoms are rarely a problem with controlled medical administration of cannabinoids. The ability to drive vehicles or to operate machinery may be impaired until a tolerance is developed. Although supporters of medical cannabis say that it is safe, further research is required to assess the long-term safety of its use.

Recreational use

Tetrahydrocannabinol (THC), the principal psychoactive constituent of the cannabis plant, has low toxicity while the LD50 (dose of THC needed to kill 50% of tested rodents) is high. Acute effects may include anxiety and panic, impaired attention, and memory (while intoxicated), an increased risk of psychotic symptoms, and possibly increased risk of accidents if a person drives a motor vehicle while intoxicated. Psychotic episodes are well-documented and typically resolve within minutes or hours. There have been few reports of symptoms lasting longer.

According to the United States Department of Health and Human Services, there were 455,000 emergency room visits associated with cannabis use in 2011. These statistics include visits in which the patient was treated for a condition induced by or related to recent cannabis use. The drug use must be "implicated" in the emergency department visit, but does not need to be the direct cause of the visit. Most of the illicit drug emergency room visits involved multiple drugs. In 129,000 cases, cannabis was the only implicated drug.

Effects of chronic use may include bronchitis, a cannabis dependence syndrome, and subtle impairments of attention and memory. These deficits persist while chronically intoxicated. Compared to non-smokers, people who smoked cannabis regularly in adolescence exhibit reduced connectivity in specific brain regions associated with memory, learning, alertness, and executive function. One study suggested that sustained heavy, daily, adolescent onset cannabis use over decades is associated with a decline in IQ by age 38, with no effects found in those who initiated cannabis use later, or in those who ceased use earlier in adulthood.

There has been a limited amount of studies that have looked at the effects of smoking cannabis on the respiratory system. Chronic heavy marijuana smoking is associated with coughing, production of sputum, wheezing, coughing, and other symptoms of chronic bronchitis. Regular cannabis use has not been shown to cause significant abnormalities in lung function.

Cannabis smoke contains thousands of organic and inorganic chemical compounds. This tar is chemically similar to that found in tobacco smoke, and over fifty known carcinogens have been identified in cannabis smoke, including nitrosamines, reactive aldehydes, and polycylic hydrocarbons, including benz[a]pyrene. Light and moderate use of cannabis is not believed to increase risk of lung or upper airway cancer. Evidence for causing these cancers is mixed concerning heavy, long-term use. In general there are far lower risks of pulmonary complications for regular cannabis smokers when compared with those of tobacco. Combustion products are not present when using a vaporizer, consuming THC in pill form, or consuming cannabis edibles.

There is serious suspicion among cardiologists, spurring research but falling short of definitive proof, that cannabis use has the potential to contribute to cardiovascular disease.Cannabis is believed to be an aggravating factor in rare cases of arteritis, a serious condition that in some cases leads to amputation. Because 97% of case-reports also smoked tobacco, a formal association with cannabis could not be made. If cannabis arteritis turns out to be a distinct clinical entity, it might be the consequence of vasoconstrictor activity observed from delta-8-THC and delta-9-THC. Other serious cardiovascular events including myocardial infarction, stroke, sudden cardiac death, and cardiomyopathy have been reported to be temporally associated with cannabis use. Research in these events is complicated because cannabis is often used in conjunction with tobacco, and drugs such as alcohol and cocaine. These putative effects can be taken in context of a wide range of cardiovascular phenomena regulated by the endocannabinoid system and an overall role of cannabis in causing decreased peripheral resistance and increased cardiac output, which potentially could pose a threat to those with cardiovascular disease.

Cannabis usually causes no tolerance or withdrawal symptoms except in heavy users. In a survey of heavy users 42.4% experienced withdrawal symptoms when they tried to quit marijuana such as craving, irritability, boredom, anxiety and sleep disturbances. About 9% of those who experiment with marijuana eventually become dependent. The rate goes up to one in six among those who begin use as adolescents, and one-quarter to one-half of those who use it daily according to a NIDA review. A 2013 review estimates daily use is associated with a 10-20% rate of dependence. The highest risk of cannabis dependence is found in those with a history of poor academic achievement, deviant behavior in childhood and adolescence, rebelliousness, poor parental relationships, or a parental history of drug and alcohol problems.

A 2013 literature review found that exposure to marijuana had biologically-based physical, mental, behavioral and social health consequences and was "associated with diseases of the liver (particularly with co-existing hepatitis C), lungs, heart, and vasculature".

Cognitive effects

A 2011 systematic review evaluated published studies of the acute and long-term cognitive effects of cannabis. THC intoxication is well established to impair cognitive functioning on an acute basis, including effects on the ability to plan, organize, solve problems, make decisions, and control impulses. The extent of this impact may be greater in novice users, and paradoxically, those habituated to high-level ingestion may have reduced cognition during withdrawal. Studies of long-term effects on cognition have provided conflicting results, with some studies finding no difference between long-term abstainers and never-users and others finding long-term deficits. The discrepancies between studies may reflect greater long-term effects among heavier users relative to occasional users, and greater duration of effect among those with heavy use as adolescents compared to later in life. A second systematic review focused on neuroimaging studies found little evidence supporting an effect of cannabis use on brain structure and function. A 2003 meta-analysis concluded that any long-term cognitive effects were relatively modest in magnitude and limited to certain aspects of learning and memory.

Impact on psychosis

Exposure to THC can cause acute transient psychotic symptoms in healthy individuals and people with schizophrenia.

A 2007 meta analysis concluded that cannabis use reduced the average age of onset of psychosis by 2.7 years relative to non-cannabis use. A 2005 meta analysis concluded that adolescent use of cannabis increases the risk of psychosis, and that the risk is dose-related. A 2004 literature review on the subject concluded that cannabis use is associated with a two-fold increase in the risk of psychosis, but that cannabis use is «neither necessary nor sufficient» to cause psychosis. A French review from 2009 came to a conclusion that cannabis use, particularly that before age 15, was a factor in the development of schizophrenic disorders.

Other potential long-term effects

A 2008 National Institutes of Health study of 19 chronic heavy marijuana users with cardiac and cerebral abnormalities (averaging 28 g to 272 g (1 to 9+ oz) weekly) and 24 controls found elevated levels of apolipoprotein C-III (apoC-III) in the chronic smokers. An increase in apoC-III levels induces the development of hypertriglyceridemia.

Pharmacology

The genus Cannabis contains two species which produce useful amounts of psychoactive cannabinoids: Cannabis indica and Cannabis sativa, which are listed as Schedule I medicinal plants in the US; a third species, Cannabis ruderalis, has few psychogenic properties. Cannabis contains more than 460 compounds; at least 80 of these are cannabinoids – chemical compounds that interact with cannabinoid receptors in the brain. As of 2012, more than 20 cannabinoids were being studied by the U.S. FDA.

The most psychoactive cannabinoid found in the cannabis plant is tetrahydrocannabinol (or delta-9-tetrahydrocannabinol, commonly known as THC). Other cannabinoids include delta-8-tetrahydrocannabinol, cannabidiol (CBD), cannabinol (CBN), cannabicyclol (CBL), cannabichromene (CBC) and cannabigerol (CBG); they have less psychotropic effects than THC, but may play a role in the overall effect of cannabis. The most studied are THC, CBD and CBN.

CB1 and CB2 are the primary cannabinoid receptors responsible for several of the effects of cannabinoids, although other receptors may play a role as well. Both belong to a group of receptors called G protein-coupled receptors (GPCRs). CB1 receptors are found in very high levels in the brain and are thought to be responsible for psychoactive effects. CB2 receptors are found peripherally throughout the body and are thought to modulate pain and inflammation.

Absorption

Cannabinoid absorption is dependent on its route of administration.

Inhaled and vaporized THC have similar absorption profiles to smoked THC, with a bioavailability ranging from 10 to 35%. Oral administration has the lowest bioavailability of approximately 6%, variable absorption depending on the vehicle used, and the longest time to peak plasma levels (2 to 6 hours) compared to smoked or vaporized THC.

Similar to THC, CBD has poor oral bioavailability, approximately 6%. The low bioavailability is largely attributed to significant first-pass metabolism in the liver and erratic absorption from the gastrointestinal tract. However, oral administration of CBD has a faster time to peak concentrations (2 hours) than THC.

Due to the poor bioavailability of oral preparations, alternative routes of administration have been studied, including sublingual and rectal. These alternative formulations maximize bioavailability and reduce first-pass metabolism. Sublingual administration in rabbits yielded bioavailability of 16% and time to peak concentration of 4 hours. Rectal administration in monkeys doubled bioavailability to 13.5% and achieved peak blood concentrations within 1 to 8 hours after administration.

Distribution

Like cannabinoid absorption, distribution is also dependent on route of administration. Smoking and inhalation of vaporized cannabis have better absorption than do other routes of administration, and therefore also have more predictable distribution. THC is highly protein bound once absorbed, with only 3% found unbound in the plasma. It distributes rapidly to highly vascularized organs such as the heart, lungs, liver, spleen, and kidneys, as well as to various glands. Low levels can be detected in the brain, testes, and unborn fetuses, all of which are protected from systemic circulation via barriers. THC further distributes into fatty tissues a few days after administration due to its high lipophilicity, and is found deposited in the spleen and fat after redistribution.

back to the liver in recirculation for metabolism. Eventually, both routes of metabolism result in the metabolism of psychoactive THC to inactive 11-COOH-THC.

Administration

Smoking has been the means of administration of cannabis for many users, but it is not suitable for the use of cannabis as a medicine. It was the most common method of medical cannabis consumption in the US as of 2013. It is difficult to predict the pharmacological response to cannabis because concentration of cannabinoids varies widely, as there are different ways of preparing it for consumption (smoked, applied as oils, eaten, infused into other foods, or drunk) and a lack of production controls. The potential for adverse effects from smoke inhalation makes smoking a less viable option than oral preparations. Cannabis vaporizers have gained popularity because of the perception among users that fewer harmful chemicals are ingested when components are inhaled via aerosol rather than smoke.Cannabinoid medicines are available in pill form (dronabinol and nabilone) and liquid extracts formulated into an oromucosal spray (nabiximols). Oral preparations are «problematic due to the uptake of cannabinoids into fatty tissue, from which they are released slowly, and the significant first-pass liver metabolism, which breaks down Δ9THC and contributes further to the variability of plasma concentrations».

The US Food and Drug Administration (FDA) has not approved smoked cannabis for any condition or disease, as it deems that evidence is lacking concerning safety and efficacy.The FDA issued a 2006 advisory against smoked medical cannabis stating: «marijuana has a high potential for abuse, has no currently accepted medical use in treatment in the United States, and has a lack of accepted safety for use under medical supervision.»Drug Trafficking Patterns to and from Eastern Africa

In the period 1995-2006, reported seizures of heroin, cannabis and cocaine in the region covered by UNODC Eastern Africaare comparatively few and do not reflect the extent of trafficking, availability and growing abuse in the region. The region is attractive to international drug trafficking syndicates as they are quick to exploit non-existent or ineffective border (land, sea and air) controls, limited cross border and regional cooperation as well as serious deficiencies in the criminal justice systems. Hence, the low seizure figures are more an indication that few resources are allocated to drug control and that international border controls are weak than a sign that no drugs are being trafficked through the region.

The region covered by UNODC Eastern Africa is accessible by sea to heroin and cannabis resin producer countries in South West and South East Asia through the ports in Djibouti, Eritrea, Kenya and Tanzania. Anecdotal evidence suggests that Somalia, currently in the process of establishing a central authority, is host to widespread illegal transactions, including drug and arms trafficking. There are two important international airports in the region, servicing the capitals' of Ethiopia and Kenya, which are used as transit points for drugs. Both airports have connections between West Africa and the heroinproducing countries in South West and South East Asia. There is also an increasing use of postal and courier services for cocaine, heroin and hashish.

A review of drug seizures from 1998 to date indicates an increase in the trafficking of heroin to eastern African countries from Pakistan, Thailand and India. Increased seizures of heroin with Nigerian connections bound for Uganda, Tanzania and Kenya through Ethiopia have been noted as well. Seizures and arrest statistics show that more Tanzanians and Mozambicans are becoming involved in the trafficking of heroin from Pakistan and Iran.

West African syndicates, with their experience in cannabis and heroin smuggling, are actively networking in Latin America, and are responsible for the emergence of cocaine trafficking and abuse in eastern Africa. As shown in graph (3), although the volume of cocaine seized in Africa is still relatively small, the situation is changing as trafficking groups extend their highly-organised networks. In most countries in the ROEA region it is possible to purchase pharmaceutical products on demand without presenting a valid prescription. Many of these products, sometimes imported without authorization, are sold by hawkers in street-markets.

Unfortunately, the situation has been worsening in the last 1015 years. In the majority of the countries in the UNODC Eastern Africa region, control and monitoring of the national drug supply and distribution channels, including precursors, are inefficient. This results not only in the ineffective control of pharmaceutical products, but also in the circulation of counterfeit medicines. Together these pose serious health and socioeconomic problems, they undermine law enforcement activities and confidence in public health services.

The emergence of Mandrax in the region has gone hand in hand with the diversion of licit drugs and essential chemical precursors into the illicit market. The control of essential chemical precursors that are either being trafficked through the UNODC Eastern Africaregion to countries producing cocaine and heroin or used in the illegal production of Mandrax, is an important part of the battle against drugs in the region. It is feared that illegal trafficking, importation and use will continue as long as there are no effective control mechanisms in the countries of the region.

History

Ancient

Cannabis, called má (meaning «hemp; cannabis; numbness») or dàmá (with «big; great») in Chinese, was used in Taiwan for fiber starting about 10,000 years ago. The botanist Hui-lin Li wrote that in China, «The use of Cannabis in medicine was probably a very early development. Since ancient humans used hemp seed as food, it was quite natural for them to also discover the medicinal properties of the plant.» Emperor Shen-Nung, who was also a pharmacologist, wrote a book on treatment methods in 2737 BCE that included the medical benefits of cannabis. He recommended the substance for many ailments, including constipation, gout, rheumatism, and absent-mindedness. Cannabis is one of the 50 «fundamental» herbs in traditional Chinese medicine.

The Ebers Papyrus (c. 1550 BCE) from Ancient Egypt describes medical cannabis. The ancient Egyptians used hemp (cannabis) in suppositories for relieving the pain of hemorrhoids.

Surviving texts from ancient India confirm that cannabis› psychoactive properties were recognized, and doctors used it for treating a variety of illnesses and ailments, including insomnia, headaches, gastrointestinal disorders, and pain, including during childbirth.

The Ancient Greeks used cannabis to dress wounds and sores on their horses, and in humans, dried leaves of cannabis were used to treat nose bleeds, and cannabis seeds were used to expel tapeworms.

In the medieval Islamic world, Arabic physicians made use of the diuretic, antiemetic, antiepileptic, anti-inflammatory, analgesic and antipyretic properties of Cannabis sativa, and used it extensively as medication from the 8th to 18th centuries.How drugs are used and are trafficked is constantly changing and the ways they are trafficked are growing in technical and organisational complexity. What is not changing is the profitability of the drugs trade. Every year EU citizens spend tens of billions of euros on illicit drugs.

The organised crime groups (OCGs) involved are becoming more specialised and more fully interconnected. And the overall rate of change is accelerating, partly as a result of globalisation. Activities related to trafficking are becoming concentrated in particular geographic areas, while instability in regions neighbouring the EU could have profound effects on the drug market in Europe.

Significant domestic demand already exists along all trafficking routes and may be growing, with drug trafficking acting as an additional destabilising factor in countries that are already faced with other serious political, social, health and economic problems. Developments on the Southern route

"Southern route"—from Afghanistan through Pakistan or Iran, via the Persian Gulf and East Africa—are of special concern, given the potentially larger role of this route in the supply of heroin and other drugs to Europe and its negative impact on countries in Africa.

Meeting the Challenges

These factors, taken individually and together, pose enormous challenges for Europol and its partner organisations, such as the European Monitoring Centre for Drugs and Drug Addiction (EMCDDA) and Interpol. These challenges are being met in a number of ways, including through:

systematic and ongoing analyses of the features of the drug trade and the business models underlying it, thus bolstering operational effectiveness and guiding the formulation of policy partnerships between national authorities, international organisations, industry, and national governments the efficient effective marshalling of resources the gathering of sound information and insights in order to shape strategic responses, meet specific challenges, and identify new opportunities to fight this scourge

Europol also supports drug raids by offering criminal intelligence analysis and operational support to law enforcement, such as through Analysis Project (AP) Cola, Europol's team of specialists and analysts dedicated to tackling cocaine trafficking.

Undermining Power and Profit

Whatever the class of drug, a central aim of the activities of Europol and its partners, beyond the apprehension of traffickers and the interdiction of supplies, is to undermine the twin motives—profit and power—that perpetuate this scourge.

Landrace strains

Cannabis seeds may have been used for food, rituals or religious practices in ancient Europe and China. Harvesting the plant led to the spread of cannabis throughout Eurasia about 10,000 to 5,000 years ago, with further distribution to the Middle East and Africa about 2,000 to 500 years ago. A landrace strain of cannabis developed over centuries. They are cultivars of the plant that originated in one specific region.

Widely cultivated strains of cannabis, such as "Afghani" or "Hindu Kush", are indigenous to the Pakistan and Afghanistan regions, while «Durban Poison» is native to Africa. There are approximately 16 landrace strains of cannabis identified from Pakistan, Jamaica, Africa, Mexico, Central America and Asia.

Modern

An Irish physician, William Brooke O'Shaughnessy, is credited with introducing cannabis to Western medicine. O›Shaughnessy discovered cannabis in the 1830s while living abroad in India, where he conducted numerous experiments investigating the drug's medical utility (noting in particular its analgesic and anticonvulsant effects). He returned to England with a supply of cannabis in 1842, after which its use spread through Europe and the United States. Cannabis was entered into the United States Pharmacopeia in 1850.

The use of cannabis in medicine began to decline by the end of the 19th century, due to difficulty in controlling dosages and the rise in popularity of synthetic and opium-derived drugs. Also, the advent of the hypodermic syringe allowed these drugs to be injected for immediate effect, in contrast to cannabis which is not water-soluble and therefore cannot be injected.

In the United States, the medical use of cannabis further declined with the passage of the Marihuana Tax Act of 1937, which imposed new regulations and fees on physicians prescribing cannabis. Cannabis was removed from the U.S. Pharmacopeia in 1941, and officially banned for any use with the passage of the Controlled Substances Act of 1970.

Cannabis began to attract renewed interest as medicine in the 1970s and 1980s, in particular due to its use by cancer and AIDS patients who reported relief from the effects of chemotherapy and wasting syndrome. In 1996, California became the first U.S. state to legalize medical cannabis in defiance of federal law. In 2001, Canada became the first country to adopt a system regulating the medical use of cannabis.

United States

Section 1300.01 Definitions relating to controlled substances:

(b) As used in parts 1301 through 1308 and part 1312 of this chapter, the following terms shall have the meanings specified:

(30) The term narcotic drug means any of the following whether produced directly or indirectly by extraction from substances of vegetable origin or independently by means of chemical synthesis or by a combination of extraction and chemical synthesis:

(i) Opium, opiates, derivatives of opium and opiates, including their isomers, esters, ethers, salts, and salts of isomers, esters, and ethers whenever the existence of such isomers, esters, ethers and salts is possible within the specific chemical designation. Such term does not include the isoquinoline alkaloids of opium.

(ii) Poppy straw and concentrate of poppy straw.

(iii) Coca leaves, except coca leaves and extracts of coca leaves from which cocaine, ecgonine and derivatives of ecgonine or their salts have been removed.

(iv) Cocaine, its salts, optical and geometric isomers, and salts of isomers.

(v) Ecgonine, its derivatives, their salts, isomers and salts of isomers.

(vi) Any compound, mixture, or preparation which contains any quantity of any of the substances referred to in paragraphs (b)(31)(i) through (v) of this section.

A 1984 amendment to 21 USC (Controlled Substances Act), Section 802 expanded and revised definition of "narcotic drug", including within term poppy straw, cocaine, and ecgonine.

US v. Stieren

John Arthur Stieren appeals from the judgment of conviction for possession of cocaine with intent to distribute and dispense under 21 U.S.C. § 841(a)(1). Stieren contends that the statute is unconstitutional because "cocaine is classified as a narcotic under Schedule II of 21 U.S.C. § 812(c), when as a matter of scientific and medical fact cocaine is not a narcotic but is a non-narcotic stimulant."

The sufficiency of the evidence is not disputed. Stieren was convicted after special agents testified that he was in possession of and attempted to sell them a large quantity of cocaine. Defendant urges that the testimony and reports by physicians and scientists demonstrate that cocaine is not a narcotic. He also cites cases which hold that cocaine is not a narcotic under the pharmacological definition of the term. State v. Erickson, 574 P.2d 1 (Alaska 1978).

It is within the legislative prerogative to classify cocaine, which is a non-narcotic central nervous system stimulant, as a narcotic for penalty and regulatory purposes. 21 U.S.C. § 802(16)(A). The use of cocaine poses serious problems for the community and has a high potential for abuse. Congress' choice of penalty reflects a societal policy which must be adhered to by the courts.2 Congress has the power to reclassify cocaine. This power has been delegated to the Attorney General. 21 U.S.C. § 811(a)(1). If cocaine is to be reclassified, defendant's arguments should be made to the legislative branch, not the courts.

We hold that Congress had a rational legislative purpose when it classified cocaine as a Schedule II narcotic drug for the purpose of imposing penalties.

History

The term "narcotic" is believed to have been coined by the Greek physician Galen to refer to agents that numb or deaden, causing loss of feeling or paralysis. It is based on the Greek word (narcosis), the term used by Hippocrates for the process of numbing or the numbed state. Galen listed mandrake root, altercus (eclata),seeds, and poppy juice (opium) as the chief examples. It originally referred to any substance that relieved pain, dulled the senses, or induced sleep. Now, the term is used in a number of ways. Some people define narcotics as substances that bind at opioid receptors (cellular membrane proteins activated by substances like heroin or morphine) while others refer to any illicit substance as a narcotic. From a U.S. legal perspective, narcotics refer to opium, opium derivatives, and their semi-synthetic substitutes, though in U.S. law, due to its numbing properties, cocaine is also considered a narcotic.

Sense of "any illegal drug" first recorded 1926, Amer.Eng. The adj. is first attested c.1600. There are many different types of narcotics. The two most common forms of narcotic drugs are morphine and codeine. Both are synthesized from opium for medicinal use. The most commonly used drug for recreational purposes created from opium is heroin. Synthesized drugs created with an opium base for use in pain management are fentanyl, oxycodone, tramadol, demarol, hydrocodone, methadone, and hydromorphone. New forms of pain medication are being created regularly. The newest drug to come out in 2014 is zohydro, an intense dosage of hydrocodone medication, the strongest yet created for pain management.

Analgesics

Analgesics are drugs that relieve pain. There are two main types: non-narcotic analgesics for mild pain, and narcotic analgesics for severe pain.

Spiritual and religious use

Some religions, particularly ethnic religions are based completely on the use of certain drugs, known as entheogens, which are mostly hallucinogens,—psychedelics, dissociatives, or deliriants. Some drugs used as entheogens include kava which can act as a stimulant, a sedative, a euphoriant and an anesthetic. The roots of the kava plant are used to produce a drink which is consumed throughout the cultures of the Pacific Ocean.

Some shamans from different cultures use entheogens, defined as «generating the divine within»to achieve religious ecstasy. Amazonian shamans use ayahuasca (yagé) a hallucinogenic brew for this purpose. Mazatec shamans have a long and continuous tradition of religious use of Salvia divinorum a psychoactive plant. Its use is to facilitate visionary states of consciousness during spiritual healing sessions.

Silene undulata is regarded by the Xhosa people as a sacred plant and used as an entheogen. Its root is traditionally used to induce vivid (and according to the Xhosa, prophetic) lucid dreams during the initiation process of shamans, classifying it a naturally occurring oneirogen similar to the more well-known dream herb Calea ternifolia.

Peyote a small spineless cactus has been a major source of psychedelic mescaline and has probably been used by Native Americans for at least five thousand years. Most mescaline is now obtained from a few species of columnar cacti in particular from San Pedro and not from the vulnerable peyote.

The entheogenic use of cannabis has also been widely practised for centuries. Rastafari use marijuana (ganja) as a sacrament in their religious ceremonies.

Psychedelic mushrooms (psilocybin mushrooms), commonly called magic mushrooms or shrooms have also long been used as entheogens.

Smart drugs and designer drugs

Nootropics, also commonly referred to as "smart drugs", are drugs that are claimed to improve human cognitive abilities. Nootropics are used to improve memory, concentration, thought, mood, and learning. An increasingly used nootropic among students, also known as a study drug, is methylphenidate branded commonly as Ritalin and used for the treatment of attention deficit hyperactivity disorder (ADHD) and narcolepsy. At high doses methylphenidate can become highly addictive. Serious addiction can lead to psychosis, anxiety and heart problems, and the use of this drug is related to a rise in suicides, and overdoses. Evidence for use outside of student settings is limited but suggests that that it is commonplace. Intravenous use of methylphenidate can lead to emphysematous damage to the lungs, known as Ritalin lung.

Some nootropics are also now beginning to be used to treat medical conditions such as Parkinson's disease, and Alzheimer's disease. They are also commonly used to regain brain function lost during aging.

Other drugs known as designer drugs are produced. An early example of what today would be labelled a ‹designer drug› was LSD, which was synthesised from ergot. Other examples include analogs of performance-enhancing drugs such as designer steroids taken to improve physical capabilities and these are sometimes used (legally or not) for this purpose, often by professional athletes. Other designer drugs mimic the effects of psychoactive drugs. Since the late 1990s there has been the identification of many of these synthesised drugs. In Japan and the United Kingdom this has spurred the addition of many designer drugs into a newer class of controlled substances known as a temporary class drug.

Synthetic cannabinoids have been produced for a longer period of time and are used in the designer drug synthetic cannabis.

Recreational drug use

Recreational drug use is the use of a drug (legal, controlled, or illegal) with the primary intention of altering the state of consciousnessthrough alteration of the central nervous system in order to create positive emotions and feelings. The hallucinogen LSD is a psychoactive drug commonly used as a recreational drug.

Some national laws prohibit the use of different recreational drugs; and medicinal drugs that have the potential for recreational use are often heavily regulated. However, there are many recreational drugs that are legal in many jurisdictions and widely culturally accepted. Cannabis is the most commonly consumed controlled recreational drug in the world (as of 2012). Its use in many countries is illegal but is legally usedin several countries usually with the proviso that it can only be used for personal use. It can be used in the leaf form of marijuana (grass), or in the resin form of hashish. Marijuana is a more mild form of cannabis than hashish.

There may be an age restriction on the consumption and purchase of legal recreational drugs. Some recreational drugs that are legal and accepted in many places include alcohol, tobacco, betel nut, and caffeine products, and in some areas of the world the legal use of drugs such as khat is common.

There are a number of legal intoxicants commonly called legal highs that are used recreationally. The most widely used of these is alcohol.

Administration of drugs

All drugs, can be administered via a number of routes, and many can be administered by more than one.

- Bolus is the administration of a medication, drug or other compound that is given to raise its concentration in blood to an effective level. The administration can be given intravenously, by intramuscular, intrathecal or subcutaneous injection.
- Inhaled, (breathed into the lungs), as an aerosol or dry powder. (This includes smoking a substance)
- Injection as a solution, suspension or emulsion either: intramuscular, intravenous, intraperitoneal, intraosseous.
- Insufflation, or snorted into the nose.
- Orally, as a liquid or solid, that is absorbed through the intestines.
- Rectally as a suppository, that is absorbed by the rectum or colon.
- Sublingually, diffusing into the blood through tissues under the tongue.
- Topically, usually as a cream or ointment. A drug administered in this manner may be given to act locally or systemically.
- Vaginally as a pessary, primarily to treat vaginal infections.

Control of drugs

There are numerous governmental offices in many countries that deal with the control and oversee of drug manufacture and use, and the implementation of various drug laws. The Single Convention on Narcotic Drugs is an international treaty brought about in 1961 to prohibit the use of narcotics save for those used in medical research and treatment. In 1971, a second treaty the Convention on Psychotropic Substances had to be introduced to deal with newer recreational psychoactive and psychedelic drugs.

The legal status of Salvia divinorum varies in many countries and even in states within the United States. Where it is legislated against the degree of prohibition also varies.

The Food and Drug Administration (FDA) in the United States is a federal agency responsible for protecting and promoting public health through the regulation and supervision of food safety, tobacco products, dietary supplements, prescription and over-the-counter medications, vaccines, biopharmaceuticals, blood transfusions, medical devices, electromagnetic radiation emitting devices, cosmetics, animal foods and veterinary drugs.

Drug Laws

Federal and state laws regulate the possession and distribution of drugs. For the most part, the drug laws of each jurisdiction are relatively uniform since most states have modeled their laws based on the federal Controlled Substances Act, 21 U.S.C. §801 et. seq., which was passed in 1970 and amended thereafter to conform with various international conventions.

Controlled Substances Act

The CSA divides drugs into five schedules, numbered I through V. Schedule I includes drugs that have no medical use, have a high potential for abuse, and for which there is no accepted safe use, except under medical supervision. Schedule I drugs include marijuana (even though some states, such as California, accept the medical use of marijuana), LSD, MDMA (Ecstasy), heroin, DMT and the like.

Schedule II drugs have a high potential for abuse, a currently-accepted medical use (as opposed to Schedule I) and a risk of "severe" dependence if abused. Schedule II drugs require a prescription, with prescriptions limited to 30 days, and include cocaine, methamphetamine, morphine, PCP, and amphetamines.

Schedule III drugs have a lower potential for abuse, currently-accepted medical uses and a risk of high psychological dependence or moderate physical dependence if abused. Anabolic steroids and intermediate-acting steroids are on this schedule.

Schedule IV includes longer-acting barbituates, and Schedule V include some preparations including codeine and opium.

Drug Sentencing

Since 1986, federal judges have sentenced defendants convicted of drug offenses to substantially lengthier prison terms. Under federal mandatory minimum sentencing laws, the type and weight of the drug, as well as the defendant's prior convictions dictate the length of the sentence. Judges no longer may consider other factors such as likelihood of recidivism. Some states have followed suit and passed laws that treat drug offenses more strictly if committed by violent felons. In California, for instance, the Three Strikes law counts a felony drug offense (or any nonviolent felony) as a third strike if the first two strikes were violent or "serious."

Critics of the federal mandatory minimum sentencing regime contend that drug sentencing laws disproportionately affect minorities. They cite as one key example the disparity in sentencing between crack and powder cocaine. Under federal law, possession of five grams of crack would result in the same prison term as 500 grams of powder. In 2002, the US Sentencing Commission found that 85% of the persons convicted of an offense involving crack cocaine were black and that judges sentenced persons convicted of crack possession to prison sentences five times longer than that for possession of powder cocaine. The Supreme Court is expected to decide whether that part of the law in constitutional by the summer of 2008.

Twelve states—Alaska, California, Colorado, Hawaii, Maine, Maryland, Montana, Nevada, New Mexico, Oregon, Rhode Island, Vermont, and Washington—have enacted medical marijuana laws, legalizing the possession and distribution of marijuana for medical reasons. In 2005, however, the Supreme Court ruled in Gonzales v. Raich, 545 U.S. 1, that the federal government has the right to prosecute federal marijuana laws, regardless of state protections for medical use. Since marijuana sales cross state borders, the Court said, the Commerce Clause gives Congress the right to regulate drug sales and use, regardless of what individual states may do.

The main categories of drug offenses, in increasing levels of punishment, are simple possession, possession with intent to distribute, manufacturing, selling or distributing, conspiracy to manufacture or sell, and "continuing criminal enterprise," a charge used against gangs, which applies when five or more people cooperated to sell drugs as an ongoing business that created "substantial" income. Federal sentences range from five years for a first offense of trafficking in certain drugs to life imprisonment for those with two or more priors who trafficked in large amounts of Schedule I and II drugs.

We provide operational support, analysis and training to help national police to tackle widescale drug trafficking.

Since the types of drugs trafficked and the routes used are constantly evolving, it is essential that countries work together in a united and coordinated way.

We assist national, regional and international law enforcement bodies to counter the illicit production, trafficking and abuse of drugs in the following ways:

Global operations against drug trafficking and assistance to ongoing investigations;

Criminal analysis of intelligence on drug trafficking routes, modus operandi and the criminal networks involved;

Comprehensive training for police worldwide to better tackle drug trafficking.

"The supply of illicit drugs everywhere around the globe is more abundant, more sophisticated and more diverse than it has ever been before."

Operations

We coordinate drug trafficking operations spanning different regions of the world, and support drug operations and investigations led by national or international agencies. They aim to disrupt the movement of specific products along routes affecting target regions or international illicit drug flows.

Our operational working meetings serve as a platform for officers worldwide to exchange information on cases where we have identified common links.

The Lionfish model of operations targets drug trafficking along every possible route: air, land and sea. First conducted in 2013 in Latin America, it has since expanded to other regions of the world and involves thousands of law enforcement officials. Read more about Operation Lionfish.

Training

Ensuring police worldwide have the knowledge and skills to prevent, investigate and disrupt drug trafficking is a key part of our drug strategy.

Training can be combined with operational support to assist member countries in planning and executive on-the-ground operations against drug trafficking.

Case study: Fiji

Following a significant increase in the volume of illegal drugs being trafficked through the country, the Fiji authorities requested INTERPOL's assistance. In May 2018, we delivered a comprehensive training course covering drugs, financial investigations and security document examination.

Police from Fiji, Papua New Guinea, Samoa, Solomon Islands, Tonga and Timor-Leste learned how to use the Relief database which provides automatic analysis of the tool marks, logos and chemical compositions of drug packages.

Global Conference on Illicit Drugs

Our first Global Conference on Illicit Drugs took place in Spain in April 2018, bringing together representatives from more than 100 countries. The meeting also gave participants the chance to review recent developments, and implications of convergences between drug trafficking and other criminal activities such as money laundering, cybercrime and weapons trafficking.

Police need timely, accurate criminal intelligence in order to understand crime trends so they can adapt their activities and policies accordingly. We support our member countries with intelligence through dedicated analysis on drug trafficking.

We generate analytical reports by combining national police information with data from other sources – such as international organizations, civil society and open sources. These help our member countries to expand their knowledge on crimes, highlight subjects of potential interest, and foster cross-border coordination.

Social behaviour is disturbed in many substance abuse and psychiatric disorders. Given the consensus that social behaviours of lower mammals may help to understand some human emotional reactions, the aim of the present work was to provide an up-to-date review of studies on the changes in social behaviour induced by drugs of abuse. Various animal models have been used to study the relationship between drugs of abuse and social behaviour. Herein, we describe the effects of different substances of abuse on the three most commonly used animal models of social behaviour: the social play test, the social interaction test and the resident–intruder paradigm. The first is the most widely used test to assess adolescent behaviour in rodents, the second is generally used to evaluate a wide repertoire of behaviours in adulthood and the latter is specific to aggressive behaviour. Throughout the review we will explore the most relevant studies carried out to date to evaluate the effects of alcohol, cocaine, opioids, 3,4-methylenedioxymethamphetamine (MDMA), cannabinoids, nicotine and other drugs of abuse on these three paradigms, taking into account the influence of different variables, such as social history, age and type of exposure. Drugs of diverse pharmacological classes induce alterations in social behaviour, although they can be contrasting depending on several factors (drug, individual differences and environmental conditions). Ethanol and nicotine increase social interaction at low doses but reduce it at high doses. Psychostimulants, MDMA and cannabinoids reduce social interaction, whereas opiates increase it. Ethanoland psychostimulants enhance aggression, whereas MDMA, opiates, cannabinoids and nicotine reduce it. Prenatal drug exposure alters social behaviour, whereas drug withdrawal decreases sociability and enhances aggression. As a whole, this evidence has improved our understanding of the social dimension of drug addiction. Drugs continue to pour into the country from numerous sources despite the efforts of the Drug Enforcement Administration (DEA), law enforcement agencies, border patrols, and the United States government. Illegal drug abuse costs American society $181 billion a year in health care costs, lost workplace productivity, law enforcement, and legal costs. Prisons are overflowing with drug-related offenders, as 330,000 prison inmates in 2012 were incarcerated for drug offenses. Over 30 percent of all offenses in 2013 were related to drug trafficking, and 22,215 cases of drug trafficking were reported to the United States Sentencing Commission in the 2013 fiscal year.

Busted drug traffickers in 2013 were primarily male, approximately 85.8 percent with an average age of 35 years; 73.7 percent were US citizens and almost half, 49.5 percent, had little to no prior criminal history. The majority of drug trafficking offenders arrested in 2013 were Hispanic, at 47.9 percent, while 26.7 percent were black, 22.3 percent were white, and 3.1 percent were other races. Almost all drug trafficking offenders sentenced in 2013 went to prison, 96.3 percent, with an average sentence length of 72 months. Sentences varied depending on the type of drug trafficked, with the biggest penalties for crack cocaine and meth, and the lightest sentences for marijuana-related offenses.

Southwestern border

Most of the illicit drugs come into the United States across the vast 2,000-mile land border between the US and Mexico, called the Southwestern border or SWB. Drug cartels in Mexico utilize drug mules, tunnels, boats, vehicles, trains, aircrafts, donkeys, and couriers to get illegal drugs into America. Mexican drug cartels make an estimated $19-$29 billion a year on drug sales in the United States. Conflicts between drug cartels over territory as well as the attempts to stop drug trafficking by law enforcement officials often results in violence, and this has caused over 55,000 deaths since the proclaimed Mexican Drug War began in 2006.

Mexico's involvement in the illicit drug trade in the United States:

Marijuana: Mexico is the number one foreign supplier of marijuana to the United States, and marijuana is thought to be the top revenue generator for Mexican drug cartels.

Cocaine: Mexico does not produce cocaine, however, Mexican cartels move Columbian cocaine through South and Central America and into the United States. An estimated 93 percent of cocaine headed to the US from South America moves through Mexico.

Methamphetamine: Mexico remains the biggest foreign supplier of methamphetamine to the United States, and Mexican drug cartels set up labs to manufacture meth on both sides of the border, controlling labs in Southern California as well as domestically.

Heroin: While Asia and the Middle East remain the biggest producers of heroin, Mexican black-tar and brown heroin is on the rise. In fact, 39 percent of heroin identified under the DEA's Heroin Signature Program (HSP) in 2008 came from Mexico, making Mexico the source country for many of the heroin abusers west of the Mississippi River.

It is no surprise then that the top five districts sentencing drug trafficking offenders were on or near the SWB in 2013:

Western District of Texas: 1,587 sentenced drug trafficking offenders

Southern District of California: 1,426 sentenced drug trafficking offenders

Southern District of Texas: 1,279 sentenced drug trafficking offenders

District of Arizona: 1,162 sentenced drug trafficking offenders

District of Puerto Rico: 687 sentenced drug trafficking offenders

Methamphetamine trafficking

The popular stimulant drug made from the ephedrine or pseudoephedrine found in cold medications and manufactured into illegal methamphetamine in illicit laboratories may have initially been primarily trafficked by motorcycle gangs up and down the West Coast but concentrated in California. Mexican drug cartels are now heavily involved, and organized crime syndicates both manufacture and distribute the finished product as well as secure the main ingredients for domestic production in numerous smaller labs around the country. Superlabs produce larger quantities of meth at a time and are generally controlled by Mexican drug cartels, regardless of the side of the border on which the labs reside.

Legislation regarding the controlled status and sale of pseudoephedrine and ephedrine products has caused drug traffickers to get more creative in the ways they obtain the main ingredient in meth. The Combat Methamphetamine Epidemic Act in 2005, required retailers to keep pseudoephedrine products behind the counter and to register sales. Traffickers began sending buyers to multiple retail outlets in the same day to buy small and legal amounts of pseudoephedrine, a process called "smurfing," which they then used in clandestine labs to produce meth.

Meth can be "cooked" virtually anywhere; however, rural and smaller labs are prevalent across the Midwest and around the United States as well. Domestic meth production may be on the rise, as meth can be cut with many common products including anhydrous ammonia, one of the main ingredients used in fertilizer by farmers.

Meth labs are highly volatile as cutting meth uses highly flammable and explosive materials. From 2007-2009, the number of domestic meth lab incidents rose from 596 to 966 across the country, especially in the South and the Midwest. Oregon, Mississippi, and several cities have passed laws making pseudoephedrine only available with a prescription, and in Oregon, meth lab incidents decreased from 400 in 2004 to just 20 in 2008.

Prices of meth have dropped 70 percent between 2007 and 2012 while purity has increased. Meth seizures at the border have jumped from just over 2,000 kilograms to more than 10,000 kilograms. With the help tutorials on the Internet, small meth labs have sprung up around the country, although estimates report that 90 percent of the meth for sale on the streets in the United States is still made in Mexico.

Marijuana and the effects of legalization

In recent years, drug channels have shifted some as the popularity of the Internet has surged. There are numerous ways to find and order illicit drugs online and even have them delivered by mail to your doorstep. Most common, perhaps, are synthetic and designer drugs that often contain legal and unregulated chemicals. The most popular among these designer drugs are synthetic cannabinoids and synthetic cathinones.

Synthetic cannabinoids, called "Spice," "K2," and "fake weed," contain high levels of tetrahydrocannabinol, or THC, the active ingredient in marijuana, although the THC in these dangerous designer drugs is often up to 100 times more potent than what you might find in traditional pot. Spice is sold as "incense" or "potpourri" in local head shops, gas stations, and on the Internet, often escaping regulation due to labeling that markets the plant-based material sprayed with synthetic drugs as "not intended for human consumption." Synthetic cathinones, called "bath salts," are hallucinogenic drugs that may mimic LSD or ecstasy, and they are sold as "jewelry cleaner" or "plant food."

In 2012, the Synthetic Drug Abuse Prevention Act was passed, regulating some of the mind-altering chemicals used to manufacture Spice and bath salts in illicit laboratories. These chemicals are often imported from China and come in hundreds of varieties. As one chemical is controlled, inventive drug distributors and producers discover and market another. The Internet is rife with ways to abuse these drugs, where to find them, and even a ranking system on which are the best.

An overdose on these designer drugs can be very unpredictable and can lead to paranoid delusions, aggression, hostility, psychosis, and anxiety as well as cause nausea, vomiting, an irregular heart rate, and heightened blood pressure and body temperatures. Poison control call centers received over a thousand calls related to adverse reactions to Spice products in the first few weeks of April 2015 alone. Spice abuse has decreased in the past few years as it becomes more difficult to obtain the psychoactive chemicals with them becoming more tightly controlled and their status switching from legal to illegal. Still one in 20 high school students admitted to using Spice in 2014.

In 2013, over 24 million Americans aged 12 and older were current illicit drug users, meaning they had abused drugs in the month prior to the national survey.

The U.S. Drug Enforcement Administration, or DEA, employs over 9,000 men and women, and strives to curb the flow of drugs into America and their distribution domestically. From 2005-2014, the DEA has successfully stemmed almost $30 billion dollars in revenue from drug traffickers.

Prison populations are full of drug offenders and abusers who committed their crimes while on drugs. In 2004, a national survey found that 32 percent of all state prisoners and 26 percent of federal prisoners admitted to being under the influence of drugs when they committed their most current offense. Additionally in 2007, approximately 1.8 million people were arrested for drug abuse offenses. Many of these offenders could benefit from treatment instead of incarceration.

How Illicit Drug Use Affects Business and the Economy

The Federal Government and business community are increasingly recognizing the negative consequences of substance abuse on the U.S. economy and the Nation's workforce. Abuse of drugs and alcohol is costly for our society and, left untreated, places a burden on our workplace, our healthcare system, and our communities. A number of reports and surveys highlight the detrimental effects substance abuse has on business productivity and competitiveness as it also increases workplace injuries and absenteeism.

The following data provide a stark illustration of consequences of drug use in our society.

Economic Costs

The economic cost of drug abuse in the United States was estimated at $193 billion in 2007,1 the last available estimate. This value includes:

$120 billion in lost productivity, mainly due to labor participation costs, participation in drugabuse treatment, incarceration, and premature death;

$11 billion in healthcare costs – for drug treatment and drug‐related medical consequences; and

$61 billion in criminal justice costs, primarily due to criminal investigation, prosecution and incarceration, and victim costs.

Labor Force

In 2009, the majority (67%) of current drug users aged 18 or older were employed, either full time (48%) or part time (19%), with the unemployed accounting for 13% and the remaining 21% not in the labor force.

Among full time workers aged 18 or older, nearly one in 12 (8%) reported past month (current) use of an illicit drug in 2009.3 Unemployed workers were twice as likely – one in six (17%) – to report current drug use in 2009.

Turnover and Absenteeism

From 2002 to 2004, full time workers aged 18 64 who reported current illicit drug use were more than twice as likely as those reporting no current illicit drug use to report they had worked for three or more employers in the past year (12.3% versus 5.1%).

In the same period, full time workers who were current drug users were more likely to report missing two or more workdays in the past month due to illness or injury, when compared with workers who were not current users (16.4% vs. 11.0%).

Full time workers who were current drug users also were about twice as likely as non users to skip one or more days of work in the past month (16.3% vs. 8.2%).

School Performance

Students who are not current marijuana users are more than twice as likely to report an average grade of "A" than those who are current users of marijuana (30.5% vs. 12.5%).

College students who use prescription stimulant medications for non medical purposes typically have lower grade point averages and are more likely to be heavy drinkers and users of other illicit drugs. They also are more likely to meet diagnostic criteria for dependence on alcohol and marijuana, skip class more frequently, and spend less time studying.

Resources Available for Employers to Create a Drug Free Workplace

Preventing drug use in the workplace and supporting employees in recovery are vital to ensuring a healthy, safe, and productive workforce. The Federal Government provides a number of resources to help employers create an alcohol and drug free policy for their companies:

Drug Free Workplace Advisor

Provides information for businesses about how to establish and maintain an alcohol and drug free workplace.

Employers' Kit to Developing a Drug Free Workplace

The Department of Health and Human Services has created this kit to assist employers in setting a drug free workplace policy.

Working Partners: Guidelines for Developing an Alcohol and Drug Free Workplace

The Department of Labor has created this guide with the help of industry partners to advise businesses wanting to create a drug free workplace policy.

State and Territory Laws

Many states have regulations that impact when, where, and how employers can implement drugfree workplace programs. Check this site for a summary of rules that apply to businesses in your state. http://www.dol.gov/asp/programs/drugs/said/StateLaws.asp

Substance Abuse Information Database

Learn about workplace substance abuse issues and develop drug free workplace programs.

Training and Educational Materials

Free posters, brochures, and presentation materials.

Sharing intelligence data

We manage what we call a Drugs Analysis File, which is a repository of intelligence shared by 114 countries on illicit regional and international drug trafficking, including:

- Transnational criminal networks, their members and associates;
- Telephone numbers, website addresses and other media linked to drug trafficking;
- Modus operandi;
- Financial information used to conceal or launder assets;
- Locations associated with criminal activities.

Unlike our criminal databases, the analysis file includes not only police data but also a wider range of information from international organizations, civil society and open sources to further identify potential links. This information helps law enforcement and government officials to make more informed decisions.

Project AMEAP assists national authorities to identify security threats and tackle organized crime groups engaged in illicit drug trafficking in Africa, the Middle East, and Asia and the Pacific.

It seeks to promote and strengthen the cooperation and the exchange of drug related intelligence between agencies, enabling countries to benefit from our global police databases. By increasing access to the flow of information generated by member countries in different regions, the likelihood of a successful investigation and prosecution is greatly improved.

The project, which is supported by the United Arab Emirates and the INTERPOL Foundation for a Safer World, comprises three major regional initiatives:

Africa

The project aims to address the trafficking of cocaine, heroin and synthetic drugs especially methamphetamine to and from Africa, and the illegal diversion of precursor chemicals for none licit usage.

We have set up a multi-disciplinary and joint agency approach that combines investigative support and capacity building. We work on the ground to help law enforcement officials to exchange data and conduct operations focusing on one or several targets in real-time, and in closed and secure environments.

Middle East and Gulf

We have created an operational platform to address the increased production and distribution of illicit drugs, in particular Captagon. This platform serves as an information and intelligence sharing mechanism for drug investigators in the region and focuses on identifying and targeting the criminal elements behind this illicit trade, about which very little is currently documented.

We also organize workshops and expert group meetings aimed at shedding some light on the Captagon market and the criminal organizations involved in its trade.

Asia and the Pacific

Criminals take advantage of technology such as the Internet/Darknet to maximize their profits in the production and distribution of synthetic drugs, such as ATS (amphetamine type stimulants) and NPS (New Psychoactive Substances, as well as to divert the precursor chemicals for the production of illicit drugs.

The project seeks to support the Asia Pacific countries in combatting drug trafficking by enhancing their operational and intelligence sharing capabilities. It specifically targets the production and trafficking of synthetic drugs and the diversion of precursor chemicals.

We organize training events and workshops, working group meetings, and we conduct joint regional and inter-regional operations to address the challenges, using the collection, exchange and analysis of data.

Why Do People Use Drugs?

People use drugs for various reasons, but they do not start taking drugs with the intention of becoming dependent on them. Although the first-time use is voluntary, continual use is often the result of physical changes in the brain.

Erik, a student in recovery from addiction, discusses why he used drugs.

Drugs affect the brain's reward system by producing an excess of dopamine, the chemical responsible for pleasurable feelings. Our brains are wired to make sure we repeat rewarding activities, including those associated with drug use. Feelings of pleasure from drug use cause the brain to associate drugs with rewards, which causes cravings.

Some reasons for drug use include:

- Feeling good
- Self-medicating
- Enhancing performance
- Fitting in

Over time, drug use can diminish self-control, making it difficult for people to stop.

Environmental Factors

Drugs provide a temporary sense of accomplishment, euphoric sensations and an overall feeling of self-confidence and satisfaction. Numerous factors at home or school can promote drug abuse.

Parental behaviors play an important role in whether a child experiments with drugs later in life. An unstable family environment with a lack of parental supervision often leads to neglected children. Quality of life can also influence drug addiction. Living in an impoverished community can increase the risk for drug abuse.

People ridden with stress and anxiety may feel the need to self-medicate with cannabis, stimulants or other drugs to lessen their worries. They assume that regular consumption of a drug will alleviate their problems. Similarly, some students and athletes take performance-enhancing drugs to keep up with the pressure of consistently playing well.

Adolescents are vulnerable to social pressure from their substance-using peers. Teens are impressionable and spend a lot of time with their peers. Those who use drugs often push their peers to experiment. According to NIDA, the majority of first-time drug users are in their teens.

Biological Factors

According to NIDA, genetic factors are responsible for 40 to 60 percent of a person's vulnerability to drug addiction. Studies show that a person's predisposition to drug addiction positively correlates to their degree of genetic similarity to a relative who has a history of drug dependence or addiction. Mental disorders and medical conditions are also risk factors.

Are you looking for help with a drug addiction?

We tailor our treatment model around you to make sure you get the best possible care.

Consequences of Drug Abuse

Substance abuse has negative consequences that affect more than just the individual. Illicit drugs cost the United States about $193 billion every year in lost productivity, health costs and crime-related costs.

Health

The most direct repercussion of drug abuse is a decline in health. Death is the ultimate price of a substance use disorder. There is a drug-induced death in the United States every 13 minutes, according to a 2014 report by the Office of National Drug Control Policy.

One of the major health concerns related to drug use is a lack of hygienic practices, which can lead to the contraction of HIV, AIDS and hepatitis.

- Cardiovascular disease
- Stroke
- Cancer
- Lung disease
- Mental disorders
- Neonatal abstinence syndrome (withdrawal symptoms in the babies of drug addicts)

In 2011, more than 1.3 million patients visited the emergency department for a drug-related incident. Cocaine was involved in more than half a million visits.

Society

Illicit drug use and production have a negative impact on society and the environment.

- Chemical toxicity risks to people who live nearby
- Risk of fire or explosion to houses in the immediate vicinity

- Long-term effects of toxic waste on the environment
- Cleaning a laboratory that produces methamphetamines is costly. Rehabilitating children who have been exposed to chemicals used to make meth requires special training and resources. This takes time and labor that officials could spend on other issues.

Drug users rarely consider the dangers of improperly disposing of drugs or paraphernalia. The disposal of needles and drug-related materials contributes to environmental pollution.

Illicit drug users need intensive treatment after prolonged drug use. In 2012, 23.1 million substance users needed treatment, according to the Office of National Drug Control Policy. Treatment for drug addiction can affect the cost of social services and government resources, increasing the burden on taxpayers.

Relationships

New behavioral patterns that stem from drug use can harm relationships. Procuring their drug of choice becomes the drug user's primary concern. This often leads them to steal from their friends, family or workplace to afford more drugs, which damages trust among their peers.

Parents who use drugs often neglect or abuse their children. Poor familial conditions are harmful to children and may pave the way for future drug use.

Teenage drug abusers rarely graduate from school as a result of poor academic performance. Their academic and social skills suffer, causing tension within the family. They often distance themselves from friends and gravitate toward their substance-using peers.

Legal

Drug addiction can predispose people to commit crimes. It is illegal to acquire or possess illicit drugs, and people often resort to theft or other crimes to pay for them.

Research shows drug use is more common among arrestees than the general population. The Office of National Drug Control Policy reported that 63 to 83 percent of people arrested in five major metropolitan areas in 2013 tested positive for at least one illicit drug. The three most common drugs present during tests were marijuana, cocaine and opiates, and many people tested positive for multiple drugs.

Furthermore, a 2004 Bureau of Justice Statistics survey among inmates in correctional facilities showed that 32 percent of state inmates and 26 percent of federal prisoners revealed that they were under the influence of drugs when they committed the offense for which they were arrested.

Seeking Help for Drug Addiction

Treating a drug use disorder is not easy. Long-term drug use can change the brain in such a way that it becomes incapable of discerning when it needs to stop. Specialized treatment can break the cycle of drug abuse and the dangerous behaviors that ensue.

Nanci Stockwell of Advanced Recovery Systems explains the importance of receiving professional treatment for drug addiction.

Treatment extends far beyond stopping drug use. In some cases, the withdrawal period may be life-threatening, hence requiring medical supervision.

- Five Steps of Substance Use Disorder Treatment
- Detoxification
- Behavioral counseling
- Medication-assisted treatment
- Evaluation and treatment for co-occurring disorders
- Long-term plan for relapse prevention
- Every patient has different treatment needs, so it is important to have a specialized treatment plan.

Some people may resist drug treatment and refuse to go to a rehabilitation facility. If necessary, family members, employers or the criminal justice system can require them to get treatment.

Behavioral Therapy

Behavioral therapies are beneficial to recovering patients because they can help change one's perspective regarding their former drug use and life. Therapists also promote healthy and positive life practices and recommend medication when necessary to aid in detox and treatment.

Outpatient Behavioral Treatment

Outpatient programs can be beneficial for people who want to be around their friends and family while they receive substance abuse treatment.

Multidimensional family therapy: This family-based approach focuses on adolescent drug use and involves parents to promote group healing.

Motivational interviewing: Using this approach, therapists help patients explore their inner motivations to change their drug-using behavior and disregard for the dangers of substance abuse.

Motivational incentives: Therapists use positive reinforcement to encourage patients to stay away from drugs.

Outpatient programs typically occur several times weekly; however, they can decrease in frequency depending on the patient's progress.

Inpatient Treatment

Inpatient treatment, also known as residential treatment, provides severely dependent patients with a safe haven and round-the-clock services. Daily therapy sessions may be beneficial to people suffering from co-occurring disorders.

Residential treatment may involve therapeutic communities where patients stay at the facility for six to 12 months. A treatment staff and other patients in recovery provide the appropriate support to deter future substance use.

Arguments for and against drug prohibition

Arguments about the prohibition of drugs, and over drug policy reform, are subjects of considerable controversy. The following is a presentation of major drugs policy arguments, including those for drug law enforcement on one side of the debate, and arguments for drug law reform on the other. Arguments for and against drug prohibition discuss which system is more effective to protects human rights, prevent drug abuse and violence, and which system is more ethical.

Efficiency

Drug laws are effective

Supporters of prohibition claim that drug laws have a successful track record suppressing illicit drug use since they were introduced 100 years ago. The licit drug alcohol has current (last 12 months) user rates as high as 80–90% in populations over 14 years of age, and tobacco has historically had current use rates up to 60% of adult populations, yet the percentages currently using illicit drugs in OECD countries are generally below 1% of the population excepting cannabis where most are between 3% and 10%, with six countries between 11% and 17%.

In the 50-year period following the first 1912 international convention restricting use of opium, heroin and cocaine, the United States' use of illicit drugs other than cannabis was consistently below 0.5% of the population, with cannabis rising to 1–2% of the population between 1955 and 1965. With the advent of the counter-culture movement from the late 1950s, where illicit drug use was promoted as mind-expanding and relatively harmless, illicit drug use rose sharply. With illicit drug use peaking in the 1970s in the United States, the «Just Say No» campaign, initiated under the patronage of Nancy Reagan, coincided with recent (past month) illicit drug use decreases from 14.1% in 1979 to 5.8% in 1992, a drop of 60%.

In March, 2007, Antonio Maria Costa, former executive director of the United Nations Office on Drugs and Crime, drew attention to the drug policy of Sweden, arguing:

Sweden is an excellent example. Drug use is just a third of the European average while spending on drug control is three times the EU average. For three decades,Sweden has had consistent and coherent drug-control policies, regardless of which party is in power. There is a strong emphasis on prevention, drug laws have been progressively tightened, and extensive treatment and rehabilitation opportunities are available to users. The police take drug crime seriously. Governments and societies must keep their nerve and avoid being swayed by misguided notions of tolerance. They must not lose sight of the fact that illicit drugs are dangerous – that is why the world agreed to restrict them.

In Europe, Sweden spends the second highest percentage of GDP, after the Netherlands, on drug control. The UNODC argues that when Sweden reduced spending on education and rehabilitation in the 1990s in a context of higher youth unemployment and declining GDP growth, illicit drug use rose but restoring expenditure from 2002 again sharply decreased drug use as student surveys indicate. In 1998, a poll run by SIFO of 1,000 Swedes found that 96% wanted stronger action by government to stop drug abuse, and 95% wanted drug use to remain illegal.

Criticizing governments that have relaxed their drug laws, Antonio Maria Costa, speaking in Washington before the launch of the World Drug Report in June 2006, said:

After so many years of drug control experience, we now know that a coherent, long-term strategy can reduce drug supply, demand and trafficking. If this does not happen, it will be because some nations fail to take the drug issue sufficiently seriously and pursue inadequate policies. Many countries have the drug problem they deserve.

Inefficiency

Drug laws are ineffective

One of the prominent early critics of prohibition in the United States was August Vollmer, founder of the School of Criminology at University of California, Irvine and former president of the International Association of Chiefs of Police. In his 1936 book The Police and Modern Society, he stated his opinion that:

Stringent laws, spectacular police drives, vigorous prosecution, and imprisonment of addicts and peddlers have proved not only useless and enormously expensive as means of correcting this evil, but they are also unjustifiably and unbelievably cruel in their application to the unfortunate drug victims. Repression has driven this vice underground and produced the narcotic smugglers and supply agents, who have grown wealthy out of this evil practice and who, by devious methods, have stimulated traffic in drugs. Finally, and not the least of the evils associated with repression, the helpless addict has been forced to resort to crime in order to get money for the drug which is absolutely indispensable for his comfortable existence.

The first step in any plan to alleviate this dreadful affliction should be the establishment of Federal control and dispensation – at cost – of habit-forming drugs. With the profit motive gone, no effort would be made to encourage its use by private dispensers of narcotics, and the drug peddler would disappear. New addicts would be speedily discovered and through early treatment, some of these unfortunate victims might be saved from becoming hopelessly incurable.

Drug addiction, like prostitution, and like liquor, is not a police problem; it never has been, and never can be solved by policemen. It is first and last a medical problem, and if there is a solution it will be discovered not by policemen, but by scientific and competently trained medical experts whose sole objective will be the reduction and possible eradication of this devastating appetite. There should be intelligent treatment of the incurables in outpatient clinics, hospitalization of those not too far gone to respond to therapeutic measures, and application of the prophylactic principles which medicine applies to all scourges of mankind.

Stephen Rolles, writing in the British Medical Journal, argues:

Consensus is growing within the drugs field and beyond that the prohibition on production, supply, and use of certain drugs has not only failed to deliver its intended goals but has been counterproductive. Evidence is mounting that this policy has not only exacerbated many public health problems, such as adulterated drugs and the spread of HIV and hepatitis B and C infection among injecting drug users, but has created a much larger set of secondary harms associated with the criminal market. These now include vast networks of organised crime, endemic violence related to the drug market, corruption of law enforcement and governments.

These conclusions have been reached by a succession of committees and reports including, in the United Kingdom alone, the Police Foundation, the Home Affairs Select Committee, the Prime Minister's Strategy Unit, the Royal Society of Arts, and the UK Drug Policy Consortium. The United Nations Office of Drugs and Crime has also acknowledged the many "unintended negative consequences" of drug enforcement.

The editor of the British Medical Journal, Dr. Fiona Godlee, gave her personal support to Rolles' call for decriminalisation, and the arguments drew particular support from Sir Ian Gilmore, former president of the Royal College of Physicians, who said we should be treating drugs "as a health issue rather than criminalising people" and "this could drastically reduce crime and improve health".

Danny Kushlik, head of external affairs at Transform, said the intervention of senior medical professionals was significant. He said: "Sir Ian's statement is yet another nail in prohibition's coffin. The Hippocratic oath says: 'First, do no harm'. Physicians are duty bound to speak out if the outcomes show that prohibition causes more harm than it reduces."

Nicholas Green, chairman of the Bar Council, made comments in a report in the profession's magazine, in which he said that drug-related crime costs the UK economy about £13bn a year and that there was growing evidence that decriminalisation could free up police resources, reduce crime and recidivism and improve public health.

A report sponsored by the New York County Lawyers' Association, one of the largest local bar associations in the United States, argues on the subject of US drug policy:

Notwithstanding the vast public resources expended on the enforcement of penal statutes against users and distributors of controlled substances, contemporary drug policy appears to have failed, even on its own terms, in a number of notable respects. These include: minimal reduction in the consumption of controlled substances; failure to reduce violent crime; failure to markedly reduce drug importation, distribution and street-level drug sales; failure to reduce the widespread availability of drugs to potential users; failure to deter individuals from becoming involved in the drug trade; failure to impact upon the huge profits and financial opportunity available to individual "entrepreneurs" and organized underworld organizations through engaging in the illicit drug trade; the expenditure of great amounts of increasingly limited public resources in pursuit of a cost-intensive "penal" or "law-enforcement" based policy; failure to provide meaningful treatment and other assistance to substance abusers and their families; and failure to provide meaningful alternative economic opportunities to those attracted to the drug trade for lack of other available avenues for financial advancement.

Moreover, a growing body of evidence and opinion suggests that contemporary drug policy, as pursued in recent decades, may be counterproductive and even harmful to the society whose public safety it seeks to protect. This conclusion becomes more readily apparent when one distinguishes the harms suffered by society and its members directly attributable to the pharmacological effects of drug use upon human behavior, from those harms resulting from policies attempting to eradicate drug use.

With aid of these distinctions, we see that present drug policy appears to contribute to the increase of violence in our communities. It does so by permitting and indeed, causing the drug trade to remain a lucrative source of economic opportunity for street dealers, drug kingpins and all those willing to engage in the often violent, illicit, black market trade.

Meanwhile, the effect of present policy serves to stigmatize and marginalize drug users, thereby inhibiting and undermining the efforts of many such individuals to remain or become productive, gainfully employed members of society. Furthermore, current policy has not only failed to provide adequate access to treatment for substance abuse, it has, in many ways, rendered the obtaining of such treatment, and of other medical services, more difficult and even dangerous to pursue.

In response to claims that prohibition can work, as argued by Antonio Maria Costa, executive director of the United Nations Office on Drugs and Crime, who drew attention to the drug policy of Sweden, Henrik Tham has written that sometimes it's domestically important to stress drug policy as successful; in the case of Sweden, where this notion is important, such claims serve "the function of strengthening a threatened national identity in a situation where the traditional 'Swedish model' has come under increasingly hard attack from both inside and outside the country." Tham questions the success of the Swedish model – "The shift in Swedish drug policy since around 1980" ...(more difficult to receive nolle prosequifor minor drug crimes) ..."towards a more strict model has according to the official point of view been successful by comparison with the earlier, more lenient drug policy. However, available systematic indicators show that the prevalence of drug use has increased since around 1980, that the decrease in drug incidence was particularly marked during the 1970s and that some indicators point towards an increase during the 1990s."

Leif Lenke and Börje Olsson from Stockholm University have conducted research that showed how drug use have followed the youth unemployment in close correlation. They noted that unlike most of Europe, Sweden did not have widespread and lingering youth unemployment until the early 1990s financial crisis, suggesting that unattractive future prospects may contribute to the increase in drug use among the young. CAN, the Swedish Council for Information on Alcohol and Other Drugs, 2009 report stated that the increase in drug use have continued since the 1990s with a slight dip in the mid-2000.

The professor emeritus in criminology at the University of Oslo, Nils Christie, pointed out Sweden as the hawk of international drug policy in a 2004 book. He said that Sweden is serving the role of being welfare alibi for, and lending legitimacy to, the US drug war. Adding that USA and Sweden have had an extraordinary influence on UNODC as the biggest donor countries. Sweden was the second biggest donor financing 8% of the UNODC budget behind the European Commission in 2006, followed by the US. In 2007 and 2008 Sweden was the fourth biggest donor, behind the European Commission, USA and Canada. In 2009 it was the third, as USA withdrew some of its funding.

An editorial in The Economist argued:

fear [of legalisation] is based in large part on the presumption that more people would take drugs under a legal regime. That presumption may be wrong. There is no correlation between the harshness of drug laws and the incidence of drug-taking: citizens living under tough regimes (notably America but also Britain) take more drugs, not fewer. Embarrassed drug warriors blame this on alleged cultural differences, but even in fairly similar countries tough rules make little difference to the number of addicts: harsh Sweden and more liberal Norway have precisely the same addiction rates.

Antonio Maria Costa's conviction that "countries have the drug problem they deserve" if they fail to follow the 'Swedish Model' in drug control has also been criticised in Peter Cohen's work – Looking at the UN, smelling a rat.

In its 2011 report, the Global Commission on Drug Policy stated that «The global war on drugs has failed, with devastating consequences for individuals and societies around the world».

Deterrence

Arguments that prohibition discourages drug use

A 2001 Australian study, of 18- to 29-year-olds by the NSW Bureau of Crime Statistics and Research suggests that prohibition deters illicit drug use. 29% of those who had never used cannabis cited the illegality of the substance as their reason for never using the drug, while 19% of those who had ceased use of cannabis cited its illegality as their reason.

Gil Kerlikowske, Director of the US ONDCP argues,

Controls and prohibitions help to keep prices higher, and higher prices help keep use rates relatively low, since drug use, especially among young people, is known to be sensitive to price. The relationship between pricing and rates of youth substance use is well-established with respect to alcohol and cigarette taxes. There is literature showing that increases in the price of cigarettes triggers declines in use."

The DEA argues "Legalization has been tried before—and failed miserably. Alaska's experiment with legalization in the 1970s led to the state's teens using marijuana at more than twice the rate of other youths nationally. This led Alaska's residents to vote to re-criminalize marijuana in 1990."

Drug Free Australia has cited the Netherlands as an example of drug policy failure because it is soft in approach. They argue that the Dutch idea of going soft on cannabis dealers, thereby creating a «separation of markets» from hard drug dealers has failed to stem the initiation to drugs such as heroin, cocaine, and amphetamines, saying that, in 1998, the Netherlands had the third highest cannabis and cocaine use in Europe. According to Barry McCaffrey of the US Office of National Drug Control Policy, Dutch tolerance has allowed the Netherlands to become a criminal epicentre for illicit synthetic drug manufacture, particularly ecstasy, as well as the home for production and worldwide export of strains of cannabis with THC reportedly 10 times higher than normal. Gil Kerlikowske has attested that, where there were once thousands of cannabis cafés there are now only several hundred. Levels of cannabis use, in 2005 only marginally higher than in 1998, while other European countries have accelerated past them, are more likely, Drug Free Australia argues, the result of a growing intolerance of cannabis in the Netherlands rather than a growing tolerance. Drug Free Australia has also argued that British reductions in cannabis use after softer legislation may be more so the result of heavy UK media exposure of the stronger evidence of links between cannabis and psychosis

Arguments that prohibition does not discourage drug use

It has been suggested that drug law reform could reduce the use of hard drugs as it has in countries such as the Netherlands. According to a 2009 annual report by the European Monitoring Centre for Drugs and Drug Addiction, the Dutch are among the lowest users of marijuana or cannabis in Europe, despite the Netherlands' policy on soft drugs being one of the most liberal in Europe, allowing for the sale of marijuana at "coffee shops", which the Dutch have allowed to operate for decades, and possession of less than 5 grams (0.18 oz).

British Crime Survey statistics indicated that the proportion of 16- to 24-year-olds using cannabis decreased from 28% a decade ago to 21%, with its declining popularity accelerating after the decision to downgrade the drug to class C was announced in January 2004. The BCS figures, published in October 2007, showed that the proportion of frequent users in the 16–24 age group (i.e. who were using cannabis more than once a month), fell from 12% to 8% in the past four years.

American teenagers are drinking and smoking less and doing fewer drugs than their predecessors in more than 40 years of tracking. Use of marijuana is down among 8th- and 10th-graders, though it is flat among high school seniors, according to the annual Monitoring the Future survey of American teens.

Arguments that cannabis is a gateway drug

The US Drug Enforcement Agency's "2008 Marijuana Sourcebook" argues that recent research supports the gateway hypothesis that certain drugs (such as cannabis) act as gateways to use of 'harder' drugs such as heroin, either because of social contact or because of an increasing search for a better high. Proponents cite studies such as that of 311 same sex twins, where only one twin smoked cannabis before age 17, and where such early cannabis smokers were five times more likely than their twin to move on to harder drugs.

Arguments that cannabis is not a gateway drug

In the American Journal of Public Health, Andrew Golub and Bruce Johnson of the National Development and Research Institute in New York wrote that young people who smoked marijuana in the generations before and after the baby boomers did not appear to be likely to move on to harder drugs.

Researchers from the independent Rand Drug Policy Research Center in Santa Monica, California, looking at data from the National Household Survey on Drug Abuse between 1982 and 1994, concluded that teenagers who took hard drugs did so whether they had first tried cannabis or not.

A twin study (of 510 same sex twin pairs) which adjusted for additional confounders such as peer drug use, found that cannabis use and associations with later hard drug use existed only for non-identical twins. The study suggested that a causal role of cannabis use in later hard drug usage is minimal, if it exists at all, and that cannabis use and hard drug use share the same influencing factors such as genetics and environment.

Health

Health arguments for drug laws

Advocates of prohibition argue that particular drugs should be illegal because they are harmful. Drug Free Australia for example argues "That illicit drugs are inherently harmful substances is attested by the very nomenclature of the 'harm reduction' movement." The U.S. government has argued that illegal drugs are «far more deadly than alcohol" saying "although alcohol is used by seven times as many people as drugs, the number of deaths induced by those substances is not far apart. According to the Centers for Disease Control and Prevention (CDC), during 2000, there were 15,852 drug-induced deaths; only slightly less than the 18,539 alcohol-induced deaths." Ratios of the harms of illicit opiates to licit alcohol and tobacco in Australia are similar, with 2 deaths per hundred opiate users per annum versus 0.22 deaths per hundred for alcohol (9 times less) per year and 0.3 for tobacco (7 times less).

The DEA has said:

Marijuana is far more powerful than it used to be. In 2000, there were six times as many emergency room mentions of marijuana use as there were in

1990, despite the fact that the number of people using marijuana is roughly the same. In 1999, a record 225,000 Americans entered substance abuse treatment primarily for marijuana dependence, second only to heroin—and not by much. ... According to the National Institute on Drug Abuse, "Studies show that someone who smokes five joints per week may be taking in as many cancer-causing chemicals as someone who smokes a full pack of cigarettes every day." Marijuana contains more than 400 chemicals, including the most harmful substances found in tobacco smoke. For example, smoking one marijuana cigarette deposits about four times more tar into the lungs than a filtered tobacco cigarette. ... The short-term effects are also harmful. They include: memory loss, distorted perception, trouble with thinking and problem solving, loss of motor skills, decrease in muscle strength, increased heart rate, and anxiety. Marijuana impacts young people's mental development, their ability to concentrate in school, and their motivation and initiative to reach goals. And marijuana affects people of all ages: Harvard University researchers report that the risk of a heart attack is five times higher than usual in the hour after smoking marijuana.

Many of the deaths from using cannabis, other than from car accidents while intoxicated or violence and aggression, are more likely to figure in the longer term, just as with tobacco, where both nicotine overdose and cannabis overdose are extremely rare or nonexistent. While ecstasy may have lower rates of immediate mortality than some other illicits, there is a growing science on the already recognized considerable health harms of ecstasy. Drug Free Australia argues that distinctions between «soft» and «hard» drugs are entirely artificial, and titling cannabis «soft» or ecstasy «recreational» does not lessen the extensive harms of these substances.

Gil Kerlikowske, director of the US Office of National Drug Control Policy (ONDCP) argues that in the United States, illegal drugs already cost $180 billion a year in health care, lost productivity, crime, and other expenditures, and that number would only increase under legalization because of increased use.

Drug Free Australia claims arguments that increased health harms of illicit drugs are the result of lack of government regulation of their purity and strength are not well supported by evidence. In Australia, which has had the highest opioid mortality per capita in the OECD, studies found that «overdose fatality is not a simple function of heroin dose or purity. There is no evidence of toxicity from contaminants of street heroin in Australia.» Drug Free Australia claims that other causes of death such as suicide, murder and accidents are an effect of the drug themselves, not of their purity or otherwise.

Addiction

Drug Free Australia argues "Regarding the freedom of choice of those addicted to a drug, it is important to recognize that addiction is defined as compulsive by its very nature and that addictions curb individual freedom." ... "As is the case with alcohol addiction, illicit drug addictions likewise serve to keep many such users functionally in poverty and often as a continued burden on friends, family and society. Where it is argued that all disabilities are a burden on society it must be recognized that most disabilities are not the result of a choice, whereas the decision to recreationally use illicit drugs is most commonly free, and with the knowledge that they may lead to an abundance of addictions."

Health arguments for drug law reform

There is evidence that many illicit drugs pose comparatively fewer health dangers than certain legal drugs. The health risks of MDMA (Ecstasy) have been exaggerated for instance, the risks from cannabis use also overstated, and health problems from the use of legal substances, particularly alcohol and tobacco, are greater, even than from cocaine use for example (occasional cocaine use does not typically lead to severe or even minor physical or social problems).

Health benefits

Many trials have shown beneficial effects associated with psychoactive drug use:

- There is evidence that MDMA (ecstasy) can treat or cure post-traumatic stress disorder and anxiety in cases of terminal illness.
- LSD has been widely researched as a therapeutic agent, and has shown effectiveness against alcoholism, frigidity and various other disorders. See Psychedelic therapy.
- Researchers at Harvard-affiliated McLean Hospital found members of a religious group regularly using peyote scored significantly better on several measures of overall mental health than did subjects who did not use the hallucinogen.
- A 2007 study, by Santos et al. found that users of ayahuasca scored better on tests measuring anxiety and hopelessness than people who did not use the drug.

Quality control

According to a World Health Organisation report: "As cannabis is an illegal drug its cultivation, harvesting and distribution are not subject to quality control mechanisms to ensure the reliability and safety of the product used by consumers. It is well recognised in developing countries, such as Kenya, that illicit alcohol production can result in the contamination with toxic by-products or adulterants that can kill or seriously affect the health of users. The same may be true of illicit drugs such as opiates, cocaine and amphetamine in developed societies."

The government cannot enforce quality control on products sold and manufactured illegally. Examples include: the easier to make derivative MDA being sold as MDMA, heroin users unintentionally injecting brick dust, quinine, or fentanyl with which their heroin had been cut; and heroin/cocaine overdoses occurring as a result of users not knowing exactly how much they are taking.

The illegality of injectable drugs leads to a scarcity of needles which causes an increase in HIV infections. An easy cure to this problem, while upholding the illegality of drugs, is the Dutch policy of distributing free needles. The money spent on both increased health costs due to HIV infections and drug prohibition itself causes a drain upon society.

Studies on the effects of prescribing heroin to addicts as practiced in many European countries have shown better rates of success than any other available treatment in terms of assisting long-term users establish stable, crime-free lives. Many patients were able to find employment, some even started a family after years of homelessness and delinquency.

Block to research

The illegality of many recreational drugs may be dissuading research into new, more effective and perhaps safer recreational drugs. For example, it has been proposed that a drug with many of the same desired effects as alcohol could be created with fewer adverse health effects.

Potency Effect

The risk of punishment when producing, selling, or using a drug that is prohibited or highly regulated leads to an added cost for anyone who still chooses to engage in illicit trade on a black market. Anyone doing business producing or trading a prohibited substance will incur the same risk of being caught regardless of how strong (potent) the substance. Thus, dealers and producers will always prefer to transport and trade drugs that are as potent as possible. It is more profitable with the same risk.

Moreover, because of this economic incentive, over time the potency of illegal drugs will increase with new methods of production. The potency effect was clearly demonstrated during alcohol prohibition in the US with the advent of highly distilled liquors like moonshine. It is also clearly evident in marijuana production today with the use of hydroponic growing methods.

The potency effect is particularly dangerous from a health perspective because lower doses can have greater effects than the user expects which can be harmful or fatal. And very often highly concentrated drugs will be "cut" with unknown substances in order to dilute their effects.

Misleading health statistics

The United States Drug Enforcement Administration (DEA) has suggested that illegal drugs are "far more deadly than alcohol", arguing that "although alcohol is used by seven times as many people as drugs, the number of deaths induced by those substances is not far apart", quoting figures from the Centers for Disease Control and Prevention (CDC), claiming «during 2000, there were 15,852 drug-induced deaths; only slightly less than the 18,539 alcohol-induced deaths.»

The DEA's use of such figures is questionable however. An article in the Journal of the American Medical Association gave the number deaths caused by alcohol in year 2000 as 85,000 – over four and a half times greater than the

DEA's preferred figure. The DEA's argument also overlooks tobacco, causing 435,000 US deaths in year 2000. And, the CDC definition of «drug-induced death» includes suicides using drugs, accidental overdose, and deaths from medically prescribed (not illegal) drugs. An analysis of drug-induced deaths for the 20-year period 1979–1998 found the vast majority attributable to accidental overdose, and suicide by drug taking, which together account for about 76 percent of all such deaths. Taking into account deaths from non-illegal drugs leaves only 21 percent of CDC «drug-induced death» figures actually due to the use of «illegal» drugs.

Claims that cannabis is far more powerful than it used to be are also dubious, with "scare figures" skewed by comparing the weakest cannabis from the past with the strongest of today. Figures regarding emergency room mentions of marijuana use can be misleading too, as «mention» of a drug in an emergency department visit does not mean that the drug was the cause of the visit.

Medical uses

A document published for the non-profit advocacy organization Europe Against Drugs (EURAD) argues that «one cannot vote for a medicine» and that a scientific approval basis is essential. It says that EU rules set out strict criteria for the acceptance of a drug for medical use:

All active ingredients have to be identified and their chemistry determined. They have to be tested for purity with limits set for all impurities including pesticides, microbe & fungi and their products. These tests have to be validated and reproduced if necessary in an official laboratory. Animal testing will include information on fertility, embryo toxicity, immuno-toxicity, mutagenic and carcinogenic potential. Risks to humans, especially pregnant women and lactating mothers, will be evaluated. Adequate safety and efficacy trials must be carried out. They must state the method of administration and report on the results from different groups, i.e. healthy volunteers, patients, special groups of the elderly, people with liver and kidney problems and pregnant women. Adverse drug reactions (ADR) have to be stated and include any effects on driving or operating machinery.

Arguments against medical uses of prohibited drugs

According to Janet D. Lapey, M.D., of Concerned Citizens For Drug Prevention, " Due to a placebo effect, a patient may erroneously believe a drug is helpful when it is not. This is especially true of addictive, mind-altering drugs like marijuana. A marijuana withdrawal syndrome occurs, consisting of anxiety, depression, sleep and appetite disturbances, irritability, tremors, diaphoresis, nausea, muscle convulsions, and restlessness. Often, persons using marijuana erroneously believe that the drug is helping them combat these symptoms without realizing that actually marijuana is the cause of these effects. Therefore, when a patient anecdotally reports a drug to have medicinal value, this must be followed by objective scientific studies."

The US Drug Enforcement Administration also says:

There is a growing misconception that some illegal drugs can be taken safely. For example, savvy drug dealers have learned how to market drugs like Ecstasy to youth. Some in the Legalization Lobby even claim such drugs have medical value, despite the lack of conclusive scientific evidence.

Arguments for medical uses of prohibited drugs

Most of the psychoactive drugs now prohibited in modern societies have had medical uses in history. In natural plant drugs like opium, coca, cannabis, mescaline, and psilocybin, the medical history usually dates back thousands of years and through a variety of cultures.

Psychedelics such as LSD and psilocybin (the main ingredient in most hallucinogenic mushrooms) are the subject of renewed research interest because of their therapeutic potential. They could ease a variety of difficult-to-treat mental illnesses, such as chronic depression, post-traumatic stress disorder, and alcohol dependency. MDMA (Ecstasy) has been used for cognitive enhancement in people with Parkinson›s disease, and has shown potential in treating posttraumatic stress disorder.

Lack of access to controlled medications

Under prohibition, millions of people find it very difficult to obtain controlled medications, particularly opiate pain-relievers. The United Nations 1961 Single Convention on Narcotic Drugs requires that opiates be distributed only by medical prescription, but this is impractical in many areas.

According to the Transnational Institute, June 2008:

According to the International Narcotics Control Board (INCB) and the World Health Organisation (WHO) there is now an unmet demand in opiates. Ironically, the current drug control regulations hamper access to controlled opiate medications for therapeutic use. Many patients are unable to access morphine, methadone or an equivalent opioid. Global medical morphine consumption would rise five times if countries would make morphine available at the level of the calculated need, according to a recent WHO estimate.

According to the New York Times, September 2007:

Under Sierra Leone law, morphine may be handled only by a pharmacist or doctor, explained Gabriel Madiye, the hospice's founder. But in all Sierra Leone there are only about 100 doctors — one for every 54,000 people, compared with one for every 350 in the United States.... "How can they say there is no demand when they don't allow it?" he [Madiye] asked. "How can they be so sure that it will get out of control when they haven't even tried it?"

Economic

Economic arguments for prohibitive drug laws

The DEA argues that "compared to the social costs of drug abuse and addiction—whether in taxpayer dollars or in pain and suffering—government spending on drug control is minimal."

Antonio Maria Costa, executive director of the United Nations Office on Drugs and Crime, has said:

The economic argument for drug legalization says: legalize drugs, and generate tax income. This argument is gaining favour, as national administrations seek new sources of revenue during the current economic crisis. This legalize and tax argument is un-ethical and uneconomical. It proposes a perverse tax, generation upon generation, on marginalized cohorts (lost to addiction) to stimulate economic recovery. Are the partisans of this cause also in favour of legalizing and taxing other seemingly intractable crimes like human trafficking? Modern-day slaves (and there are millions of them) would surely generate good tax revenue to rescue failed banks. The economic argument is also based on poor fiscal logic: any reduction in the cost of drug control (due to lower law enforcement expenditure) will be offset by much higher expenditure on public health (due to the surge of drug consumption). The moral of the story: don't make wicked transactions.

Gil Kerlikowske, current director of the US ONDCP, argues that legalizing drugs, then regulating and taxing their sale, would not be effective fiscally.

The tax revenue collected from alcohol pales in comparison to the costs associated with it. Federal excise taxes collected on alcohol in 2007, totaled around $9 billion; states collected around $5.5 billion. Taken together, this is less than 10 percent of the over $185 billion in alcohol-related costs from health care, lost productivity, and criminal justice. Tobacco also does not carry its economic weight when we tax it; each year we spend more than $200 billion on its social costs and collect only about $25 billion in taxes.

Former directors of the ONDCP, John P. Walters and Barry McCaffrey have accused billionaires George Soros, Peter Lewis and John Sperling of bankrolling the pro-pot or drug legalisation movement. «These people use ignorance and their overwhelming amount of money to influence the electorate", Walters said. Billionaire US financier, George Soros said in his autobiography, «I would establish a strictly controlled distribution network through which I would make most drugs, excluding the most dangerous ones like crack, legally available.» . The drug legalization lobby›s vigorous and well funded promotion in media and schools of a ‹safe use of illegal drugs› message indicates that drug prohibition is in the midst of a pitched battle waged by those who are accepting not only of the drug user but who also strongly promote an acceptance of drug use itself.

Prohibition of hemp industry

Opposition to the legalization of hemp, which uses plants of the cannabis genus for commercial purposes, centres on the fact that those wanting to legalize the use of cannabis for recreational and medical purposes themselves present it as their Trojan horse for that very purpose:

Alex Shum, importers of hemp fabric, "feel that the way to legalize marijuana is to sell marijuana legally. When you can buy marijuana in your neighbourhood shopping mall, IT'S LEGAL! So, they are going to produce every conceivable thing out of hemp.

In a Huffington Post interview, Mark Kleiman, the "Pot Czar" of Washington state, said he was concerned that the National Cannabis Industry Association would favor profits over public health. He also said that it could become a predatory body like the lobbying arms of the tobacco and alcohol industries. Kleiman said: «The fact that the National Cannabis Industry Association has hired itself a K Street suit [lobbyist] is not a good sign.»

Economic arguments for drug law reform

The United States efforts at drug prohibition started out with a $350 million budget in 1971, and was in 2006 a $30 billion campaign. These numbers only include direct prohibition enforcement expenditures, and as such only represent part of the total cost of prohibition. This $30 billion figure rises dramatically once other issues, such as the economic impact of holding 400,000 prisoners on prohibition violations, are factored in.

The war on drugs is extremely costly to such societies that outlaw drugs in terms of taxpayer money, lives, productivity, the inability of law enforcement to pursue mala in se crimes, and social inequality. Some proponents of decriminalization say that the financial and social costs of drug law enforcement far exceed the damages that the drugs themselves cause. For instance, in 1999, close to 60,000 prisoners (3.3% of the total incarcerated population) convicted of violating marijuana laws were behind bars at a cost to taxpayers of some $1.2 billion per year. In 1980, the total jail and prison population was 540,000, about one-quarter the size it is today. Drug offenders accounted for 6% of all prisoners. According to the Federal Bureau of Prisons, drug offenders now account for nearly 51%.

It has been argued that if the US government legalised marijuana it would save $7.7 billion per year in expenditure on enforcement of prohibition. Also, that marijuana legalization would yield tax revenue of $2.4 billion annually if it were taxed like all other goods and $6.2 billion annually if it were taxed at rates comparable to those on alcohol and tobacco.

The creation of drug cartels

Mass arrests of local growers of marijuana, for example, not only increase the price of local drugs, but lessens competition. Only major retailers that can handle massive shipments, have their own small fleet of aircraft, troops to defend the caravans and other sophisticated methods of eluding the police (such as lawyers), can survive by this regulation of the free market by the government

... it is because it's prohibited. See, if you look at the drug war from a purely economic point of view, the role of the government is to protect the drug cartel. That's literally true.

Effect on producer countries

The United States' "War on Drugs" has added considerably to the political instability in South America. The huge profits to be made from cocaine and other South American-grown drugs are largely because they are illegal in the wealthy neighbouring nation. This drives people in the relatively poor countries of Colombia, Peru, Bolivia and Brazil to break their own laws in organising the cultivation, preparation and trafficking of cocaine to the States. This has allowed criminal, paramilitary and guerrilla groups to reap huge profits, exacerbating already serious law-and-order and political problems. Within Bolivia, the political rise of current president Evo Morales is directly related to his grassroots movement against US-sponsored coca-eradication and criminalization policies. However, coca has been cultivated for centuries in the Andes. Among their various legitimate uses, coca leaves are chewed for their mild stimulant & appetite suppression effects, and steeped as a tea which is known to reduce the effects of human altitude sickness. Rural farmers in the poor regions in which coca has historically been cultivated often find themselves at the difficult and potentially violent intersection of government-sponsored eradication efforts, illegal cocaine producers & traffickers seeking coca supplies, anti-government paramilitary forces trafficking in cocaine as a source of revolutionary funding, and the historical hardships of rural subsistence farming (or its typical alternative – abandoning their land and fleeing to an urban slum). In some regions, farmers' coca and other crops are frequently destroyed by U.S.-sponsored eradication treatments (usually sprayed from the air with varying degrees of discrimination), whether or not the farmers directly supply the cocaine trade, thereby destroying their livelihoods. Agricultural producers in these countries are pushed further to grow coca for the cocaine trade by the dumping of subsidised farming products (fruit, vegetables, grain etc.) produced by Western countries (predominantly US and EU agricultural surpluses) (see BBC reference, below), which reduces the prices they could otherwise receive for alternate crops such as maize. The net effect can be a depression of prices for all crops, which can both make the farmer›s livelihood more precarious, and make the cocaine producers› coca supplies cheaper.

After providing a significant portion of the world's poppy for use in heroin production, Afghanistan went from producing practically no illegal drugs in 2000 (following banning by the Taliban), to cultivating what is now as much as 90% of the world's opium. The Taliban is currently believed to be heavily supported by the opium trade there.

Furthermore, the sale of the illegal drugs produces an influx of dollars that is outside the formal economy, and puts pressure on the currency exchange keeping the dollar low and making the export of legal products more difficult.

Prohibition of hemp industry

The War on Drugs has resulted in the outlawing of the entire hemp industry in the United States. Hemp, which is a special cultivar of Cannabis Sativa, does not have significant amounts of psychoactive (THC) substances in it, less than 1%. Without even realizing the plant had been outlawed several months prior, Popular Mechanics magazine published an article in 1938 entitled The New Billion-Dollar Crop anticipating the explosion of the hemp industry with the invention of machines to help process it. Recently, governmental refusal to take advantage of taxing hemp has been a point of criticism. Hemp has a large list of potential industrial uses including textiles, paper, rope, fuel, construction materials, and biocomposites (for use in cars for example). Hemp has some drawbacks, however, one being that the long fibers in hemp are only a part of the outer bast, and this has contributed to hemp having only modest commercial success in countries (for example in Canada) where it is legal to harvest hemp.

The seed of the hemp plant is highly nutritious. Rare for a plant, it contains all essential amino acids. Rare for any food, it is a good source of alpha-linolenic acid, an omega 3 fatty acid which is deficient in most diets.

Crime, terrorism and social order

Arguments for prohibitive drug laws

While concerns are sometimes expressed that the "war on drugs" can never be won, there is a failure to recognize that other justifiably costly policing wars such as "blitzes" on speeding can likewise never be won. Such blitzes reduce and contain speeding, as with policing of illicit drug use. Failure to police speeding drivers simply allows inordinate harm to be inflicted on other individuals. Speeding is not legalized simply because it can never be eradicated.

There is an argument that much crime and terrorism is drug related or drug funded and that prohibition should reduce this.

Former US president George W. Bush, in signing the Drug-Free Communities Act Reauthorization Bill in December 2001, said, «If you quit drugs, you join the fight against terror in America.»

The US Office of National Drug Control Policy (ONDCP) says that drug-related offences may include violent behavior resulting from drug effects.

The US Drug Enforcement Administration claims:

Crime, violence and drug use go hand in hand. Six times as many homicides are committed by people under the influence of drugs, as by those who are looking for money to buy drugs. Most drug crimes aren't committed by people trying to pay for drugs; they're committed by people on drugs.

The U.S. government began the Drug Use Forecasting (DUF) program in 1987 to collect information on drug use among urban arrestees. In 1997, the National Institute of Justice expanded and reengineered the DUF study and renamed it the Arrestee Drug Abuse Monitoring (ADAM) program. ADAM is a network of 34 research sites in select U.S. cities.

DUF research indicates that:

- Frequent use of hard drugs is one of the strongest indicators of a criminal career.
- Offenders who use drugs are among the most serious and active criminals, engaging in both property and violent crime.

- Early and persistent use of cocaine or heroin in the juvenile years is an indicator of serious, persistent criminal behavior in adulthood.
- Those arrested who are drug users are more likely than those not using drugs to be rearrested on pretrial release or fail to appear at trial.

Criminal behavior can importantly be the direct result of drug use which can cause emotional/brain damage, mental illness and anti-social behavior. Psychoactive drugs can have a powerful impact on behavior which may influence some people to commit crimes that have nothing to do with supporting the cost of their drug use. The use of drugs changes behavior and causes criminal activity because people will do things they wouldn›t do if they were rational and free of the drug›s influence. Cocaine-related paranoia is an example. If drug use increases with legalization, so will such forms of related violent crime as assaults, drugged driving, child abuse, and domestic violence.

That higher prices make the trade lucrative for criminals is recognized but countered by the argument that capitulating to illicit drug use on these grounds makes no more sense than capitulating to those who continue to traffic in human lives, a more expensive business because of its illegality and therefore more lucrative for the criminal, but necessary for the rights of vulnerable citizens.

The Office of National Drug Control Policy says that the idea that our nation's prisons are overflowing with otherwise law-abiding people convicted for nothing more than simple possession of marijuana is a myth, "an illusion conjured and aggressively perpetuated by drug advocacy groups seeking to relax or abolish America's marijuana laws." ONDCP state that the vast majority of inmates in state and federal prison for marijuana have been found guilty of much more than simple possession. Some were convicted for drug trafficking, some for marijuana possession along with one or more other offenses. And many of those serving time for marijuana pleaded down to possession in order to avoid prosecution on much more serious charges. In the US, just 1.6 percent of the state inmate population were held for offences involving only marijuana, and less than one percent of all state prisoners (0.7 percent) were incarcerated with marijuana possession as the only charge. An even smaller fraction of state prisoners were first time offenders (0.3 percent). The numbers on the US federal prisons are similar. In 2001, the overwhelming majority of offenders sentenced for marijuana crimes were convicted for trafficking and only 63 served time for simple possession.

Detective superintendent Eva Brännmark from the Swedish National Police Board, in a speech given to Drug Free Australia's first international conference on illicit drug use, said:

The police have been able to solve other crimes, e.g. burglaries, thefts and robberies, by questioning people arrested for using drugs. Some even provide information about people who are selling drugs, and the police have seized large amounts of drugs as a result of information from people brought in for a urine test. Many interrogations of drug abusers have also resulted in search warrants and the recovery of stolen property.

The argument that drug addicts of certain drugs are forced into crime by prohibition should first and foremost highlight the fact that this argument presupposes and underlines the addictive nature of some illicit drugs (which legalization proponents often downplay), addictive enough to create a viable criminal supply industry. Secondly, the harms of increased addictive drug use, which as previously outlined would be a consequence of legalization and its cheaper prices, far outweigh the current crime harms of prohibition. It is worth pointing out, this argument is not useful for substances such as LSD and mescaline, with no addictive properties.

Although criminal punishments vary with rooting out drug usage, it is not the foremost eradication technique to resolve drug abuse issues. In order to combat these issues, the application of treatment and support group resources coupled with community support and understanding, has far higher long-term potential to cure the ever-growing epidemic plaguing the nation, especially in rural areas.

Arguments for drug law reform

Violence and profits of drugs traffickers

Prohibition protects the drug cartel insofar as it keeps the distribution in the black market and creates the risk that makes smuggling profitable. As former federal narcotics officer Michael Levine states in relation to his undercover work with Colombian cocaine cartels, from Lamar

"I learned that not only did they not fear our war on drugs, they counted on it to increase the market price and to weed out the smaller, inefficient drug dealers. They found U.S. interdiction efforts laughable. The only U.S. action they feared was an effective demand reduction program. On one undercover tape-recorded conversation, a top cartel chief, Jorge Roman, expressed his gratitude for the drug war, calling it «a sham put on for the American taxpayer» that was actually «good for business».

Critics of drug prohibition often cite the fact that the end of alcohol prohibition in 1933 led to immediate decreases in murders and robberies to support the argument that legalization of drugs could have similar effects. Once those involved in the narcotics trade have a legal method of settling business disputes, the number of murders and violent crime could drop. Robert W. Sweet, a federal judge, strongly agrees: "The present policy of trying to prohibit the use of drugs through the use of criminal law is a mistake". When alcohol use was outlawed during prohibition, it gave rise to gang warfare and spurred the formation of some of the most well known criminals of the era, among them the infamous Al Capone. Similarly, drug dealers today resolve their disputes through violence and intimidation, something which legal drug vendors do not do. Prohibition critics also point to the fact that police are more likely to be corrupted in a system where bribe money is so available.

Police corruption due to drugs is widespread enough that one pro-legalization newsletter has made it a weekly feature.

Drug money has been called a major source of income for terrorist organizations. Critics assert that legalization would remove this central source of support for terrorism. While politicians blame drug users for being a major source of financing terrorists, no clear evidence of this link has been provided. US government agencies and government officials have been caught trafficking drugs to finance US-supported terrorist actions in events such as the Iran-Contra Affair, and Manuel Noriega but the isolated nature of these events precludes them from being major sources of financing.

Corruption

Human rights organizations and legal scholars have claimed that drug prohibition inevitably leads to police corruption On 2 July 2010, former Interpol President Jackie Selebi was found guilty of corruption by the South African High Court in Johannesburg for accepting bribes worth US$156,000 from a drug trafficker. After being charged in January 2008, Selebi resigned as president of Interpol and was put on extended leave as National Police Commissioner of South Africa.

Stigma of conviction

Despite the fact that most drug offenders are non-violent, the stigma attached to a conviction can prevent employment and education.

Children being lured into the illegal drug trade

Janet Crist of the White House Office of National Drug Control Policy mentioned that the anti-drug efforts have had «no direct effect on either the price or the availability of cocaine on our streets». Additionally, drug dealers show off expensive jewellery and clothing to young children. Some of these children are interested in making fast money instead of working legitimate jobs. Drug decriminalization would remove the «glamorous Al Capone-type traffickers who are role-models for the young».

The lack of government regulation and control over the lucrative illegal drug market has created a large population of unregulated drug dealers who lure many children into the illegal drug trade. The U.S. government's most recent 2009 National Survey on Drug Use and Health (NSDUH) reported that nationwide over 800,000 adolescents ages 12–17 sold illegal drugs during the previous 12 months preceding the survey. The 2005 Youth Risk Behavior Survey by the U.S. Centers for Disease Control and Prevention (CDC) reported that nationwide 25.4% of students had been offered, sold, or given an illegal drug by someone on school property. The prevalence of having been offered, sold, or given an illegal drug on school property ranged from 15.5% to 38.7% across state CDC surveys (median: 26.1%) and from 20.3% to 40.0% across local surveys (median: 29.4%).

Despite more than $7 billion spent annually towards arresting and prosecuting nearly 800,000 people across the country for marijuana offenses in

2005, the federally funded Monitoring the Future Survey reports about 85% of high school seniors find marijuana "easy to obtain." That figure has remained virtually unchanged since 1975, never dropping below 82.7% in three decades of national surveys.

Environmental

With respect to drug crop cultivation, eradication efforts in line with prohibitionist drug policies ultimately force coca, poppy, and marijuana growers into more remote, ecologically sensitive areas. These crops, which are generally grown away from urban centers and state presence, tend to deplete forestland and expand the agricultural frontier. Out of fear of eradication, cultivators are incentivized to accelerate production cycles in order to obtain the highest yield in the shortest period of time; the pace and methods used by growers neglect measures to promote sustainability, exacerbating the environmental impact. Drug cultivators typically opt to produce in areas with ecosystems with abundant plant biomass to better conceal their operations. Ultimately, this practice leads to increased deforestation which contributes to a greater influx of greenhouse gases into the atmosphere. Moreover, the aerial spraying of herbicides such as glyphosate used in eradication and control efforts have been shown to have negative effects on environmental and human health.

The "balloon effect" also operates further up the drug commodity chain in countries where drugs are trafficked rather than cultivated. Like eradication programs, interdiction pushes traffickers into remote areas where they exacerbate preexisting pressures on forestland. Traffickers use slash and burn practices to convert forest into arable land for cash crop production for the purposes of money laundering as well as the construction of clandestine roads and airstrips. The war on drugs and prohibitionist policies only serve to aggravate the already detrimental impacts of narco-trafficking on Central American forests. Intensified ecological devastation across cultivation and trafficking zones is yet another negative unintended consequence of emphasis on supply-side narcotic reduction borne by poor countries.

Legal dilemmas

Several drugs such as dimethyltryptamine, morphine and GHB are illegal to possess but are also inherently present in all humans as a result of endogenous synthesis. Since some jurisdictions classify possession of drugs to include having the drug present in the blood in any concentration, all residents of such jurisdictions are technically in possession of multiple illegal drugs at all times.

User cost of drugs

When the cost of drugs increases, drug users are more likely to commit crimes in order to obtain money to buy the expensive drugs. Legalizing drugs would make drugs reasonably cheap.

Arguments for inconsistent drug laws

In response to the issue of consistency with regard to drug prohibition and the dangers of alcohol former director of the ONDCP John P. Walters, has said, "It's ludicrous to say we have a great deal of problems from the use of alcohol so we should multiply that with marijuana".

Arguments against inconsistent drug laws

Since alcohol prohibition ended and the War on Drugs began there has been much debate over the issue of consistency among legislators with regard to drug prohibition. Many anti-prohibition activists focus on the well-documented dangers of alcohol (such as alcoholism, cystisis, domestic violence, brain and liver damage). In addition to anecdotal evidence, they cite statistics to show more deaths caused by drunk driving under the influence of alcohol than by drivers under the influence of marijuana, and research which suggests that alcohol is more harmful than all but the most «dangerous» drugs. When the level of harm associated with the other drugs includes harm that arises solely as a result of the drugs illegality rather than merely that danger which is associated with actually using the drugs, only heroin, cocaine, barbiturates and street methadone were shown to be more harmful than the legal drug alcohol.

A 2002 DAWN report, for the USA records two possible drug-induced deaths where marijuana was the only drug found. Legal drugs however, have been the cause of more than half a million deaths a year: 480,000 from tobacco smoking-related illnesses and 80,000 from alcohol abuse. Together, tobacco and alcohol cause about 20% of all yearly deaths in the USA.

It is argued that inconsistency between the harm caused and the legal status of these common drugs undermines the declared motives of the law enforcement agencies to reduce harm by prohibition, for example of marijuana.

In February 2009, the UK government was accused by its most senior expert drugs adviser Professor David Nutt of making political decisions with regard to drug classification, for example in rejecting the scientific advice to downgrade ecstasy from a class A drug. The Advisory Council on the Misuse of Drugs (ACMD) report on ecstasy, based on a 12-month study of 4,000 academic papers, concluded that it is nowhere near as dangerous as other class A drugs such as heroin and crack cocaine, and should be downgraded to class B. The advice was not followed. Jacqui Smith, then Home Secretary, was also widely criticised by the scientific community for bullying Professor David Nutt into apologising for his comments that, in the course of a normal year, more people died from falling off horses than died from taking ecstasy. Professor Nutt was later sacked by Jacqui Smith›s successor as Home Secretary Alan Johnson; Johnson saying "It is important that the government's messages on drugs are clear and as an advisor you do nothing to undermine public understanding of them. I cannot have public confusion between scientific advice and policy and have therefore lost confidence in your ability to advise me as Chair of the ACMD."

Consistency between drugs

In the United States, defendants convicted of selling crack cocaine receive equal sentences to those convicted of selling 100 times the same amount of powder cocaine. This disparity was lessened during the Obama administration when the Fair Sentencing Act 2010 changed the ratio to 18 to 1. The majority of offenders convicted for selling crack are poor and/or black, while the majority of those convicted for selling cocaine are not.

Same policy for distinct drugs

Many drug policies group all illegal drugs into a single category. Since drugs drastically vary in their effects, addictive potential, dosages, methods of production, and consumption the arguments either way could be seen as inconsistent.

Race and enforcement of drug laws

It has been alleged that current drug laws are enforced in such a way as to penalize non-whites more harshly and more often than whites, and to penalize the poor of all races more harshly and more often than the middle and upper classes. For example, up until 2012, crack cocaine carried penalties one hundred times more severe than cocaine despite the fact that these drugs are essentially identical. Especially in urban black communities, convictions were nearly exclusively for crack, while cocaine use is statistically much higher among affluent whites.

Civil rights

Civil rights arguments for prohibitive drug laws

Article 33 of the United Nations Convention on the Rights of the Child reads:

States Parties shall take all appropriate measures, including legislative, administrative, social and educational measures, to protect children from the illicit use of narcotic drugs and psychotropic substances as defined in the relevant international treaties and to prevent the use of children in the illicit production and trafficking of such substances.

Drug Free Australia argues:

The notion that illicit drug use is a victimless crime and that everyone should be free to do what they want with their body disregards the web of social interactions that constitute human existence. Affected by an individual's illicit drug use are children, parents, grandparents, friends, colleagues, work, victims of drugged drivers, crime victims, elder abuse, sexual victims etc. Illicit drug use is no less victimless than alcoholism.

Drug Free Australia gives the example that in 2007 one in every nine children under the age of 18 in the United States lived with at least one drug dependent or drug abusing parent. 2.1 million children in the United States live with at least one parent who was dependent on or abused illicit drugs.

The Christian Institute argues that there is no point in having criminal laws unless those caught breaking them will at least face prosecution. Less serious offenses, such as failing to complete a census form, may also attract a criminal record, so the contention that criminalizing drug use is draconian can be seen as overstatement.

"Parental substance dependence and abuse can have profound effects on children, including child abuse and neglect, injuries and deaths related to motor vehicle accidents, and increased odds that the children will become substance dependent or abusers themselves. Up-to-date estimates of the number of children living with substance-dependent or substance-abusing parents are needed for planning both adult treatment and prevention efforts and programs that support and protect affected children."

Drug Free Australia concludes any democratic society that deems the use of a certain drug to present unacceptable harm to the individual user, to present unacceptable harm to the users' surrounding community or to transfer too great a burden to the community will seek legislation which will curb that particular freedom of the individual.

Sweden's centre-right alliance government Moderate Party advocates «Zero tolerance for crime", arguing:

Few things restrict people's freedom as much as the consequences of violence, drugs and criminality in society.

.Many people argue that only drug dealers should be fought and not the drug users themselves. But this rests on the fundamental error that big-time drugs smugglers and dealers hawk illicit drugs to new consumers. This is most often not the case. Rather it is the users themselves that are mostly responsible for recruiting new users through networks of friends or relatives demonstrating that users need to be targeted as the recruiters of new drug use, and that an emphasis on early rehabilitation for young users is the best answer to curbing widespread dealing. Sweden›s mandatory rehabilitation program has resulted in the lowest drug use levels in the developed world.

The freedom of choice of those addicted to a drug is also questioned, recognizing that addiction is defined as compulsive by its very nature and that addictions in and of themselves curb individual freedom. Likewise, the proposal that addictive drugs should be legalized, regulated and opened to «free market dynamics» is immediately belied by the recognition that the drug market for an addict is no longer a free market – it is clear that they will pay any price when needing their drug.

Civil rights arguments for drug law reform

Cognitive liberty

Authors such as Aldous Huxley and Terence McKenna believed that what persons do in private should not be regulated by the government. It is argued that persons should be able to do whatever they want with their bodies, including the recreational use of drugs, as long as they do not harm others. Such arguments often cite the harm principle of philosopher John Stuart Mill who urged that the state had no right to intervene to prevent individuals from doing something that harmed them, if no harm was thereby done to the rest of society: ‹Over himself, over his own body and mind, the individual is sovereign› and ‹The only purpose for which power can be rightfully exercised over any member of a civilized community, against his will, is to prevent harm to others. His own good, either physical or moral, is not sufficient warrant.› The argument is that drug use is a victimless crime and as such the government has no right to prohibit it or punish drug consumers, much like the government does not forbid overeating, which causes significantly more deaths per year. This can be equated with the quest for freedom of thought.

Spiritual and religious

We're playing with half a deck as long as we tolerate that the cardinals of government and science should dictate where human curiosity can legitimately send its attention and where it can not. It's an essentially preposterous situation. It is essentially a civil rights issue, because what we're talking about here is the repression of a religious sensibility. In fact, not a religious sensibility, the religious sensibility.

Some religious groups including the União do Vegetal, the Native American Church, the Bwiti religion and the Rastafari movement (see religious and spiritual use of cannabis) use psychoactive substances as sacrament in religious rituals. In some religious practice, drugs are sometimes used as a conduit to an oceanic feeling or divine union, equated with mysticism or entheogenic (‹that which causes God to be within an individual›) experiences. In others, the ‹entactogenic› qualities of drugs are used to enhance feelings of empathyamong congregations.

Personal development and exploration

Some people believe that altered states of consciousness enable many people to push the boundaries of human experience, knowledge, and creativity. There is thus a moral imperative to experiment with drugs in terms of human progress, teleological development, or just increased artistic creativity; such ideas are central to Cognitive Liberty, Stoned Ape Hypothesis and Aldous Huxley's The Doors of Perception.

In PiHKAL, Alexander Shulgin, argues that the psychedelics help us learn about ourselves; indeed that is where the name "psychedelic" (mind expanding) comes from.

I am completely convinced that there is a wealth of information built into us, with miles of intuitive knowledge tucked away in the genetic material of every one of our cells. Something akin to a library containing uncountable reference volumes, but without any obvious route of entry. And, without some means of access, there is no way to even begin to guess the extent and quality of what is there. The psychedelic drugs allow exploration of this interior world, and insights into its nature.

Moral and ethical reasons

Many people, including some religious groups, argue that the war on drugs is itself immoral.

In 2007, Richard Brunstrom, the Chief Constable of North Wales, one of Britain's most senior police officers, said "If policy on drugs is in future to be pragmatic not moralistic, driven by ethics not dogma, then the current prohibitionist stance will have to be swept away as both unworkable and immoral, to be replaced with an evidence-based unified system (specifically including tobacco and alcohol) aimed at minimisation of harms to society."

The author and physician Andrew Weil has commented on the peculiar attitude and emotional bias of some people who think «drug taking is bad», but who nevertheless consume alcohol, and formulate the unhelpful conception «We drink. Therefore alcohol is not a drug.»

The UK drug policy reform group Release believe that the stigma attached to drug use needs to be removed. Release›s actions have included challenging such stigmatisation with its «Nice People Take Drugs» advertising campaign.

Political

Sending out signals

Arguments for sending out signals

Some argue that sending out signals should be a consideration of drug policy. Previous UK Home Office Minister Vernon Coaker argued «is not part of any system with respect to drugs ... not only trying to send messages out to people who misuse drugs but also about trying to send messages out to people out there in the community?»

In response to the UK government's official drugs advisory body's opposition to cannabis reclassification (upwards, from a class C to a class B drug) in 2008, prime minister Gordon Brown said: "I believe that if we're sending out a signal, particularly to teenagers – and particular those at the most vulnerable age, young teenagers – that in any way we find cannabis acceptable, given all we know about the way that cannabis is being sold in this country, that is not the right thing to do. There's a stronger case now for sending out a signal that cannabis is not only illegal, it's unacceptable."

Arguments against sending out signals

The Science and Technology Select Committee appointed by the House of Commons to inquire into the Government›s handling of scientific advice, risk and evidence in policy making agreed with Transform Drug Policy Foundation's view that "Criminal law is supposed to prevent crime, not 'send out' public health messages". Transform warned that sending out signals could backfire by "fostering distrust of police and public health messages amongst young people". The Select Committee's report said "The Government's desire to use the Class of a particular drug to send out a signal to potential users or dealers does not sit comfortably with the claim that the primary objective of the classification system is to categorise drugs according to the comparative harm associated with their misuse. It is also incompatible with the Government's stated commitment to evidence based policy making since it has never undertaken research to establish the relationship between the Class of a drug and the signal sent out and there is, therefore, no evidence base on which to draw in making these policy decisions."

Political calculation

Arguments for political calculation

John Donnelly, writing for the Boston Globe on the presidential race of 2000, suggested that the candidates' silence on drug policy may stem from a widely shared belief that any position even hinting at reducing penalties for drug use would be political suicide. Charles R. Schuster, director of the National Institute on Drug Abuse under Presidents Reagan and Bush (Snr.), was reported as saying in 1997, "Talking sense about drug policy in today's climate of opinion can be political suicide."

Drug policy academic Mark A.R. Kleiman has argued:

There are things we can do about drug policy that would reduce the number of people in prison, and the extent of drug abuse and drug related crime. Legalization isn't one of them because there's not public support for it. And if we acknowledge the fact that, from the point of view of the majority of the population it's a loser, then it's not as if we can talk them out of that, so I think the legalization debate is mostly a distraction from doing the real work of fixing our drug policies

Scott Morgan reports how he once attended a discussion of Peter Reuter and David Boyum's book An Analytic Assessment of U.S. Drug Policy, in which the authors admitted ignoring the legalization option in their analysis. Boyum claimed that there was no legitimate political support for ending the drug war and that he and Reuter had therefore confined themselves to recommendations that they thought were politically viable.

Arguments against political calculation

Two teenagers deaths in March 2010 triggered nationwide concern about the drug mephedrone in the UK. The Advisory Council on the Misuse of Drugs (ACMD) recommended a ban on 29 March, which was quickly passed into law, but the decision was criticised for being politically rather than scientifically driven and led to the resignation of the ACMD›s Eric Carlin, the eighth member of the council to leave in five months in protest at what was seen as political interference. Toxicology reports released later in May 2010 revealed that the boys had never taken the drug.

Professor Colin Blakemore, professor of neuroscience at the University of Oxford, said: "This shocking news should be a salutary lesson to tabloid journalists and prejudiced politicians who held a gun to the heads of the ACMD and demanded that this drug should be banned before a single autopsy had been completed ... The politicians talk about using drug classification as a way of sending 'messages' to young people. I fear that the only message that will be sent by the hasty decision on mephedrone is that the drug laws deserve no respect."

Professor David Nutt, the former chairman of the ACMD, said: "the previous government's rush to ban mephedrone never had any serious scientific credibility – it looks much more like a decision based on a short-term electoral calculation. This news demonstrates why it's so important to base drug classification on the evidence, not fear, and why the police, media and politicians should only make public pronouncements once the facts are clear."

Public opinion on prohibitive drug laws

A direct example of societal attitudes driving the International Drug Conventions is the 1925 speech by the Egyptian delegate M. El Guindy to the 1925 Geneva Convention forum which prohibited cannabis – largely reproduced in Willoughby, W. W.; In the late 19th and early 20th century drug use was regarded by the public «as alone a habit, vice, sign of weakness or dissipation», similar to the view of those who could not control their use of the licit drug alcohol. The use of illicit drugs has been prohibited internationally since 1912, an entire century, because of international agreement that the general community has a greater right to protect itself from the harms of illicit drug use than does an individual user to use a harmful substance recreationally.

Currently there is still greater public support for the continued prohibiting of illicit drug use than there is for legalizing and regulating the use of these substances. In the United States 82% of those polled by the Family Research Association in 1998 were opposed to the legalization of heroin and cocaine in the same manner as alcohol is legal. In October 2009 a Gallup poll found that 54% of those polled were against the legalization of cannabis. In Australia, which has had the highest levels of illicit drug use in Organisation for Economic Co-operation and Development (or OECD) countries for more than a decade, according to a 2007 survey, 95% of Australians do not support the legalization of heroin, cocaine and amphetamines, and 79% do not support the legalization of cannabis.

It can be argued that the negative attitudes to illicit drug use which issued in the international drug Conventions, with prohibitions against their use 100 years ago, still exist today. Taking again statistics from Australia, 97% disapprove of the regular use of heroin, 96% disapprove the regular use of amphetamines or cocaine, and 76.5% disapprove of the regular use of cannabis. In any democracy where "the will of the people" is respected by its political representatives, the prohibition of these substance might well be expected to remain intact.

Public opinion on drug law reform

According to Transform Drug Policy Foundation, over the past decade there has been strong shift in public opinion in favour of drug policy reform. This shift has taken place despitesuccessive government's reluctance to consider or debate the subject, or even call to for an independent inquiry.

A national telephone survey conducted in 1993 found that between 52% and 55% of Australians believed that growing and possessing cannabis for personal use should be legalised.

An ICM poll of 1201 people for The Guardian in 1998 found that 47% believed that the illegality of drugs actually encourages young people to try them.

46% of UK adults in a 2002 Guardian poll (of 1075) felt that drug addicts who register themselves as such should have access to certain illegal drugs via prescription.

An ICM poll of 1008 UK adults (aged 16+) for The Guardian in 2008 found that 38% would support a scheme, similar to that established in Portugal and Spain, whereby it is not a criminal offence to possess and use drugs privately.

Following President Barack Obama's win of the 2008 presidential election, Change.gov hosted a service on their website named the Citizen›s Briefing Book allowing United States citizens to give their opinion on the most important issues in America, and allow others to vote up or down on those ideas. The top ten ideas are to be given to Obama on the day of his inauguration, January 20, 2009. The most popular idea according to respondents was "Ending Marijuana Prohibition", earning 92,970 points and obtaining a total of 3,550 comments. The second most popular hope, by contrast, was «Commit to becoming the «Greenest» country in the world.» with 70,470 points.

Marijuana has seen a renaissance in its utopian representation in films such as the suburban satire American Beauty (1999, dir. Sam Mendes) and the stoner comedy Pineapple Express (2008, dir. David Gordon Green). Another venue for contemporary criticism of marijuana prohibition is television, such as the SHOWTIME series Weeds (2005–2012, dev. Jenji Kohan); the HBO series True Blood (2008–2014, dev. Alan Ball); and adult animation shows such as South Park, Family Guy, and American Dad!.

David Simon, creator of the television series The Wire, in 2011 told U.S. Attorney General Eric Holder that he›d «give him another season of the HBO show for an end to the war on drugs." Holder had invited show stars Wendell Pierce, Sonja Sohn, and Jim True-Frost to Washington on behalf of an anti-drug public relations campaign and at the time called on Simon and Ed Burns for another season or a movie of the show. Simon replied via a letter to a newspaper offering the trade.

Another option is a short-term residential program where patients undergo detoxification and receive intensive counseling to steer them toward a community-based treatment program.

Recovery housing provides monitored and short-term stays for patients who are transitioning to an independent life.

Support Groups

Support groups are paramount to successful treatment. Groups such as Narcotics Anonymous follow the 12-step model and provide those in recovery with a platform to share their experiences. Patients meet other people in similar situations, and the group holds everyone accountable for maintaining sobriety.

With the appropriate support and treatment, a person suffering from drug addiction can recover and enjoy a substance-free life.

Bibliography

- Geoffrey Burchfield (1997). Meredith Hopes (ed.). "What's your poison: caffeine". Australian Broadcasting Corporation. Archived from the original on 26 July 2009. Retrieved 15 January 2014.
- Richard Lovett (24 September 2005). "Coffee: The demon drink?". Archived from the original on 11 April 2014. Retrieved 2014-05-01.
- "Drug". Dictionary.com Unabridged. v 1.1. Random House. 20 September 2007. Archived from the original on 14 September 2007 – via Dictionary.com.
- "Drug Definition". Stedman's Medical Dictionary. Archived from the original on 2014-05-02. Retrieved 2014-05-01 – via Drugs.com.
- H.P., Rang; M.M, Dale; J.M., Ritter; R.J., Flower; G., Henderson (2011). "What is Pharmacology". Rang & Dale's pharmacology (7th ed.). Edinburgh: Churchill Livingstone. p. 1. ISBN 978-0-7020-3471-8. a drug can be defined as a chemical substance of known structure, other than a nutrient of an essential dietary ingredient, which, when administered to a living organism, produces a biological effect
- Atanasov AG, Waltenberger B, Pferschy-Wenzig EM, Linder T, Wawrosch C, Uhrin P, Temml V, Wang L, Schwaiger S, Heiss EH, Rollinger JM, Schuster D, Breuss JM, Bochkov V, Mihovilovic MD, Kopp B, Bauer R, Dirsch VM, Stuppner H (December 2015). "Discovery and resupply of pharmacologically active plant-derived natural products: A review". Biotechnol Adv. 33 (8): 1582–614. doi:10.1016/j.biotechadv.2015.08.001. PMC 4748402. PMID 26281720.
- "Drug". The American Heritage Science Dictionary. Houghton Mifflin Company. Archived from the original on 14 September 2007. Retrieved 20 September 2007 – via dictionary.com.
- Mahoney A, Evans J (6 November 2008). "Comparing drug

classification systems". AMIA Annual Symposium Proceedings: 1039. PMID 18999016.

- World Health Organization (2003). Introduction to drug utilization research (PDF). Geneva: World Health Organization. p. 33. ISBN 978-92-4-156234-8. Archived (PDF)from the original on 2016-01-22.
- Bergström, CA; Andersson, SB; Fagerberg, JH; Ragnarsson, G; Lindahl, A (16 June 2014). "Is the full potential of the biopharmaceutics classification system reached?". European Journal of Pharmaceutical Sciences. 57: 224–31. doi:10.1016/j.ejps.2013.09.010. PMID 24075971.
- "Archived copy". Archived from the original on 2015-03-28. Retrieved 2015-03-16.
- Crocq MA (June 2003). "Alcohol, nicotine, caffeine, and mental disorders". Dialogues Clin. Neurosci. 5 (2): 175–185. PMC 3181622. PMID 22033899.
- "Recreational Drug". The Free Dictionary. Retrieved 16 March 2015.
- Fox, Thomas Peter; Oliver, Govind; Ellis, Sophie Marie (2013). "The Destructive Capacity of Drug Abuse: An Overview Exploring the Harmful Potential of Drug Abuse Both to the Individual and to Society". ISRN Addiction. 2013: 450348. doi:10.1155/2013/450348. PMC 4392977. PMID 25938116. Archived from the original on 11 September 2015. Retrieved 15 April 2015.
- "MHRA Side Effects of Medicines." Archived 2014-05-02 at the Wayback MachineMHRA Side Effects of Medicines,
- Harper, Douglas. "drug". Online Etymology Dictionary.
- Tupper KW (2012). "Psychoactive substances and the English language: "Drugs," discourses, and public policy". Contemporary Drug Problems. 39 (3): 461–492. doi:10.1177/009145091203900306.
- "About Registration: Medicines and Prescribing". Health and Care Professions Council. Archived from the original on 2016-01-13. Retrieved 22 January 2016.
- "Glossary of MHRA terms – P". U.K. Medicines and Healthcare products Regulatory Agency. Archived from the original on 2008-11-14. Retrieved 2008-11-05.
- ""Generic Drugs", Center for Drug Evaluation and Research, U.S. Food and Drug Administration" (PDF). Fda.gov. Archived (PDF) from the original on 29 August 2017. Retrieved 11 October 2017.
- Entheogen, [dictionary.com], archived from the original on 2012-02-13, retrieved 2012-03-13
- Valdés, Díaz & Paul 1983, p. 287.
- Sobiecki, Jean-Francois (July 2012). "Psychoactive Spiritual Medicines and Healing Dynamics in the Initiation Process of Southern Bantu Diviners". Journal of Psychoactive Drugs. 44 (3): 216–223. doi:10.1080/02791072.2012.703101. PMID 23061321.